D1562004

Colloquial

Swedish

The Colloquial Series

Series adviser: Gary King

The following languages are available in the Colloquial series:

Afrikaans
Albanian
Amharic
Arabic (Levantine)
Arabic of Egypt
Arabic of the Gulf
and Saudi Arabia
Basque
Bulgarian
*Cambodian
*Cantonese
*Chinese
Croatian and Serbian
Czech
Danish
Dutch
Estonian
Finnish
French
German
Greek
Gujarati
Hindi
Hungarian
Indonesian
Italian
Japanese
Korean
Latvian
Lithuanian
Malay
Mongolian
Norwegian
Panjabi
Persian
Polish
Portuguese
Portuguese of Brazil
Romanian
*Russian
Slovak
Slovene
Somali
*Spanish
Spanish of Latin America
Swedish
*Thai
Turkish
Urdu
Ukrainian
*Vietnamese
Welsh

Accompanying cassette(s) (*and CDs) are available for all the above titles. They can be ordered through your bookseller, or send payment with order to Taylor & Francis/Routledge Ltd, ITPS, Cheriton House, North Way, Andover, Hants SP10 5BE, UK, or to Routledge Inc, 29 West 35th Street, New York NY 10001, USA.

COLLOQUIAL CD-ROMs
Multimedia Language Courses
Available in: Chinese, French, Portuguese and Spanish

Colloquial
Swedish

The Complete Course for Beginners
Second edition

Philip Holmes and Gunilla Serin

London and New York

First published 1990
by Routledge
11 New Fetter Lane, London EC4P 4EE

Simultaneously published in the USA and Canada
by Routledge
29 West 35th Street, New York, NY 10001

Reprinted 1993 (twice), 1995
Revised edition published 1996
Reprinted 1998, 1999, 2001

Routledge is an imprint of the Taylor & Francis Group

Illustrations by Matthew Crabbe

Typeset in Times by Philip Holmes
Printed and bound in Great Britain by
Clays Ltd, St Ives plc

British Library Cataloguing in Publication Data
A catalogue record for this book is available from the British Library

Library of Congress Cataloging in Publication Data
A catalog record for this book is available from the Library of Congress

ISBN 0-415-13716-0 (book)
ISBN 0-415-13717-9 (cassette)
ISBN 0-415-13718-7 (book and cassette course)

Contents

Acknowledgements

We extend our grateful thanks to Olle Kjellin for advice on the presentation of stress, Gunnel Clarke for many valuable suggestions notably in the section on Accents, to Roger and Taija Nyborg for help with the stress markings and for proof-reading the text, to Michael Cooper for help with the vocabulary, to Oscar Forsberg for writing the letter from Jocke in Lesson 18, and to Ian Hinchliffe for allowing us to use ideas and examples from *Essentials of Swedish Grammar.*

We thank all our students over the years for teaching us so much, and particularly Phil's first-year students who have taken such a positive interest in improving this book. Special thanks go to Wendy Davies for the user's insight.

Phil Holmes and Gunilla Serin
Hull and Stockholm
February 1996

Acknowledgements

Using this book

We have designed this book for anyone wishing to acquire basic conversational Swedish, that is the grammar, pronunciation and intonation as well as basic vocabulary and a range of phrases necessary for communicating different needs. We also provide you with some background information about Sweden, its regions, history, traditions and way of life.

Each of the eighteen lessons contains three passages – a 'Text', a 'Dialogue' and a 'Factual text'.

In the 'Text' you learn about the lives of a group of characters: Rebecca, an English student spending a year at Stockholm University, Bill Morris, an English export representative travelling in Sweden, and the Swedish Forsberg family of Jan, Eva and Joakim holidaying in the South of Sweden and then pursuing their daily lives. Other characters appear in the story from time to time

The 'Dialogue' is to provide you with a number of ways of meeting conversational needs arising in everyday situations you are likely to encounter, such as, for example, 'Asking for things' or 'Expressing likes and dislikes'. It is often followed by further notes on other constructions you can use.

In each lesson you will find numbered language notes which explain, for example, aspects of word order, inflexion and agreement as well as providing all kinds of colloquial constructions and other useful information. By referring to the 'Grammatical index' you can use the book as a concise reference grammar, though lack of space precludes a great amount of detail. More detailed sources of reference are Philip Holmes and Ian Hinchliffe, *Swedish. A Comprehensive Grammar*, Routledge, 1993, or Philip Holmes and Ian Hinchliffe, *Essentials of Swedish Grammar*, Hull Swedish Press, 1991. Another substantial set of exercises are *Swedish Exercises for use on PCs* by the same authors with Chris Hall, Hull Swedish Press, 1995.

You are provided with a list of vocabulary after each text and dialogue. You should note particularly that a word is explained only on the first occasion it appears, though all the words used are to be found in the 'Swedish–English glossary' at the end of the book. A relatively large vocabulary is used in the book, and by the time you reach the end of the book you should have learned some 2,000 words in all. For these reasons it is a good idea to learn new words as they appear. About 1,000 words appear in the 'Concise English–Swedish glossary'.

The 'Factual text' is primarily for reading comprehension and to provide you with some background on Sweden and its culture. You should not normally need to translate the text. It is sufficient for you to get the gist of the meaning and guess some of the words. Only the most difficult vocabulary is, therefore, provided after these texts.

In the lessons there are exercises of many different kinds. Some 120 short exercises are to be found in the book which make use of the vocabulary employed in the texts. A 'Key to exercises' is found at the end of the book so that you can check your answers.

In Lessons 1 to 9 there are 'Pronunciation' exercises, which are also found on the cassette so you can compare your pronunciation with that of native speakers.

A feature of Swedish that makes it relatively easy to learn is its *vocabulary.* There is a core vocabulary of Germanic words that are familiar to us (**arm**, **fot**, **finger**, **knä**, **son**, **lamm**, etc.) as well as many loanwords from German (**fru**, **krig**, **betala**, **fönster**, **spegel**, **språk**), English (**jobb**, **potatis**, **baby**, **cykel**, **jeans**) and French (**trottoar**, **fåtölj**, **paraply**, **scen**, **frisör**).

There are also a number of grammatical similarities with English: e.g. adjectives are placed before the noun: **en kall vinter**, **den kalla vintern** (a cold winter, the cold winter).

Adjectives compare by adding an ending: **rik** – **rikare** – **rikast** (rich – richer – richest) or by using **mer**, **mest**: **mer typisk**, **mest typisk** (more typical, most typical).

Verbs have a **-d/-t** ending in the past tense: **vi badade**, **jag kysste Eva** (we bathed, I kissed Eva), or change the stem vowel: **de sitter**, **de satt** (they sit, they sat).

Swedish verbs are, incidentally, much simpler than those in most European languages in that they have the same form throughout each tense: **jag/du/han/hon/vi/ni/de simmar** (I/you/he/she/we/you/they swim).

Some of the apparent problems in learning Swedish are:

Pronunciation – initially this appears difficult, but it is in fact very regular once you have learned a few rules. The difference between short and long vowels is crucial to accurate pronunciation. Use the account at the beginning of the book for reference. You will find that pronunciation is also practised systematically in the early lessons.

Stress – which words are stressed in the sentence – and *accent* – Swedish has two word accents – are the keys to your being clearly understood. There is a general account of stress and accent at the beginning of the book, not all of which you will need to assimilate immediately, but which should prove useful to refer back to later.

In the text and dialogue in the first five lessons we have also marked the length of the vowels and consonants in those words in the sentence that receive stress. Note that in the vocabulary lists to these lessons on the contrary the pronunciation of the new words is shown as if these were pronounced individually (i.e. not in a sentence).

Word order and sentence structure – it is possible to learn to speak Swedish and make oneself understood without paying any great attention to word order and different ways of constructing sentences. But if you wish to continue beyond a very basic level, and perhaps even ultimately to learn to write Swedish, then it is necessary to devote some time to the problems of word order right from the start. It will then avoid real difficulties later. The teaching of Swedish word order is nowadays often based on a positional scheme originally produced by the Danish linguist Paul Diderichsen which breaks the sentence down into seven positions for different sentence elements (subject, object, etc.). This book is no exception, though we have adopted a rather more user-friendly approach. See the 'Note on grammatical terms' for a quick 'brush-up' on the basic terms used.

Lycka till! (Good luck!)

Note on grammatical terms

Most of the grammatical terms used in this book should be familiar to anyone who has learned the rudiments of a modern foreign language (or even English) at school, but for those who feel the need of a quick 'brush-up' we provide some English examples marked with terms found in the book. These include only one new term.

Parts of the sentence

John	searched	the room	with great care.
SUBJECT	VERB	OBJECT	MPT-EXPRESSION (MANNER)

MPT-expressions are words or phrases denoting Manner, Place or Time, i.e. how, where or when the action takes place.

The girl	is	a student	at the university.
She	is	young.	
SUBJECT	VERB	COMPLEMENT	MPT-EXPRESSION (PLACE)

A complement is an adjective or noun, often describing the subject, which is necessary to complete the sense of the sentence after an 'empty' verb, e.g. 'is', 'becomes'.

It	never	rained	in summer.
SUBJECT	ADVERB	VERB	MPT-EXPRESSION (TIME)

Putting the adverb into this sentence changes the meaning of the entire sentence. Try taking it out!

The football	hit	him.
SUBJECT	VERB	OBJECT

Not all grammatical subjects are people. Not all grammatical objects are things. Both subjects and objects can be pronouns. In example 4 the verb has no object; in example 5 the verb must have an object.

Main clauses and sub(ordinate) clauses

Main clauses are groups of words (usually containing a minimum of a subject and verb) that may stand on their own as a sentence:

She	walked.
SUBJECT	VERB

Yesterday	Eva	walked	quickly	to school.
MPT-EXPR.	SUBJECT	VERB	MPT-EXPR.	MPT-EXPR.
(TIME)		(MANNER)		(PLACE)

Examples 1–5 above are also main clause sentences.

Subordinate (sub) clauses are groups of words (which also usually contain a subject and verb) which form part of a main clause sentence:

She walked faster *when she saw the headmistress.*
SUB CLAUSE

MAIN CLAUSE SENTENCE

When she saw the headmistress she walked faster.
SUB CLAUSE

Some sub clauses, such as the one in examples 8 and 9 which is itself an MPT–expression (time), can be placed at the beginning or end of the main clause sentence.

She saw the headmistress *who was standing by the gym.*
SUB CLAUSE

The headmistress, *who was standing by the gym,* saw her.
SUB CLAUSE

Some sub clauses describe part of the main clause sentence (often its subject or object) and may therefore come in the middle of the sentence.

Note on forms used in vocabulary lists

The vocabulary lists after the texts and dialogues provide key information about the different forms of the Swedish words:

Nouns

In vocabulary lists:	*Indefinite singular*	*Singular + end article (definite)*	*Indefinite plural*
klocka -n -or	**en klocka**	**klockan**	**klockor**
bil -en -ar	**en bil**	**bilen**	**bilar**
äpple -t -n	**ett äpple**	**äpplet**	**äpplen**
hus -et -	**ett hus**	**huset**	**hus** (no pl. ending)
fågel -n fåglar	**en fågel**	**fågeln fåglar**	

man, mannen, män For irregular nouns all forms are given.

Adjectives

In vocabulary lists:	*Indefinite with N-words*	*Indefinite with T-words*	*Plural & definite*
rolig -t -a	**rolig**	**roligt**	**roliga**
gratis -	**gratis**	**gratis**	**gratis** (indeclinable)
bred, brett, breda	For irregular adjectives all forms are given		
hota/d -t -de	For past participle forms: stem + ending		
inskriv/en -et -na	For past participle forms: stem + ending		

Verbs

The verb stem (= imperative form) is indicated with / and the infinitive, present and past tense endings are given, from which it is possible to predict the remaining forms, e.g.

In vocabulary lists:	*Infinitive* (to call)	*Present* (call/s)	*Past* (called)	*Supine (for perfect, pluperfect)* (has, had called)
kalla/ -r -de	**kalla**	**kallar**	**kallade**	**kallat**
böj/a -er -de	**böja**	**böjer**	**böjde**	**böjt**
köp/a -er -te	**köpa**	**köper**	**köpte**	**köpt**
tro/ -r -dde	**tro**	**tror**	**trodde**	**trott**
skriv/a -er skrev	**skriva**	**skriver**	**skrev**	**skrivit**
gå/ -r gick gått	For irregular verbs the supine is also given.			

Note on the second edition (1996)

A number of alterations have been made to the texts and dialogues which include updating of facts in the factual texts and inclusion of a new exercise on nouns with end articles in Lesson 5. An index is now included, and the tapes have been re-recorded with new material.

Pronunciation, stress and accents

The Alphabet

The Swedish alphabet has 29 letters, three more letters than the English alphabet, and these different letters all come at the end. Notice the order:

a b c d e f g h i j k l m n o p q r s t u v w x y z å ä ö

Of these, the letter **w** (pronounced as **v**) is found only in names and foreign loan words: **Wasa, wellpapp, WC**. Words beginning with **w** are found under **v** in dictionaries.

Pronunciation

Vowels

Swedish has a large number of different vowel sounds. What follows deals with stressed vowels only. Notice first that:

1 The distinction between long and short stressed vowels is great: long vowels are very, very long, short ones quite short.

2 **å** and **ö** both have lip rounding.

3 Long **o** and long **u** have extreme lip-rounding causing a **w**-like end-phase. Both long **i** and long **y** have very high and front tongue positions. Long **y** has open lip rounding and a **j**-like end-phase (*Note*: Swedish **j** sounds like the 'y' in English 'beyond'). Long **i** has a **j**-like end-phase.

ooo^{w} **uuu**^{w} **yyy**^{j} **iii**^{j}

4 Pronunciation of **ä** and **ö** before **r** is more open than in other positions.

5 Stressed syllables are always long: short stressed vowel + long consonant (two or more consonants) or long stressed vowel + short consonant; unstressed syllables are always short. The long segments are shown by underlining in this book.

Pronunciation of stressed vowels – approximate equivalents:

long **a**	'a' in English 'father, dark'	**hat**
short **a**	open 'a' in Northern English 'hat, hand'	**hatt**
long **å**	'a' in English 'all' but with lip-rounding	**mås**
short **å**	'o' in English 'hot'	**måste**
long **o**	'oo' in English 'doom, moon' with extreme lip-rounding and **w**-like end-phase (see also note on **o**, p.9)	**bot**
short **o**	'oo' in English 'book' with slightly less extreme lip-rounding (see also note on **o**, p.9)	**bott**
long **u**	Something like 'u' in French 'lu' but with lip-rounding and **w**-like end-phase	**ful**
short **u**	'u' in English 'full', lax lip-rounding	**full**
long **e**	No equivalent. Cf. French 'é' in 'été'	**vet**
short **e**	'e' in English 'pen, best'	**vett**
long **ä**	'ea' in English 'bear', but longer	**lät**
short **ä**	'e' in English 'pen, best' (same as short **e**)	**lätt**
long **i**	'ea' in English 'beat' but longer, more closed and with **j**-like end-phase	**fin**
short **i**	'i' in English 'hit, miss'	**finns**
long **y**	No equivalent. Cf. German 'ü' in 'Tür'. Open lip-rounding with **j**-like end-phase	**byt**
short **y**	No equivalent. Cf. German 'ü' in 'dünn'	**bytt**
long **ö**	No equivalent. Cf. French 'eu' in 'peu' but much longer with lip-rounding	**nöt**
short **ö**	'u' in English 'hurt', though much shorter	**nött**

Practise saying the following personal names and place names:

i	*long vowel*	*short vowel*	**e**	*long vowel*	*short vowel*
	Frida	**Birgit**		**Eva**	**Bengt**
	Lisa	**Ingrid**		**Berit**	**Jens**
	Siv	**Britta**		**Sten**	**Petter**

	Stig	**Nils**		**Lena**	**Ebba**
a	*long vowel*	*short vowel*	**y**	*long vowel*	*short vowel*
	Karin	**Dagmar**		**Tyra**	**Yngve**
	Jan	**Annika**		**Lydia**	**Ylva**
	Karl	**Janne**		**Ryd**	**Sylvia**
	Skara	**Halland**		**Ystad**	**Yngsjö**
u	*long vowel*	*short vowel*	**å***	*long vowel*	*short vowel*
	Rut	**Ulla**		**Håkan**	**Måns**
	Sune	**Gun**		**Åsa**	**Ånge**
	Uno	**Ulf**		**Småland**	**Hålland**
	Ture	**Lund**		**Åmål**	**Tåstrup**
ä	*long vowel*	*short vowel*	**ö**	*long vowel*	*short vowel*
	Sälen	**Rättvik**		**Södra**	**Stöllet**
	Mälaren	**Säffle**		**Öland**	**Östen**
ä before r			**ö before r**		
	long vowel	*short vowel*		*long vowel*	*short vowel*
	Pär	**Märta**		**Töreboda**	**Mörtsunda**
o*	*long vowel*	*short vowel*			
	Mora	**Bosse**			
	Boden	**Blomgren**			
	Ola	**Olle**			

* Unlike the examples given here, many words with **o** spellings are pronounced with a short **å**: **Olga, Oskar, Ronneby, Stockholm.** Some are pronounced with a long **å**: **Solna, Mona, Roland.**
When long the pronunciation **o** is more common (e.g. **Mora**), when short the pronunciation **å** is more common (e.g. **Oskar**).

Vowel length

Rules for determining the length of stressed vowels from written Swedish:

Vowels followed by a single consonant letter are long:	**går**
Vowels followed by a double consonant or two consonant letters (denoting a voiceless cluster) are short and the consonant(s) long:	**gått**
Vowels *not* followed by a consonant (open syllable) are long:	**gå**

But note the following points:

- These rules do not apply to words ending in –**m**, –**n** where the **m** and **n** are often long already (= **mm, nn**), cf. **den, hem** and see p.97.
- The common words **arm, charm, arbete** have short **a**. Compare the pronunciation of English 'arm'.
- Unstressed vowels are always short: the **a** in **skriva**, the **e** [ə] in **röker**.

In this book you will sometimes see the symbol ə. This represents the unstressed sound of 'a' in English 'about', 'er' in English 'father', etc.

Consonant sounds

Many of the consonant letters are pronounced approximately as in English. These include: **b, d, f, h, l, m, n, p, t, v, x**.

Some specific problem consonants and consonant groups are dealt with in the lessons, but learners should note the following for now:

1 Pronunciation of **g-, k-, sk-** varies according to the type of vowel following. 'Soft' **g-, k-, sk-** precedes the vowels **e, i, y, ä, ö**:

g- is pronounced as Swedish **j** or English consonant 'y' in 'yell': **Göran, gymnasium, gin**.

k- is something like 'ch' in English 'church', though softer: **köpa, kära, kyrka**.

sk- is something like English 'sh' in 'shirt' but with distinct lip-rounding: **skina, skön, skära**.

There are large variations of **sk-** pronunciation depending on dialect and speaker.

Like **sk-** go words beginning with **sj-, skj-, stj-**: **sju, skjorta, stjäla**.

'Hard' **g-, k-, sk-** precedes the vowels **o, u, a, å**: These are pronounced as in English 'gate', 'keep', 'skill': **gata, gul, god, kaka, kål, ko, skall, skor, skugga**.

2 **s** is always unvoiced 's', as in English 'loss', *never* voiced 'z', as in 'please': **Lisa, stycke, ros, musik, stum, lösa**.

3 **-rs** is like 'sh' in English 'rush' but with lip-rounding: **fors, Lars, störst**.

4 **-rt** is like 't' in English 'daughter', but with the tongue further back against the palate with lips rounded: **bort, fart, kört.**

5 **t** is always pronounced far forward, with the tongue just behind the front teeth: **bott, titta, stor.**

Stress

In Swedish – as in English – there is an important distinction between words that have stress in the sentence and those that do not. All the words that are significant for the meaning are stressed (see list below). This is called *sentence stress,* and these words are indicated in the text and dialogue to Lessons 1–5 (sometimes also in vocabulary lists) to help students to acquire the rhythm of natural spoken Swedish. But different syllables within these stressed words may also be stressed. This is known as *word stress.* The method shown for marking stress on words in the texts is illustrated here:

Hon är nitton år.	She is 19 years old.

Only the stressed words in the sentence are marked. Thus in this example:

The long consonant **tt** follows a short stressed vowel **i**:	**nitton**
The short consonant **r** follows a long stressed vowel **å**:	**år**
Unstressed vowels are not marked (here **o, ä**):	**hon, är**

What follows is a series of lists for reference:

- of those types of words in the sentence which have sentence stress (and therefore long or short stressed vowels)
- of those types of words which are usually unstressed
- of two-word stress
- of stressed and unstressed syllables
- of stressed and unstressed prefixes and suffixes

Stressed in the sentence

Nouns

Anna har köpt ett hus.	Anna has bought a house.
Huset har en altan.	The house has a balcony.

Verbs

When there is *no* object, complement or expression of manner, place, time (MPT-expression):

Eva äter och dricker.	Eva is eating and drinking.
Eva dricker kaffe. OBJ	Eva drinks coffee.

and:

Hon blev sjuk. COMP	She fell ill.
Han är polis. COMP	He is a policeman.

Note: **är** is pronounced like Swedish short **e**.

Expressions of manner, place, time (MPT-expressions)

Nu bor hon i Stockholm. MPT MPT	Now she lives in Stockholm.
Stänger affären tidigt idag? MPT MPT	Does the shop shut early today?

Unstressed in the sentence

Pronouns and v-words (interrogatives)

jag (*pron.* ja), **du, han, hon, den, det** (*pron.* de), **vi, ni, de** (*pron.* dom) (I, you, he, she, it, it, we, you, they)

mig (*pron.* mej), **dig** (*pron.* dej), **sig** (*pron.* sej), **honom, henne, oss, er, dem** (*pron.* dom) (me, you, himself *etc.*, him, her, us, you, them) (except when they come at the front of the sentence or for contrast:

Jag älskar honom. **Honom älskar jag.**	I love him. Him I love.
min, din, sin, hans, hennes, **dess, vår, er, deras**	my, you, his *etc.*, his, her, its, our, your, their
man, en, ens, nån	one, one, one's, some
vem, vad (*pron.* va), **när, hur**	who, what, when, how
Vad sa du?	What did you say?

Conjunctions

och (*pron.* å), **men, att** (*pron.* å), **om, när, därför, som**	and, but, that, if, when, because,which
Han sa, att han drack gin och tonic.	He said that he drank gin and tonic.

Adverbs

inte, nog, väl, ju	not, probably, surely, of course
Hon vill inte.	She doesn't want to.
De är inte hemma.	They aren't home.
Han kommer nog.	He will probably come.

Two-word stress

Where two or more words belong together in one unit of meaning the last word in the phrase is stressed.

Preposition + Noun

(Titta) i boken. Look in the book.	**(De kommer) i dag.** They're coming today.

Indefinite article + Noun

en bil
a car

ett hus
a house

Verb + Particle

gå ut
go out

hälsa på
visit

Verb$_1$ + Verb$_2$

Jag ska gå.
I'll go

De hade kommit.
They had arrived.

Infinitive marker + Verb

att gå
to go

att komma
to come

Verb + Complement

(Han) är lång.
He is tall.

(Hon) är student.
She is a student.

än/som + the word compared

(Han är längre) än Olle.
He is taller than Olle.

(Han är lika ung) som hon.
He is as young as she is.

Pronoun + Pronoun

det här
this

min egen
my own

Time, Measurement

klockan tre
three o'clock

(två) koppar kaffe
two cups of coffee

Numeral + Numeral

trettioåtta
thirty-eight

First name + Surname

Lasse Nilsson

Stressed/unstressed syllables

Of non-compounds with more than one syllable, about two-thirds have stress on the first syllable and one third on a different syllable.

Stress on first syllable: **nyckel** (key), **vinter** (winter), **köper** (buys), **hallon** (raspberry), **gåta** (riddle)

Stress on another syllable:

- prefixes be-, för-: **bestrida** (deny), **betala** (pay), **försök** (attempt).
- suffix -era: **parkera** (park), **studera**, (study).
- foreign loans: **restaurang** (restaurant), **revy** (revue), **universitet** (university).
- foreign suffixes: **regissör** (director), **gymnast** (gymnast), **musikant** (musician).

Compounds (words made up of two (or more) words) have stress on the first and last part of the compound. In Stockholm-Swedish the first stress has a falling tone; the last stress has a rising tone:

↘ ↗	↘ ↗	↘ ↗
husnyckel	**centrallasarett**	**Metallindustriarbetarförbundet**
(house key)	(central hospital)	(Metal Workers' Union)

Some problem words

Many words that are familiar from English (some of which are found in this book) are stressed differently from English:

familj, figur, institution, intresserad, juli, katolsk, klimat, kultur, miljon, passagerare, portion, program, restaurang, student, toalett, traditionell, universitet, vegetation, choklad, demokrat, demonstration, journalist, litteratur, religion, referens, chaufför

Stressed prefixes

o-, miss-, van-, gen-, an-, er-,	**olycklig, ankomma**
sam-, sär-, und-	**samarbeta**
till-, upp-, av-, in-, över-, under-	**avlida, övergå**

Stressed suffixes

-bar, -skap, -sam, -het, -dom,	**brottslighet, sjukdom**
-lek, -aktig, -mässig, -al, -ant,	**storlek, elegant**
-at, -ell, -era, -eri, -i,	**formell, kommentera**
-ik, -in, -ism, -ist, -it, -itet, -iär, -on,	**universitet**
-os, -tion, -s(s)ion, -är, -ör,	**kvalifikation, frisör**
-inna, -essa	**prinsessa**

Unstressed prefixes

be-, för-	**betala, förstå**
de-, in-, im-, inter-, kon-, ko-, pre-	**intressant**
syn-, sym-, trans-, a-, mono-	**syntes, monopol**

Unstressed suffixes

-ig, -lig, -(n)ing, -ande, -ende, -else	**sandig, parkering**
-are, -ast	**lärare, lättast**
-a (verb), -en (verb past participle)	**tala, skriven**
-or, -ar, -er (noun plural endings)	**flickor, bilar, parker**
-it (verb supine)	**sprungit**
-is, -isk, -iker, -re (comparative), -erst	**godis, tragisk**
-en (end article), -er (verb present)	**bilen, åker**

Accents

We saw above that compound words always have two stresses:

hus|nyckel	**central|lasarett**	**stor|stads|parti**
house key	central hospital	city party

When two stresses occur in one word, they take on a special tone pattern. This 'melody' is different in different parts of the country. In Central Sweden the voice goes down on the first stress and up on the last. It is this falling-rising melody that makes Swedes sound as if they are singing when they speak! It is generally called Accent 2.

↘ ↗	↘ ↗	↘ ↗	↘ ↗
hus|nyckel	**skol|bok**	**barn|mat**	**lokal|tåg**
house key	school book	baby food	local train

Quite a number of words other than compounds also have this melody when they are stressed. This means that the melody rises on an *unstressed* syllable after the stressed syllable, which is unusual in languages that have stress (you can hear it in English as spoken in Wales). Listen for this rise when you hear Swedes speak.

↘ ↗	↘ ↗	↘ ↗	↘↗	↘ ↗
gammal	**flicka**	**svenska**	**tala**	**stolar**
old	girl	Swedish	speak	chairs

The rise on the unstressed syllable makes the words sound Swedish, but often learners of Swedish make the mistake of thinking that every stressed word should have this word melody. Many words of two syllables do, it is true, but as many do *not*. These include words that have become two-syllable words because the definite ending (end article) **-en** or **-et** has been added to the noun. In fact, it is as if this ending were not part of the word. These words have only one rise (Accent 1).

↗	↗	↗
bil/en	**hus/et**	**barn/en**
the car	the house	the children

However, in the word

↘ ↗
flicka/n
the girl

which contained two syllables even before the **-n** was added (see above) the falling-rising tone remains.

Another syllable that does not permit the falling-rising tone is the present tense ending **-er**:

↗	↗	↗
skriv/er	**köp/er**	**läs/er**
write(s)	buy(s)	read(s)

These words only have a single rise (Accent 1). So you will be right most of the time if you use the falling-rising tone in two-syllable words with a stressed syllable, but remember that the definite ending and the present tense ending **-er** do not allow this.

Other words that end in **-er** (also in **-en** and **-el**) have to be learnt individually.

For now, learn to pronounce the words for 'sugar, water, bicycle' with Accent 1 (a single rise):

↗	↗	↗
socker	**vatten**	**cykel**

Words (other than compounds) where the stress comes on a syllable other than the first generally have Accent 1 as in the words for 'try, park, cigarettes'.

↗	↗	↗
försöka	**parkera**	**cigarretter**

Compounds, which we started with, always have a fall and a rise, whatever their lengths and shapes. Notice that there may be a long wait before the rise:

↘ ↗	↘ ↗
skrot|bilen	**smyg|läser**
the scrap car	reads secretly
↘_____↗	↘_______________↗
choklad|cigaretter	**Metall|industri|arbetar|förbundet**
chocolate cigarettes	Metal Workers' Union

This is because here the rise comes, not on the 'forbidden' syllables, but on the last part of the compound.

There are exceptions among compounds as well. But if you learn *not* to use Accent 2 (falling-rising) in the names of countries (e.g. **England, Sverige, Frankrike**), listen especially for how people pronounce names (e.g. **Svensson, Persson, Bergman**) and towns (e.g. **Visby, Karlstad,**

Delsbo), and use Accent 1 in the words **trädgård** (garden) and **verkstad** (workshop), then you will do nearly as well as any Swede any day of the week (**måndag, tisdag, onsdag, torsdag, fredag, lördag, söndag** also with Accent 1)!

1 Vem är det?

Who is it?

In this lesson we will look at:

- verbs in the present tense
- personal pronouns
- gender of nouns
- two types of question
- how to give short answers
- pronunciation of vowel sounds
- how to ask for things and say thanks
- how rarely Swedes use capital letters

Text 1

Vem är det?

Who is it?

Vem är det?	Who is it?
Det är Sven.	It's Sven.
Och vem är det?	And who is that?
Det är Rebecca.	It's Rebecca.
Är de på en fabrik?	Are they in a factory?
Nej, det är de inte.	No, they're not.
De är på en högskola.	They are at a university.
Vad gör Rebecca?	What's Rebecca doing?
Hon studerar.	She is studying.
Vad gör Sven?	What's Sven doing?
Han läser.	He's reading.

Äter han ett äpple?	Is he eating an apple?
Nej, han äter ett päron och en persika.	No, he's eating a pear and a peach.
Äter han en smörgås också?	Is he eating a sandwich too?
Ja, det gör han.	Yes, he is.
Är det en liten smörgås?	Is it a small sandwich?
Nej, det är en stor smörgås.	No, it's a large sandwich.
Han är hungrig.	He's hungry.

Some final consonants are dropped

Notice the following words in which the last consonant is not pronounced:

vad	what, *pron.* va	**är**	is/are, *pron.* e
det	it, *pron.* de	**och**	and, *pron.* å

Having dropped these particular final consonants, run the words together:

Det är en smörgås. It is a sandwich, *pron.* deensmörrgåss

Notice that **de** (they) is pronounced *dåmm* but **det** is pronounced *de*.

Notice also pronunciation of **gör** where the **g** sounds like an English 'y' or Swedish **j** (cf. **ja**): **Vad gör Rebecca?** (What is Rebecca doing?, va yer . . . ?)

Verbs and pronouns

Swedish verbs are the same throughout each tense and do not change for person or number:

Singular		*Plural*	
jag är	I am	**vi är**	we are
du är	you *(sing.)* are	**ni är**	you (*pl.*) are
han är	he is	**de är**	they are
hon är	she is		
den är	it is (with N-words – see below)		
det är	it is (with T-words – see below)		
man är	one is		

Pronunciation when stressed:

jag is pronounced ja
han is pronounced hann
hon is pronounced honn

man is pronounced mann
det is pronounced de
de is pronounced dåmm
(sometimes also written **dom**)

N-words and T-words

Swedes say **en fabrik** and **en smörgås**, but **ett päron.** The indefinite article, which corresponds to 'a(n)' in English, has two forms, **en** and **ett**. Nouns that take **en** have N-gender (also called non-neuter gender or **en**-gender), and nouns that take **ett** have T-gender (also called neuter gender or **ett**-gender). The gender, N or T, determines other grammatical forms we will look at later. Three-quarters of all nouns in Swedish are N-gender, as are most nouns describing people, higher animals, days and parts of the day. But nouns describing things may be of either gender, and their gender is unpredictable from their meaning. It is useful, therefore, to learn the gender (i.e. the indefinite article) with each noun. Later more clues will be learned to help you predict the gender. When the word 'it' **(den/det)** refers back to a noun already mentioned, then it must agree in gender:

Han äter *en* smörgås. *Den* är stor. — He is eating a sandwich. It's big.
Hon äter *ett* äpple. *Det* är stort. — She is eating an apple. It's big.

But if the gender is not known, or if the noun is given in the sentence, then **det** is used irrespective of gender:

Vem är *det*? *Det* är Rebecca. — Who is it? It's Rebecca.
Vad är *det*? *Det* är en smörgås. — What is it? It's a sandwhich.
***Det* är ett äpple.** — It's an apple.

Two types of question

Exactly as in English, there are two types of question. One simply changes the order of verb and subject around (inversion):

Statement	*Question*
Det är en liten pojke.	**Är det en liten pojke?**
It's a little boy.	Is it a little boy?

Hon har ett rum.	**Har hon ett rum?**
She has a room.	Has she a room?

These are called *yes/no questions* as the answer is often yes or no (Swedish **ja/nej**). The other kind of question also changes the order of subject and verb, but begins with an interrogative pronoun or *v-word* (most of them begin with a **v** in Swedish). These are called *v-questions:*

Vad	**är**	**det?**	**Vad**	**heter**	**du?**
What	is	it?	What	are	you called?
V-WORD	VERB	SUBJECT	V-WORD	VERB	SUBJECT
Vem	**är**	**det?**			
Who	is	it?			
V-WORD	VERB	SUBJECT			

Exercise 1

Translate into Swedish:

1 Is it a pear? 2 What's that? 3 It's a peach. 4 Has she got an apple? 5 Is it a university? 6 No, it's a factory. 7 It's an apple. 8 Is it Rebecca? 9 No, it's Sven. 10 Is he hungry?

Verbs – the present tense

Most verbs end in **-(e)r** in the present tense:

studera/r	studies, study, is studying	present tense in **-r**
komm/er	comes, come, is coming	present tense in **-er**
bo/r	lives, live, is living	present tense in **-r**
gör/	does, do, is doing	present tense in **-r**
ha/r	has, have, is having	present tense in **-r**
ät/er	eats, eat, is eating	present tense in **-er**
läs/er	reads, read, is reading	present tense in **-er**

The part of the verb to which the present tense ending and other endings are added is called the stem, i.e. **studera/, ät/, läs/.**

Gör is irregular in that its stem already ends in **-r**: **gör/**, so no extra **r** is added for the present tense.

Notice that there is no continuous tense in Swedish:

She is studying (= She studies).	**Hon studerar.**
What is he doing?	**Vad gör han?**

Exercise 2

Make these statements into yes/no questions:

1 De studerar. 2 Hon kommer. 3 Ni har ett päron. 4 Det är Sven. 5 Det är en stor högskola.

Exercise 3

Translate into Swedish:

1 They are reading. 2 We are studying. 3 She is living in (Swedish: i) Stockholm. 4 Are you (*sing.*) studying? 5 Are they coming?

Short answers

If someone asks you 'Is it a factory?', you may, of course, answer 'Yes, it's a factory' or you may give a short answer 'Yes, it is', or 'No, it isn't.' Notice how these are constructed in Swedish:

Yes, it is.	**Ja, det är det.**
No, it isn't.	**Nej, det är det inte.**
Are you hungry?	**Är du hungrig?**
Yes, I am.	**Ja, det är jag.**
No, I'm not.	**Nej, det är jag inte.**
Has he got a room?	**Har han ett rum?**
Yes, he has.	**Ja, det har han.**
No, he hasn't.	**Nej, det har han inte.**

Structure: **Ja/Nej, det** + verb + subject pronoun (+ **inte**).

If the verb in the question is not the verb 'to be' (**vara**), 'to have' (**ha**) or a modal verb (e.g. **ska, vill**) then the short answer uses a form of **göra**:

Talar du svenska?	**Ja, det gör jag.**
Do you speak Swedish?	Yes, I do.

Exercise 4

Translate into Swedish:

1 Yes, you are. 2 No, they're not. 3 Yes, I have. 4 No, she hasn't. 5 Yes, it is. 6 No, we haven't. 7 Yes, he is. 8 No, I'm not.

Pronunciation 1

Vowels

Practise saying the following pairs of words with long vowels. Do not worry about the meaning of the words.

A	–	Å	Å	–	O
bal		**bål**	**mås**		**mos**
bada		**båda**	**mån**		**mon**
gata		**gåta**	**båda**		**Boda**
hav		**håv**	**åk**		**ok**
tag		**tåg**	**rån**		**ron**
bas		**bås**	**tår**		**Tor**

I	–	Y	Y	–	U
bita		**byta**	**lys**		**lus**
Lisa		**lysa**	**tryta**		**truta**
silar		**sylar**	**tyr**		**tur**
ris		**rys**	**bryn**		**brun**
tider		**tyder**	**ytan**		**utan**

Dialogue 1

På kafeterian

In the café

A group of students are having a coffee break

SVEN: Jag skulle vilja ha en kopp kaffe och en bulle. Vill du också ha kaffe, Erik?

ERIK: Nej, tack. Jag tar en läsk och en ostsmörgås. Vad vill du ha, Nils?

MATTIAS: Har ni öl?

EXPEDITEN: Ja, lättöl har vi.

NILS: Kan jag få ett glas lättöl och en smörgås med ägg och ansjovis.

LISA: Vad kostar en skinksmörgås?

EXPEDITEN: Tjugo kronor.

LISA: Då tar jag en kopp te och en kaka.

CARINA: Jag tar också en kopp te, tack.
EXPEDITEN: *(tar in beställningen)* Varsågod!
ERIK: Tack så mycket!

Vocabulary

på, at, in
kafeteria -n -or, cafeteria, café
grupp -en -er, group
student -en -er, student
fika/ -r -de (*colloquial*), have a coffee break
skulle vilja ha, would like
vilja vill ville velat, want (to)
ha/ -r hade haft, have
kaffe -t, coffee
kopp -en -ar, cup
bulle -n -ar, bun
tack, please/thank you
också, also
ta/ -r tog, take
smörgås -en -ar, sandwich
läsk -en, soft drink
med, with
ostsmörgås -en -ar, cheese sandwich
öl -et, beer
lättöl -et, light beer
kan jag få, can I have
kunna kan kunde kunnat, can, be able
då, then
ägg -et -, egg
ansjovis -en -ar, anchovy
skinksmörgås -en -ar, ham sandwich
krona -n -or, *unit of currency* (100 öre = 1 krona)
glas -et -, glass
åtta, eight
kosta/ -r -de, cost
te -et, tea
kaka -n -or, cake
ta/ tar tog in, bring in
beställning -en -ar, order
varsågod, here you are
tack så mycket, thank you very much

Pronunciation: **med** (*pron.* me), **mycket** (*pron.* mycke)

Exercise 5

When looking for somewhere to eat you may see the sign **Servering** which generally means 'cafeteria'. For simple fare you can choose a **korvkiosk** which sells **varmkorv** among other things or a **gatukök** which may have a wider range, but you will probably have to stand outside. For a coffee or tea and a seat go to a **konditori (kondis, kafé** or **'fik'**) and for a meal choose a **restaurang**. Inside you may have to queue at the **självservering**. Remember to look at the **matsedel** first and to take your **bricka, tallrik, glas** and **bestick**. The best buy may be **dagens rätt** often **med smör, bröd, mjölk eller lättöl eller kaffe**. When you have collected your food you stop at the **kassa**. What must you not do under the sign **Rökning förbjuden**? Do not forget when leaving to go to the **Brickinlämning**.

Can you guess what these things are in English?

How to ask for things

Notice the different ways used in the dialogue for asking for things:

Har ni (du) . . . ?	Have you got . . . ?
Kan jag få . . . tack?	Can I have . . . please?
Jag skulle vilja ha . . .	I want . . .
Jag tar . . .	I will have *lit.* take . . .

Notice also:

Vad kostar . . . ?	What does . . . cost?

Varsågod! Tack!

There are many variations on the theme of **tack**, which means both 'thank you' and – at the end of a sentence – 'please'. Some of these are:

Kan jag få en kopp kaffe, tack?	Can I have a cup of coffee, please?
Tack, tack!	Thank you.
Tack så mycket!	Thank you very much.
Tack ska du ha!	Thank you so much.
Ja, tack. Nej, tack.	Yes, please. No, thank you.

Varsågod! like the German 'Bitte!' indicates that someone is giving you something, holding a door open, or otherwise expects you to do something.

Här har du kaffe. Varsågod!	Here's the coffee. Please help yourself!
Varsågod och stig in!	Do please come in!
Varsågod och sitt!	Please take a seat.

It can also be used impolitely in a demand:

Varsågod och gör som jag säger!	Do as I say!

Exercise 6

Ask politely in Swedish for: a ham sandwich and a glass of beer, a cup of tea and a bun, a cup of coffee and a cake, a cheese sandwich and a glass of beer. Say 'Here you are' and 'Thank you very much'.

No genitive 'of' with quantities

With quantities English has 'of', but Swedish has no genitive:

en kopp kaffe	a cup of coffee
ett glas vin	a glass of wine
en flaska öl	a bottle of beer
ett kilo ost	a kilo of cheese
en liter fil	a litre of yoghurt

Compound nouns

Two ways of saying the same thing are:

en smörgås med ost	**en ostsmörgås**
en smörgås med skinka	**en skinksmörgås**

Note: -a is dropped at the end of the first noun in the last example and similar cases

Factual text 1

Sverige

Sweden

Storbritannien är ett land, men det omfattar England, Skottland, Wales och Nordirland. I Sverige bor svenskar, och de talar mest svenska. I Storbritannien bor engelsmän, skottar, walesare och irländare, och de talar mest engelska. Sverige har en kung. Storbritannien har en drottning. Sveriges huvudstad heter Stockholm. Storbritanniens huvudstad heter London. Sverige är ett industriland. Storbritannien är också ett industriland. Sverige har mycket skog. Storbritannien har ganska lite skog. I Sverige har man ofta mycket snö på vintern.

I Storbritannien har man sällan mycket snö på vintern. I Sverige har man ibland sol på sommaren. I Storbritannien har man regn både på vintern och på sommaren!

Vocabulary

omfatta/ -r -de, comprise
svensk -en -ar, Swede
tala/ -r -de, speak
mest, mostly
svenska -n, Swedish (language)
drottning -en -ar, queen
huvudstad -en -städer, capital
kung -en -ar, king
het/a -er hette hetat, be called
mycket, a lot, much
skog -en -ar, forest
ganska, rather, quite
sällan, rarely, seldom
(en) sol, sun
ibland, sometimes
både . . . och . . ., both . . . and . . .

Exercise 7

Answer in Swedish (using, where applicable, short answers):

1 Är Sverige ett land? 2 Vad är Storbritannien? 3 Vad talar engelsmän? 4 Vad talar svenskar? 5 Har Sverige en kung? 6 Vad heter Sveriges huvudstad? 7 Är Sverige ett industriland? 8 Har Storbritannien mycket skog? 9 Har Sverige snö på vintern? 10 Har England snö på vintern? 11 Har man mycket sol i Storbritannien på sommaren?

Capital letters

Notice that small letters are used in Swedish in many cases where English has a capital:

- weekdays, months, festivals: **måndag** (Monday), **januari** (January), **midsommar** (Midsummer)

- nouns and adjectives denoting nationality, language, religion and political affiliation: **engelsman** (Englishman), **amerikan** (American), **svensk** (Swede), **katolik** (Catholic), **socialdemokrat** (Social Democrat)

- titles with names: **herr Ek** (Mr Ek), **doktor Lind** (Dr Lind)

2 Rebecca, en student

Rebecca, a student

In this lesson we will look at:

- verbs in the infinitive and present tense
- the gender of nouns and the articles
- time expressions
- straight and inverted word order
- numerals from 1 to 12
- the pronunciation of **g-**, **k-**, **sk-**
- how to say yes and no
- how to greet people
- word order in questions
- patterns in statements and questions
- a country in the north

Text 2

Rebecca, en student

Rebecca, a student

Rebecca är student. Hon är nitton år och kommer från England. Hon läser svenska på universitetet i London, men just nu bor hon i Stockholm. Hon har en lägenhet på Flöjtvägen i Rinkeby. På morgonen åker hon tunnelbana till universitetet. Vad gör hon där? Hon går på en föreläsning eller sitter på biblioteket och antecknar. Ibland skriver hon en uppsats eller gör en översättning. Ofta börjar hon redan klockan åtta på morgonen. Rebecca hatar väckarklockan. Den ringer klockan sex.

Vocabulary

en, a, an (with N-words)
student -en -er, student
hon, she
är, is/are
nitton, nineteen
år -et -, year
komma, kommer, kom, come
från, from
läs/a -er -te, read, study
universitet -et -, university
men, but
just nu, at present
bo/ -r -dde, live
lägenhet -en -er, flat
på morgonen (*pron.* morronnen), in the morning
åk/a -er -te, travel (by)
tunnelbana -n, tube, underground
till, to
gör/a gör gjorde gjort, do, make
där, there
gå/ -r gick på, go to
föreläsning -en -ar, lecture
eller, or
sitt/a -er satt, sit
bibliotek -et -, library
anteckna/ -r -de, make notes
skriv/a -er skrev, write
ibland, sometimes
uppsats -en -er, essay
översättning -en -ar, translation
börja/ -r -de, begin
redan, as early as
klockan åtta, at eight o'clock
hata/ -r -de, hate
väckarklocka -n -or, alarm clock
den, it
ring/a -er -de, ring
sex, six

Verbs, present and infinitive

As has been shown in Lesson 1, in the present tense Swedish verbs nearly always end in **-r**. All regular verbs end in **-r** or **-er** throughout the present tense:

When the stem ends in a vowel the verb adds **+r**:
börja/r (begins), **gå/r** (goes), **bo/r** (lives).

When the stem ends in a consonant the verb adds **+er**:
åk/er (travels), **skriv/er** (writes).

Regular infinitive forms end either in **-a** or another vowel:
börja/ (to begin), **åk/a** (to travel), **läs/a** (to read), **bo/** (to live).

Notice the irregular infinitive of the verb **vara** (to be), present tense **är**, and the irregular present tense of **gör/a** (to do, make), i.e. **gör/**, which already has **-r** in the stem.

Rebecca's route to the University on the Stockholm Metro

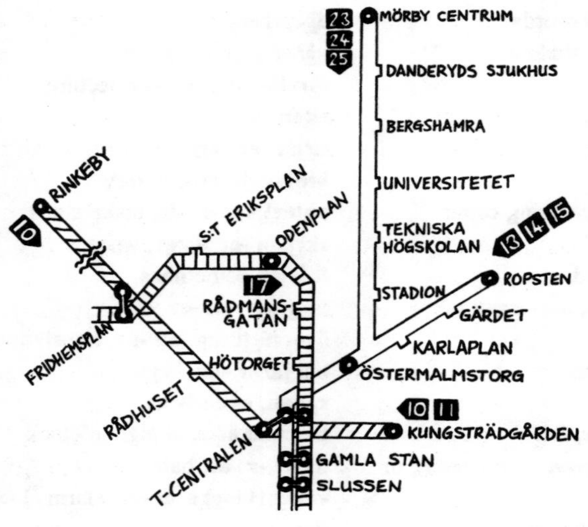

Exercise 1

Fill in the missing verb forms:

Infinitive	*Present tense*	*Infinitive*	*Present tense*
. . .	**har**	**komma**	. . .
. . .	**läser**	**heta**	. . .
. . .	**hatar**	**åka**	. . .
. . .	**gör**	**skriva**	. . .

Exercise 2

What is the Swedish for:

1 He's reading. 2 He's a student. 3 They're travelling. 4 We live in Stockholm. 5 I live in England. 6 I'm travelling to London. 7 We have a flat. 8 I'm studying Swedish. 9 They come from London. 10 The alarm clock rings at eight o'clock. 11 She starts at six o'clock in the morning. 12 They hate the alarm clock.

Nouns, gender and articles

The indefinite articles (English 'a', 'an') are **en** (with N-words) or **ett** (with T-words):

***en* student**	*a* student	***ett* år**	*a* year
***en* lägenhet**	*a* flat	***ett* universitet**	*a* university

To say 'the flat', 'the year' add the definite article **-en** or **-et** (*Note*: one **t**!) to the end of the noun. It is, therefore, known as the *end article*.

lägenhet*en*	*the* flat	**år*et***	*the* year

Notice that if the noun ends in a vowel the end article added is **-n** or **-t**:

en tunnelbana	a tube	**ett schema**	a timetable
tunnelbana*n*	the tube	**schema*t***	the timetable

No article is used before nouns denoting a person's nationality, occupation, religious or political affiliation:

Nils är lärare.	Nils is a teacher.
Olof är svensk.	Olof is a Swede.
Anders är katolik.	Anders is a Catholic.
Eva är socialdemokrat.	Eva is a Social Democrat.

This applies to all nouns referring to a person or object representing a class or group:

Har du bil?	Have you got a car?

But an article *is* used in cases where the noun is qualified, i.e. made more precise:

Han är en god katolik/ en duktig lärare.	He is a good Catholic/ a good teacher.
Han har en ny bil.	He has a new car.

Exercise 3

Fill in the missing forms of the nouns:

Indefinite	*Form with end article*	*Indefinite*	*Form with end article*
en uppsats	...	...	**fabriken**
en lägenhet	...	...	**bullen**
ett land	...	...	**året**
en dag	...	...	**skinkan**
ett äpple	...	...	**pojken**
en flicka	...	...	**industrin**
en kaka	...	...	**tunnelbanan**
ett kilo	...	...	**klockan**
en kopp	...	...	**vinet**

Time expressions

på morgonen (*pron.* mo<u>rr</u>onnen)	in the morning(s)
på eftermiddagen (*pron.* eftermi<u>dd</u>ann)	in the afternoon(s)
på kvällen	in the evening(s)
på natten	during the night
klockan åtta	at eight o'clock

(No preposition is used in Swedish before clock times.)

Word order, straight and inverted

Compare the following statements:

Front	*Verb*	*(Subject)*	*etc.*
(a) **Hon**	**bor**	–	**i London.**
(b) **Just nu**	**bor**	**hon**	**i Stockholm.**
(c) **På morgonen**	**åker**	**hon**	**till universitetet.**
(d) **Ofta**	**börjar**	**hon**	**klockan åtta.**

If the sentence begins with the subject (as in (a)) this is called *straight word order,* i.e. subject – verb. If it begins with a non-subject (as in (b), (c), (d)) the subject is placed immediately after the verb and this is called *inverted word order.* The most common non-subjects beginning the sentence are expressions of time and place (as in (b), (c)). English also begins sentences with non-subjects, but does not invert after them:

Often she	begins	at 8 o'clock.
SUBJ	VERB	

Exercise 4

Translate the following statements into Swedish:

1 She comes from England. 2 Often she travels to Stockholm. 3 She travels by tube. 4 In the mornings she studies Swedish. 5 Just now she is at the university. 6 She is beginning just now. 7 Sometimes she sits in the library. 8 At 8 o'clock she takes the tube. 9 At six o'clock the alarm clock rings.

Numerals (1–12)

0 **noll**		
1 **en, ett***	5 **fem**	9 **nio** (*pron.* *niə*)
2 **två**	6 **sex**	10 **tio** (*pron.* *tiə*)
3 **tre**	7 **sju**	11 **elva**
4 **fyra**	8 **åtta**	12 **tolv**

Note*: Because of the two genders. When counting: **ett, två, tre . . .

Pronunciation 2

Consonants g-, k-, sk-

Practise saying the following words, all personal names and place names.

'soft' g-
place names: **Gerum, Gislaved, Gyttorp, Gäddede, Göteborg**
personal names: **Gert, Gösta, Göran**

'hard' g-
place names: **Gamleby, Godby, Gubbängen, Gåsholm, Grimstad**
personal names: **Gottfrid, Gustav, Gudrun, Greta**

'soft' k-
place names: **Kedjeåsen, Kivik, Kyrkhult, Källvik, Kölby**
personal name: **Kerstin**

'hard' k-
place names: **Kalmar, Kolmården, Kumla, Kållered**
personal names: **Karin, Konrad, Kurt, Kåre, Kristina**

'soft' sk-
place names: **Skeppsvik, Skillingaryd, Skyttorp, Skänninge, Skövde**

'hard' sk-
place names: **Skara, Skogby, Skurup, Skånela**

Dialogue 2

Ett möte på universitetet

A meeting at the university

Sven asks Rebecca about herself

SVEN: Hej, Sven heter jag.
REBECCA: Hej.
SVEN: Vad läser du?
REBECCA: Jag läser svenska.
SVEN: Jaså. Du är inte svensk, va?
REBECCA: Nej, jag kommer från England.
SVEN: Men du förstår väl svenska?
REBECCA: Ja visst, lite grann. Jag studerar svenska i London.
SVEN: Jaså. Varifrån i England kommer du?
REBECCA: Bradford.
SVEN: Men nu bor du i Stockholm, eller hur?
REBECCA: Ja.
SVEN: Var i Stockholm?
REBECCA: Jag bor i Rinkeby.
SVEN: Jaha. Vad heter du förresten?
REBECCA: Rebecca Wood.
SVEN: Varför sitter du egentligen här, Rebecca?
REBECCA Jag pratar ju med dig.

Vocabulary

möte -t -n, meeting
hej, hello
va, *lit.* what
förstå/ -r förstod, understand
ja visst, of course
lite grann, a little, a bit
studera/ -r -de, study
jaså, oh, really
nej, no
varifrån, where . . . from?
eller hur *here:* don't you (cf. French 'n'est-ce pas?')
ja, yes
var, where?
jaha, I see
förresten, by the way, incidentally
egentligen, actually
här, here
prata/ -r -de, talk
ju, of course (see p.125)
dig (*pron.* dej), you (*object*)

Yes, no

There are a number of words for agreement and disagreement in the dialogue:

ja	yes
nej	no
javisst	yes, of course (stronger agreement)
jaså	oh really/I see/you don't say (registers surprise)
jaha	oh really (registers merely that you are listening)

Note also:

jo	yes (answering a negative question; cf. French 'si'):

Läser du inte svenska?	Don't you study Swedish?
Jo, det gör jag!	Yes, I do!

Greetings

Hej 'Hello', 'Hi there' is the usual friendly greeting. **Goddag** (*pron.* godda) 'How do you do?' or 'Good morning' etc. is the formal equivalent. On parting, use **hej då, hej, hej,** or **hej så länge** 'Bye for now', 'Be seeing you'. **Adjö** (*pron.* ajö) 'Goodbye' is the formal equivalent.

V-words (interrogatives)

Some v-words, or interrogative pronouns, are found in the dialogue:

vad? (*pron.* va)	what?
varifrån?	where . . . from?
var . . . ifrån?	where . . . from?

Others are:

var?	where?
vem?	who?

Notice also the following interrogatives, without **v-**:

hur?	how?
när?	when?

Word order in questions

The two types of question both have inverted (i.e. verb – subject) word order. Notice the difference however:

yes/no questions (to which the answer is **ja/nej**):

Verb	*Subject*	
Är	**du**	**student?**
Läser	**du**	**svenska?**

In yes/no questions the verb comes at the beginning. Notice that in English questions often involve 'do' or 'does', while Swedish requires only a simple verb form:

Do you read Swedish?	**Läser du svenska?**
Does she live in Stockholm?	**Bor hon i Stockholm?**

v-questions (using a v-word):

Front	*Verb*	*Subject*
Var	**bor**	**du?**
Vad	**gör**	**du?**
Varifrån	**kommer**	**du?**

In v-questions the v-word comes at the beginning.

Patterns in statements and questions

Statements and questions fit into a pattern for the sentence, which will help you to create Swedish sentences with accurate word order:

Sentence type:	*Front*	*Verb*	*(Subject)*	*etc.*
Statements				
Straight	**Hon** SUBJECT	**bor**	–	**i Stockholm.**
Inverted	**Nu**	**bor**	**hon**	**i Stockholm.**
V-questions				
Inverted	**Var** V-WORD	**bor**	**hon?**	
Yes/no questions				
Inverted		**Bor**	**hon**	**i Stockholm?**
Commands				
		Skriv	–	**till henne!**

Note: 1 In statements and v-questions the verb comes second after either a subject or a non-subject.
2 In yes/no questions the verb comes first and is not preceded by a subject or non-subject.

Exercise 5

Translate the following questions into Swedish:

1 Are they reading? 2 Do they live in Stockholm? 3 Do you understand? 4 What are they called? 5 Where are you staying? 6 What are you reading? 7 What are they doing? 8 Where does he come from? 9 Who is she? 10 When are they coming? 11 Are you speaking to Rebecca? 12 Is she reading? 13 Does he understand Swedish?

Exercise 6

Complete your part of the following conversation:

BJÖRN: Hej! DU: . . .
BJÖRN: Vad heter du? DU: . . .

BJÖRN: Vad studerar du? DU: . . .
BJÖRN: Hur gammal (='old') är du? DU: . . .
BJÖRN: Var kommer du ifrån? DU: . . .
BJÖRN: Och var bor du? DU: . . .

Factual text 2

Ett land i norr

A country in the north

Sverige ligger i Norden, som är en del av norra Europa. Andra nordiska länder är Norge, Finland, Danmark, Island och Färöarna. Sverige har bara 8,75 miljoner invånare, men det är till ytan ett mycket stort land, två och en halv gånger så stort som Storbritannien. Det är mycket stora skillnader mellan norr och söder. I Norrland, som hela den norra delen av Sverige heter, bor mycket få människor, bland dem många samer och finnar. 75% av alla svenskar bor i städer och byar med mer än 200 invånare. Stora städer är Stockholm (700 000), Göteborg (450 000) och Malmö (250 000). De ligger i södra och mellersta Sverige. Sverige är ett långt och smalt land. I norr kan man se midnattssolen varje sommar, men på vintern är det mörkt här nästan hela dagen och mycket kallt. Häruppe kan man se järvar, björnar och vargar. I söder är klimatet mildare och vegetationen rikare. Sverige har glaciärer i norr och höga fjäll - det högsta berget, Kebnekajse, är 2117 meter - men landet ligger mest under 300 meter. Här finns många älvar och sjöar – bland dem tre av Europas största – Vänern, Vättern och Mälaren. Sverige är också ett skogsland – över 50% av landet är täckt av skog. Många turister tycker att det är ett vackert land.

Vocabulary

Färöarna, the Faroes
ligg/a -er låg, be (lie)
Norden, Scandinavia
bara, only
invånare -n -, inhabitant
till ytan, in area
stor -t -a, big
gång -en -er, time
skillnad -en -er, difference
mellan, between
som, which, that
del -en -ar, part
få, few
människa -n -or, person, people

bland, among
same -n -r, Lapp, Sami
by -n -ar, village
mellersta, central
smal -t -a, narrow
varje, every
mörk -t -a, dark
nästen hela dagen, almost all day
järv -en -ar, wolverine
björn -en -ar, bear
varg -en -ar, wolf
mildare, milder
rikare, richer
fjäll -et -, mountain, fell
högst -a, highest
berg -et -, mountain
älv -en -ar, river
sjö -n -ar, lake
största, biggest
täckt av, covered with
tyck/a -er -te, think, consider
vacker -t vackra, beautiful

Exercise 7

Sätt ett kryss i rutan: (Place a cross in the box)	**rätt** (*right*)	**fel** (*wrong*)
Sverige har 700 000 invånare.	☐	☐
England är två och ett halvt gånger så stort som Sverige.	☐	☐
Göteborg och Malmö ligger i södra Sverige.	☐	☐
Den norra delen av Sverige heter Norrland.	☐	☐
Alla svenskar bor i städer och byar.	☐	☐
Sverige ligger i södra Europa.	☐	☐
I norr kan man se midnattssolen varje sommar.	☐	☐
Det finns många älvar och sjöar i landet.	☐	☐
Vänern heter en av Europas största sjöar.	☐	☐
Kebnekajse är 200 meter högt.	☐	☐

Sweden - major towns and regions

3 Att resa

Travelling

In this lesson we will look at :

- adverbs and their position in the sentence
- the **s**-genitive
- days of the week and parts of the day
- numerals from 13 to 1,000
- the negatives **inte, ej, icke**
- how to pronounce **sj-, stj-, skj-, sch-, -si-, -ti-, tj-, kj-**
- time by the clock
- verbs for motion and travel
- two-verb constructions
- communications in Sweden

Text 3

Att resa

Travelling

Bill Morris är representant för en engelsk firma som tillverkar plasthandtag. Bill säljer firmans produkter utomlands. Han reser ofta till Skandinavien i affärer. Nu är det måndag morgon och Bill ska iväg till Stockholm. Först tar han tunnelbanan till flygplatsen Heathrow utanför London. Den ligger nästan en timme från stadens centrum. Sedan flyger han direkt till Arlanda, Stockholms flygplats. Med flyg tar resan England – Sverige bara två timmar. Bill kommer till Stockholm på morgonen. Men hans väska kommer inte. Redan klockan halv fyra på eftermiddagen träffar Bill representanter för ett svenskt företag. Företaget köper ofta av Bill. Efteråt tar han in på ett hotell på

Vasagatan. På kvällen går Bill inte på restaurang för väskan med hans kläder är fortfarande i Köpenhamn!

Vocabulary

representant -en -er, representative
engelsk -t -a, English
firma -n -or, firm
tillverka/ -r -de, manufacture, produce
plasthandtag -et -, plastic handle
sälj/a -er sålde sålt, sell
produkt -en -er, products
utomlands, abroad
res/a -er -te, travel
Skandinavien, Scandinavia
i affärer, on business
nu, now
måndag -en -ar, Monday
ska(ll) iväg till, is off to
skola ska(ll) skulle skolat, shall, will
först, first
flygplats -en -er, airport
utanför, outside
timme -n -ar, hour
centrum, town centre
sedan (*usually pron.* sen), then, after that
flyg/a -er flög, fly
direkt, direct
med flyg, by air
resa -n -or, journey
hans, his
väska -n -or, suitcase
klockan halv fyra, at half past three
träffa/ -r -de, meet
företag -et -, company
köp/a -er -te, buy
ofta, often
av, *here*: from
efteråt, afterwards
ta/ -r tog tagit in på, book into, put up at
hotell -et -, hotel
restaurang -en -er, restaurant
för, because, for
kläder -na, clothes
fortfarande, still
Köpenhamn, Copenhagen

Pronunciation

Remember: **det** (*pron.* de), **de** (*pron.* dåm), **till** (*pron.* ti), **med** (*pron.* me), **sedan** (*pron.* sen), **dagen** (*pron.* dan: sometimes also written **dan**), **måndagen** (*pron.* månndan), **eftermiddagen** (*pron.* eftermiddan). In older texts **ska** is written **skall**.

Adverbs

Words like **alltid** (always), **ofta** (often), **inte** (not), **aldrig** (never), **sällan** (seldom) are adverbs of a kind that influence the meaning of the entire clause or sentence. In English such words may go either before or after the first verb (VERB1):

Bill never takes a taxi. — ADV VERB1
Bill can never take a taxi. — VERB1 ADV

In Swedish main clauses they always go directly *after* VERB1:

Bill tar aldrig taxi. — VERB1 ADV
Bill kan aldrig ta taxi. — VERB1 ADV

Exercise 1

Make the following statements negative by inserting **inte.**

1 Det är ett företag. 2 Hon bor i Stockholm. 3 Hon heter Maria. 4 De studerar svenska. 5 Jag tar kaffe. 6 Jag vill ha en kopp te. 7 Vi träffar representanter. 8 Han åker buss. 9 Han bor där.

Exercise 2

What is the Swedish for:

1 He never travels abroad. 2 He often takes the tube. 3 He always takes a taxi. 4 It always takes an hour. 5 They never buy plastic handles from Bill. 6 He doesn't fly to Sweden. 7 They don't manufacture plastic handles. 8 He doesn't take the tube to Arlanda. 9 It takes almost two hours to Copenhagen by air. 10 He always puts up at a hotel.

Position of adverbs in the sentence

Adverbs can now be added to the pattern for the Swedish sentence:

Front	*Verb₁*	*(Subject)*	*Adverb*	*etc.*
1 **Han**	**tar**	–	**aldrig**	**taxi.**
2 **Bill**	**reser**	–	**ofta**	**inom Norden.**
3 **De**	**köper**	–	**sällan**	**kläder.**
4 **På kvällen**	**går**	**han**	**alltid**	**på restaurang.**

Notice that in the statement in example 4, where the verb and subject are inverted, the adverb comes *directly after* the subject. This happens in questions too:

Åker du inte till Oslo? V S ADV	Aren't you travelling to Oslo?
Dricker du aldrig kaffe? V S ADV	Do you never drink coffee?

On occasions there may be more than one adverb:

Han tar ju aldrig taxi. V ADV_1 ADV_2	He never takes a taxi, of course.

Exercise 3

Insert the negative **inte** in the following questions.

1 Har man tunnelbana i Bradford? 2 Kommer ni från England? 3 Är du svensk? 4 Börjar vi klockan åtta? 5 Läser hon svenska? 6 Förstår de engelska? 7 Bor du i staden? 8 Åker vi buss? 9 Ligger stationen i centrum?

The s-genitive

Like English, Swedish often adds an **-s** to the noun to indicate the genitive:

Sveriges huvudstad	Sweden's capital, the capital of Sweden
firmans produkter	the firm's products
Bills resa	Bill's journey
stadens centrum	the centre of (the) town
Mattias' far	Mattias's father

From these examples we can see that:

(a) There is no apostrophe with the **s** in Swedish.
(b) **s**-genitives in Swedish often correspond to English 'of' genitives.
(c) The genitive **s** is added after the end article in Swedish.
(d) A noun following a noun with an **s**-genitive *never* takes an end article:
firma*ns* representanter *the* representatives of the firm
(e) Words already ending in **-s** often add an apostrophe instead of an **-s**.

Exercise 4

Translate into Swedish:

1 the firm's products 2 London's airport 3 an hour's journey 4 the representatives of the company 5 the student's flat 6 the university of Stockholm 7 the girl's essay

Days of the week and parts of the day

Days of the week (**veckodagar**):

söndag, måndag, tisdag, onsdag, torsdag, fredag, lördag
(*pron.* sönnda, månnda, tista, onsta, torsta, freda, lörda)
Notice that Swedish does not use capital letters.

Other useful expressions:

på måndag	on Monday (next)
i måndags (*pron.* månndass)	last Monday
nästa måndag	on Monday (next)
vecka -n -or	week
månad -en -er	month
år -et -	year
nästa månad/år	next month/year

Parts of the day:

morgon -en morgnar	morning
kväll -en -ar	evening
förmiddag -en -ar	later morning
afton -en aftnar	early evening
eftermiddag -en -ar	afternoon
natt -en nätter	night
ett dygn	a day and a night

Others:

i morse	(earlier) this morning
igår	yesterday
idag (*pron.* ida)	today
imorgon (*pron.* imorron)	tomorrow
imorgon bitti	tomorrow morning (early)
imorgon eftermiddag (*pron.* imorron eftermidda)	tomorrow afternoon

på morgonen	in the morning
på eftermiddagen	in the afternoon

Numerals (13–1,000)

13	**tretton**	30	**tretti(o)**
14	**fjorton** (*pron.* fjoton*)	40	**fyrti(o)** (*pron.* fötti*)
15	**femton**	50	**femti(o)**
16	**sexton**	60	**sexti(o)**
17	**sjutton**	70	**sjutti(o)**
18	**arton***	80	**åtti(o)**
19	**nitton**	90	**nitti(o)**
20	**tjugo** (*pron.* tjugo/tjugə/ tjugu/tjugi)	100	**(ett) hundra**
		156	**hundrafemtiosex**
21	**tjugoett** (*pron.* tjuguett/tjuett)	200	**tvåhundra**
25	**tjugofem**	1000	**(ett) tusen** (no comma)

Note*: Remember pronunciation of **-rt (see p.11)

Pronunciation 3

Consonants sj-, stj-, skj-, sch-, -si-, -ti-; tj-, kj-

Practise saying the following words containing the sounds indicated which are all pronounced the same as 'soft' sk- (see Pronunciation 2):

sj-	place names:	**Sjukarby, Själevad, Sjötorp**
	others:	**sjabbig, sjal, sjok, sjunde, sjuk, sjåp, själ, själv, sjöman**
stj-	place name:	**Stjärnholm**
	others:	**stjälk, stjärt**
skj-		**skjul, skjuta**
sch-		**schack, schas, schimpans, schlager, schottis, schäfer**
-si-		**division, explosion, fusion, pension**
-ti-		**produktion, inspektion, station, operation**

Practise saying the following words containing the sounds indicated which are pronounced the same as 'soft' **k-** (see Pronunciation 2):

tj- **tjej, tjock, tjäna, tjugo, tjata**
kj- **kjol**

The train timetable for Bill's journey to Oslo

70 Stockholm–Hallsberg–Karlstad–Oslo tab 61
12 juni 1995 – 7 jan 1996

Tågnummer 51 IN		
Period		23/10-7/1
Måndag-Fredag		M-F
Lördag		L
Sön- o Helgdag		SoH
fr **Stockholm C**	G	7.36
fr SthlmSyd Fl.berg	G	7.47
fr Södertälje Syd	G	8.00
fr Flen		|
fr Katrineholm C	G	8.53
t **Hallsberg**		9.25
fr Örebro C 64		*9.00*
fr **Hallsberg** G		9.30
t Degerfors C		10.05
fr Degerfors C	G	10.06
t Kristinehamn		10.22
fr Kristinehamn	G	10.24
t **Karlstad C**		10.48
fr Karlstad C G		10.55
t Kil		11.08
fr Kil		11.10
t **Arvika**		11.45
fr **Arvika**		11.47
t **Charlottenberg**		12.12
fr **Charlottenberg**		12.15
t Kongsvinger		12.42
t Liljestrøm		13.45
t **Oslo S**		14.05

Reslustkort ger **Rött Pris** på **Röda avgångar:**
G L, SoH, dock ej 24/6, 24/12,25/12,31/12

Dialogue 3

På Statens Järnvägar

On Swedish Railways

Bill is travelling by train to Oslo

BILL: Kan jag få en enkel till Oslo?
EXPEDITEN: Man måste ha sittplatsbiljett. När vill du åka?
BILL: Sju och trettiosex imorgon bitti. Eller finns det någon röd avgång förresten?
EXPEDITEN: Nej, röda avgångar till Oslo har vi bara på lördagar och söndagar tyvärr.
BILL: Vad synd, men då får jag väl ta sju-tåget då.
EXPEDITEN: Rökare eller icke-rökare?
BILL: Icke-rökare, tack.
EXPEDITEN: Då blir det 559 (femhundrafemtionio) kronor.
BILL: Går det bra med kort?
EXPEDITEN: Ja, då. Skriv här.
BILL: Vilket spår går tåget från?
EXPEDITEN: Det står på tavlan därborta. Spår tolv, tror jag.
BILL: Tack så mycket!

(*On the train*)
BILL: Förlåt! Vilken plats har jag?
KONDUKTÖREN: Det står här på biljetten. Vagn 65 (sextifem), plats 37 (trettisju). Det är längre fram i tåget. Du ska till Oslo. Byte i Hallsberg.
BILL: Och finns det restaurangvagn på tåget?
KONDUKTÖREN: Det gör det. Den är längre bak i tåget.
BILL: När kommer vi till Hallsberg?
KONDUKTÖREN: Kl 09.25. (nio och tjugofem)
BILL: Och när är vi framme i Oslo?
KONDUKTÖREN: Kl 14.05. (fjorton noll fem)
BILL: Tack för hjälpen!

Vocabulary

biljettlucka -n -or, ticket window

enkel, single (cf. **tur och retur** = return)

röd avgång, cheap rate (*lit.* red departure)
tyvärr, unfortunately
vad synd!, what a pity!
sittplatsbiljett -en -er, seat reservation
sjutåget, the seven o'clock train
rökare, smoker
icke-rökare, non-smoker
hur länge . . .?, how long . . .?
gäll/a -er -de, be valid, apply
lågpris, low price
bli/ -r blev blivit, be, become
kort -et -, (credit) card
vilken vilket vilka, which (*often pron.* vicken, vicket, vicka)
spår -et -, platform (*lit.* track)
tåg -et -, train
tavla -n -or, (notice)board
konduktör -en -er, ticket collector, guard
plats -en -er, place (*here*: seat)
stå/ -r stod stått, stand (*here*: be written)
biljett -en -er, ticket
vagn -en -ar, carriage
restaurangvagn -en -ar, restaurant car
längre fram, further on, forwards
längre bak, further back
ska till, is going to
byte, change
är framme (see p.106), arrive
hjälp-en (*pron.* jälp), help

Exercise 5

At the **järnvägsstation** Bill looks for the list of **Avgående tåg**. On the **plattform** he asks another passenger if this is the **tåg mot Oslo**. Then he looks at the sign showing **Var i tåget står vagnen** but he doesn't really understand this and has to ask the conductor on the train where he should sit. On his travels he may need to leave his **bagage** (*pron.* bagaasj) at the **effektförvaring**. On his train the ticket collector may well ask for **samtliga biljetter** or, for example, for the tickets of **nypåstigna i Hallsberg**.

Can you guess what these are in English?

Inte, ej, icke

There are three negatives in Swedish.

Inte is by far the most common word for 'not' in spoken and written language:

Jag röker inte.	I don't smoke.
Katarina dricker inte öl.	Katarina doesn't drink beer.

Ej is often found on signs:

Ej rökning.	No smoking.
Ej ingång.	No entrance.
Ej upp (ned).	Not up (down). (on escalators)

Icke is often found in compounds:

icke-rökare	non-smoker
icke-våld	non-violence
icke-kristen	non-Christian

Time by the clock

Notice the following expressions:

klockan nio	(at) nine o'clock
halv nio	half past eight
åtta och tretti	half past eight
kvart i nio	quarter to nine
kvart över nio	quarter past nine
tjugo minuter i nio	twenty (minutes) to nine
tjugo minuter över nio	twenty (minutes) past nine
fem minuter i halv nio	twenty-five past eight
fem minuter över halv nio	twenty-five to nine
midnatt	midnight
fm = förmiddag	a.m.
em = eftermiddag	p.m.
Hur mycket är klockan?	What is the time?
Klockan (Hon. Den) är tio.	It is ten o'clock.
Hur dags . . .? (*pron.* hurdakks)	What time . . .?

Official notices use the 24-hour clock:

13.25 = **tretton och tjugofem** = **tjugofem minuter över ett**
= **fem i halv två**

Exercise 6

Translate into Swedish:

1 eleven o'clock 2 half past three 3 quarter to seven 4 twenty-five past eight 5 It is five o'clock. 6 quarter past two 7 five minutes to twelve 8 23.25 9 What time does Bill fly to London?

Verbs for motion and travel

The usual verb meaning 'go' or 'travel' is **åk/a -er -te**:

Hon åker	**tåg.**	She's going by	train.
Hon åker	**buss.**	She's going by	bus.
Hon åker	**båt.**	She's going by	boat.
Hon åker	**tunnelbana.**	She's going by	tube.
Hon åker	**bil.**	She's going by	car.
Hon åker	**skidor.**	She's skiing.	
Hon åker	**skridskor.**	She's skating.	

Notice also:

Hon tar tåget *etc.*	She's taking the train *etc.*
Det tar två timmar med flyg.	It takes two hours by air.

res/a -er -te often indicates long distance or foreign travel:

Han reser utomlands.	He travels abroad.
Hon reser för firman.	She travels for the firm.

gå/ -r gick gått is a 'false friend' with very specific uses, primarily 'to walk':

Vi går till staden.	We walk to town.
Jag måste tyvärr gå nu.	Unfortunately I have to leave now.
Olle går ofta på bio på kvällen.	Olle often goes to the cinema in the evening.

Sometimes, when there is a modal verb with an expression indicating direction no second verb is needed:

Bill ska till Stockholm.	=	**Bill ska resa till Stockholm.**
Vi måste hem nu.	=	**Vi måste åka (gå) hem nu.**

Two-verb constructions

When, as in the dialogue above, two verbs are used together, VERB$_1$ is often a modal verb like **kan** (can, am able), **måste** (must, have to), or

ska (shall, will). Modals are different in that most of them do not have a present tense ending in **-r**. VERB$_2$ is then an infinitive:

Kan jag få en enkel till Lund? Can I have a single to Lund?
VERB$_1$ VERB$_2$

Other modals:

Man måste ha sittplatsbiljett. You must have a seat reservation.
VERB$_1$ VERB$_2$

Ska det vara icke-rökare? Would you like non-smoking?
VERB$_1$ VERB$_2$

Like modals go several other verbs with a similar function:

När tänker du åka? When are you thinking of travelling?
VERB$_1$ VERB$_2$

If the verbs are added to the pattern for the sentence, then the pattern looks like this:

Front	*Verb$_1$*	*(Subject)*	*Adverb*	*Verb$_2$*	*etc.*
Man	**måste**	—	**alltid**	**ha**	**biljett.**
När	**tänker**	**du**	—	**åka?**	
	Kan	**jag**	—	**få**	**en enkel till Lund?**
Vi	**är**	—	**ju**	—	**framme kl 13.25.**

Exercise 7

Make the following into two-verb constructions in the correct tenses (VERB$_1$ in present, VERB$_2$ in infinitive):

1 Jag (ska) (åker) till London imorgon. 2 Bill (tänker) (fortsätter = *continue*) till Oslo. 3 (Måste) det (är) icke-rökare? 4 (Kan) jag (får) en enkel till Märsta, tack? 5 Vi (ska) (köper) kaffe imorgon. 6 Du (måste) (studerar) idag. 7 (Vill) du (kommer) till Sverige?

Factual text 3

Sverige̲s kommunikationer

Communications in Sweden

Sverige är ett mycket stort land, med väldiga avstånd mellan olika landsdelar. Bilar dominerar som transportmedel. Det finns nära 3 miljoner bilar i landet. Vägarna är bra, och svenskarna kör för det mesta försiktigt. Det händer mycket få olyckor trots en snabb ökning av privatbilismen de senaste åren.

På 1970-talet gick bensinpriset upp kraftigt, och på 1980-talet började SJ med låga biljettpriser. Numera är tåg med billigare priser utmärkta med rött i tidtabellerna (så kallade röda avgångar). Man tar antingen intercitytåg, expresståg eller lokaltåg. Tågen är stora och rymliga men oftast inte lika snabba som engelska eller franska tåg. Ett nytt expresståg, X2000, går mellan vissa städer.

I Stockholm med omgivning har SL (Storstockholms lokaltrafik) både bussar, tunnelbanetåg och pendeltåg. Många som arbetar i affärer och på kontor i centrum pendlar med T-banan eftersom det är svårt att köra bil där. Det är också relativt billigt att köpa SLs månadskort som gäller både buss, tunnelbana och pendeltåg. I södra Sverige går också billiga lokaltåg – de så kallade 'pågatågen' – mellan olika städer och byar i västra Skåne. Spårvagnar finns kvar numera endast i Göteborg och Norrköping. Ute på landet måste man ofta åka landsvägsbuss, eftersom många små järnvägar inte finns kvar längre. Efter långa diskussioner har Sverige och Danmark beslutat bygga en bro över Öresund mellan de två länderna.

Vocabulary

väldig -t -a, enormous
avstånd -et -, distance
landsdel -en -ar, parts of the country
nära, almost
väg -en -ar, road
kör/a kör -de, drive
för det mesta, for the most part
försiktigt, carefully
händ/a -er hände, happen, occur
olycka -n -or, accident
trots, despite
ökning -en -ar, increase
privatbilism -en, private motoring
de senaste åren, in recent years
kraftigt, powerfully; *here*: rapidly
antingen . . . eller, either . . . or

rymlig -t -a, roomy, spacious
lika . . . som . . ., as . . . as . . .
fransk -t -a, French
omgivning -en -ar, environs
pendeltåg -et -, commuter train
affär -en -er, shop
svår -t -a, difficult
kontor -et -, office
pendla/ -r -de, commute
T-bana -n = tunnelbana -n, the tube
arbeta/ -r -de, work
billig -t -a, cheap
'pågatågen', trains named after the best known word in Skåne dialect, **påg = pojke**
spårvagn -en -ar, tram
på landet, in the country(side)
eftersom, as, because
endast, only
finnas kvar, remain, still exist
järnväg -en -ar, railway; ***here***: railway line

Exercise 8

Answer the following questions in English on the factual text:

1 What are the roads like in Sweden? 2 Why are there so few road accidents, despite the large number of cars? 3 Why has the number of rail passengers increased? 4 What are Swedish trains like in comparison to British trains? 5 Why do most Stockholmers take the tube? 6 What are 'pågatåg'? 7 Where can you still find trams? 8 Why do you have to resort to buses in many rural areas?

4 I Skåne

In Skåne

In this lesson we will look at:

- two-verb constructions with adverbs
- objects, MPT-expressions and the sentence pattern
- possessive pronouns
- the plural forms of nouns
- the indefinite declension of adjectives
- how to pronounce **s, j, r** and other consonants
- how to use **du** and **ni** in addressing people
- how to translate the verb 'to be'
- points of the compass
- ordinal numbers
- words for months and dates
- the town of Lund
- how to express centuries and decades
- compounding and abbreviation

Text 4

I Skåne

In Skåne

Familjen Forsberg brukar alltid ta semester i juli. I år besöker de Skåne, ett svenskt landskap som var en del av Danmark för bara trehundra år sedan, och där man talar en särskild dialekt.

Forsbergs kör långsamt längs kusten, stannar då och då och vandrar i små, mysiga fiskebyar och tittar på gamla slott och kyrkor. De vill äta lunch på ett traditionellt skånskt gästgiveri. Man brukar servera god mat där. I Skåne bör man äta smörgåsbord. Både Jan och Eva Forsberg äter väldiga portioner, men deras son Joakim beställer en hamburgare. Efter lunch åker de över Skåneslätten, förbi vackra gårdar med halmtak. På kvällen kommer de till staden Lund som ligger i västra Skåne. Här tänker de övernatta, för Eva vill se på domkyrkan och hennes man måste absolut gå i en stor bokhandel. Joakim är inte alls intresserad av kultur – han tänker leta efter nya skivor. Vid Stortorget finns en utmärkt skivaffär.

Vocabulary

familj -en -er, family
bruka/ -r -de, usually (do something)
semester -n semestrar, holiday
juli, July
besök/a -er -te, visit
landskap -et -, province
för . . . sedan (*usually pron.* sen), ago
där, where, there
särskil/d -t -da, special, particular
dialekt -en -er, dialect
långsamt, slowly
längs, along
kust -en -er, coast
stanna/r -de -t, stop
då och då, now and then
vandra/ -r -de, wander
mysig -t -a, cosy, charming
fiskeby -n -ar, fishing village
titta/r -de -t, look
slott -et -, castle
kyrka -n -or, church
ät/a -er åt ätit, eat
lunch -en -er (*pron.* lunsj), lunch
traditionell -t -a, traditional
skånsk -t -a, (of Skåne)
gästgiveri -et -er, country inn
servera/ -r -de, serve
god gott goda, good (of food, cf. **bra**)
mat -en, food
böra bör borde bort, ought to
smörgåsbord -et -, smörgåsbord
väldig -t -a, enormous
portion -en -er, portion, helping
deras, their
son -en söner, son
beställ/a -er -de, order, book
hamburgare -n -, hamburger
över, across
slätt -en -er, plain
förbi, past
gård -en -ar, farm
halmtak -et -, thatched roof
tänk/a -er -te, think, intend
övernatta/ -r -de, stay the night
domkyrka -n -or, cathedral
hennes, her
man -nen män, husband, man
absolut, definitely, really
bokhandel -n, bokhandlar, bookshop
inte alls, not . . . at all
intresserad av, interested in
kultur -en -er, culture
leta/ -r -de efter, look for
vid, on

torg -et -, square
ny nytt nya, new
skiva -n -or, record
utmärkt -a, excellent
skivaffär -en -er, record shop

Two-verb constructions and adverbs

Two-verb constructions and adverbs like **inte** were discussed in Lesson 3. In a number of sentences in Text 4 both are found, and we can now establish a pattern for sentences that have both:

Front	$Verb_1$	*(Subject)*	*Adverb*	$Verb_2$	*etc.*
Forsbergs	**brukar**	–	**alltid**	**ta**	**semester i juli.**
Jan	**måste**	–	**absolut**	**gå**	**i en stor bokhandel.**
I år	**vill**	**de**	**gärna**	**besöka**	**Lund.**
	Brukar	**han**	**alltid**	**köra**	**långsamt?**

Notice that in the last two examples, with inverted word order, the subject and adverb both come between VERB_1 and VERB_2.

Objects and MPT-expressions; the sentence pattern

Objects often go towards the end of the sentence:

De talar *en särskild dialekt.* De vill äta *lunch.*
Forsbergs tittar på *gamla slott.* De brukar servera *god mat.*
Joakim beställer *en hamburgare.* Han tänker leta efter *skivor.*
I år besöker de *Skåne.* Där talar man *skånska.*

But sometimes one may also wish to say *how, where* or *when* something happens, and for this an expression of manner, place or yime – an MPT-expression – is used. These MPT-expressions usually come after the object in the sentence:

Forsbergs brukar ta *semester* *i juli.*
OBJ TIME

Man talar *en särskild dialekt* *i Skåne.*
OBJ PLACE

De serverar *god mat* *där.*
OBJ PLACE

Jan kör *långsamt*.
MANNER

Sometimes more than one MPT-expression is necessary, in which case the order at the end of the sentence is often (but not always): manner – place – time (MPT):

Jan kör *långsamt* *längs kusten* *på kvällen*.
MANNER PLACE TIME

MPT-expressions are sometimes adverbs, eg. **här**, **där** or **långsamt**, but are often preposition + noun: **på måndag**, **i morgon**, **i Lund**, **på tåget**, **över slätten**, **med bil**.

An MPT-expression may also be placed at the beginning of the sentence (*Note*: only one at a time!), in which case it causes inversion of the verb and subject:

I Skåne	**bör**	**man**	**äta smörgåsbord.**
PLACE	VERB	SUBJ	
Här	**tänker**	**de**	**övernatta.**
PLACE	VERB	SUBJ	
Först	**tar**	**han**	**tunnelbana.**
TIME	VERB	SUBJ	

A sentence that has all of the parts discussed so far would adhere to the following pattern:

1	2	3	4	5	6	7
Front +	*Verb*$_1$ +	*(Subject)* +	*Adverb* +	*Verb*$_2$ +	*Object/ Complement*	+ *MPT-expression*

Any part of the sentence can come at the front, e.g. subject, MPT, object, etc.

Exercise 1

Re-arrange the order of the words divided by oblique strokes to complete the sentence. To check, fit the words into the above pattern.

1 Du alltid/måste/göra som jag säger!
2 Jan bil/brukar/aldrig/köra på semester
3 Här inte/övernatta/tänker/de.
4 Eva ofta/vill/titta på/gamla kyrkor.
5 Man serverar/i Skåne/god mat/alltid.

Some possessive pronouns

Compare the following subject pronouns with their possessive equivalents. Notice that Swedish has the same form for the possessive pronoun and the possessive adjective, i.e. **hennes** can mean both 'her' and 'hers'.

Subject pronouns		*Possessive pronouns*	
han	he	**hans**	his
hon	she	**hennes**	her(s)
den, det	it	**dess**	its
de	they	**deras**	their(s)

Han har en bil. He has a car

Hans bil är röd. His car is red.

Bilen är hans. The car is his.

Hon har en pojke. She has a boy.

Hennes pojke heter Joakim. Her boy is called Joakim.

Pojken är hennes. The boy is hers.

De äger ett hotell. They own a hotel.

Deras hotell ligger i Skåne. Their hotel is in Skane.

Hotellet är deras. The hotel is theirs.

Nouns, plural forms

A number of nouns in the plural have already been encountered in passing, especially in the factual texts. From these it can be seen that there are five main plural endings: **skiv*or*** (records), **varg*ar*** (wolves), **affär*er*** (businesses), **apple*n*** (apples), **fjäll(-)** (mountains). Plurals can now be systematised:

Singular	*Singular + end article*	*Plural*	*Modifications*	*Plural ending*
en kyrka	**kyrkan**	**kyrkor**	drops **-a**	**+ -or**
en flicka	**flickan**	**flickor**	drops **-a**	**+ -or**
en buss	**bussen**	**bussar**		**+ -ar**
en skotte	**skotten**	**skottar**	drops **-e**	**+ -ar**
en turist	**turisten**	**turister**		**+ -er**
en maskin	**maskinen**	**maskiner**		**+ -er**
en sko	**skon**	**skor**		**+ -r**
ett äpple	**äpplet**	**äpplen**		**+ -n**
ett tåg	**tåget**	**tåg**		no ending

ett slott	**slottet**	**slott**	no ending
en walesare	**walesaren**	**walesare**	no ending
(en) mat	**maten**	no plural	–

Lesson 5 shows you how to predict plural endings from clues.

Exercise 2

Find the plural forms of the following nouns used in earlier texts:

1 en timme 2 en invånare 3 en björn 4 en by 5 en miljon 6 en sjö 7 ett år 8 en portion 9 en finne 10 ett land

Adjectives, indefinite declension

So far in the texts only a few adjectives have been found. These can be arranged according to the nouns they qualify:

With N-word, singular (basic form)	*With T-word, singular*	*With plurals (both N- and T-words)*
en svensk flicka (a Swedish girl)	**ett svensk*t* företag** (a Swedish company)	**svensk*a* lokaltåg** (Swedish local trains)
en stor firma (a large firm)	**ett stor*t* land** (a large country)	**stor*a* gårdar** (large farms)

From this table it can be seen that adjectives with T-words add **-t** to the basic form, and those with plurals of both genders add **-a** to the basic form. The basic form is the form (without any endings) that is used with N-words. Matching the adjective to the noun is known as adjective agreement. Notice that there must also be agreement when the adjective comes after a verb:

Flickan är svensk. (The girl is Swedish.)	**Företaget är svensk*t*.** (The firm is Swedish.)	**Gårdarna är stor*a*.** (The farms are big.)
Firman är stor. (The firm is large.)	**Landet är stor*t*.** (The country is large.)	**Skivorna är ny*a*.** (The records are new.)

Most Swedish adjectives simply add **-t** or **-a** (not both!), but one or two display slight variations:

with N-words	*with T-words*	*with plurals*	
vacker	**vackert**	**vackra**	(drops an **e** in the plural)
gammal	**gammalt**	**gamla**	(drops an **a** in the plural, as well as an **m**)

Some adjectives are indeclinable, i.e. they add no endings at all:

en bra skola	**ett bra företag**	**bra popskivor**
(a good school)	(a good company)	(good pop records)

Exercise 3

Here are some frequent adjectives:

lång long
underbar wonderful
vänlig friendly
dyr expensive, dear
rolig fun(ny)
varm hot
fattig poor
låg low
trevlig pleasant
tråkig boring

Now fill in the adjective in its correct indefinite form in the following:

1 en (trevlig) dialekt 2 ett (vacker) slott 3 (underbar) kyrkor 4 ett (hög) fjäll 5 en (vänlig) svensk 6 en (varm) dag 7 (kall) öl 8 ett (rik) folk 9 (fattig) studenter 10 (tråkig) popskivor

Exercise 4

Fill in the adjective in its correct indefinite form in the following:

1 Firman är (stor). 2 Företaget är (stor). 3 Deras produkter är (dyr). 4 Kaffet är (varm). 5 Domkyrkan var (underbar). 6 Slottet var (gammal). 7 Resan var mycket (lång). 8 Studenter är ofta (rolig). 9 Klimatet är (kall). 10 Är Skåneslätten (tråkig)?

Pronunciation 4

Consonants s, j, r, -rs,-rg, -lg, -ng

Practise saying the following words:

s (*never* like English ‘z’!) **Lisa läsa stycke ros musik bestämt spis**

j (like English 'y-')	**jaja jul Jan Jimmy Jenny jeans**
r (trilled)	**rum röra dörr norr bra arm arbete**
-rs (like English 'sh')	**fors Lars varsågod störst första**
-rg (like rj)	**Borg Berg arga**
-lg (like lj)	**älgen helg svalg**
-ng	**Inga pengar gånger sjunger**

Dialogue 4

På hotellet

At the hotel

The Forsbergs are booking into a hotel

JAN FORSBERG: Har ni möjligen två rum för i natt? Vi vill gärna ha ett dubbelrum till oss och ett enkelrum till vår son.

PORTIERN: Javisst, det går säkert bra. Vi ska se här. Ska det vara med dusch och toalett?

EVA FORSBERG: Ja, helst.

PORTIERN: Vi har två rum på tredje våningen, tror jag. Ja, rum nummer 308 (trehundraåtta) och 314 (trehundra fjorton).

JOAKIM: Finns det teve på rummet, för det är ett musikprogram ikväll som jag måste se?

PORTIERN: Ja, det finns teve på alla rum här. Elva kanaler.

JAN: Och frukost, hur dags börjar ni servera den?

PORTIERN: Vi börjar redan klockan 7 (sju).

JAN: Då vill vi gärna beställa väckning imorgon klockan sju. Vi ska iväg rätt tidigt.

EVA: Förresten, finns det ett postkontor i närheten? Jag måste skicka ett vykort.

PORTIERN: Ja, posten ligger precis om hörnet på Knut den Stores torg. Vill ni skriva namn och adress här . . .? Då så kan ni följa med mig – hissen är den här vägen.

EVA: Vill ni vara så snäll och hjälpa mig med väskan?

Vocabulary

möjligen, possibly
rum rummet -, room
i natt, tonight
vill gärna ha, would very much like
dubbelrum, double room
oss, us
enkelrum, single room
vår -t -a, our
säkert, certainly
Det går bra. That will be all right.
dusch -en -ar (*pron.* dusj), shower
toalett -en -er, toilet
helst, preferably
tro/ -r -dde, believe
teve -n TV-apparater, TV
program -met -, programme
kanal -en -er, channel
hur dags? (*pron.* hurdakks), what time?
frukost -en -ar, breakfast
väckning -en, morning alarm call
rätt, right; *here*: quite, rather
tidigt, early
postkontor -et -, post office
närhet -en, vicinity
skicka /-r -de, send
vykort -et -, picture postcard
precis om hörnet, just round the corner
namn -et -, name
adress -en -er, address
då så, now then
följ/a -er -de, follow
hiss -en -ar, lift
den här, this
väg -en -ar, *here*: way

Exercise 5

If you cannot afford a hotel you may stay at a **pensionat** or a **vandrarhem**. You will probably need to find the **matsal** and the **herrtoalett (herrar)** or **damtoalett (damer)**. To get to your room you may need the **hiss**. Hang up your coat in the **garderob** and remember when using the bath taps to distinguish between **kar** and **dusch** otherwise you may get your hair wet unnecessarily!

Can you guess what these are in English?

Du and ni

Ni is always used to address several people. Until the 1960s only people who were close friends or family used **du** to address one another individually. And **ni** could not always be used in the singular, since it could be regarded as condescending. In many circumstances the third person, with titles and names was, therefore, the only acceptable form of address (e.g. **Vill herr Johansson hjälpa mig?** 'Would you help me, Mr Johansson?'). Then the '**du-reform**' of the late 1960s made it possible to use **du** to almost anyone. In some cases – as in Dialogue 4 – **ni** is now the equivalent of English 'Sir' or 'Madam' and is making a comeback as a polite singular form, particularly in shops and restaurants and when addressing older people.

Please

In Lesson 1 the word **tack** at the end of a sentence meant 'please'. In the dialogue above there is an expression corresponding to 'please' at the beginning of a sentence, 'Please will you . . .':

Vill du/ni vara (så) snäll och . . .

This means literally 'Will you be so kind and . . .'

Any of the following constructions can be used in similar requests in the form of questions:

Kan du/ni vara så snäll och ge mig en smörgås?
Skulle du/ni kunna vara (så) snäll och ge mig en smörgås?
Skulle du/ni vilja vara (så) snäll och ge mig en smörgås?
Skulle du/ni kunna hjälpa mig?

In Lesson 5 you will see how to form commands using the imperative form of the verb.

Translating the verb 'to be'

Notice that in the dialogue two verbs are used to translate the verb 'to be' in preference to **vara**, namely **finnas** and **ligga**. (There are others, which we will come to later.)

finnas (finns fanns funnits) usually indicates that something exists or does not exist:

Det finns inte.	It does not exist.
Finns det något öl kvar?	Is there any beer left?

ligga ligger låg legat indicates that something is located or placed, often horizontally. Its basic meaning is 'to lie':

Boken ligger på bordet.	The book is (lies) on the table.
Lund ligger i Skåne.	Lund is (lies) in Skåne.

So, when Eva asks the hotel receptionist **Finns det ett postkontor i närheten?**, she means 'does one exist?' The receptionist's answer indicates the location of the post office: **Det ligger om hörnet.** 'It is (located) round the corner.'

Points of the compass

Two ways of indicating points of the compass have been described earlier. Here is a summary of all the methods:

- using an adjective: **norra, södra, östra, västra** 'northern', etc.; **norra Sverige** 'Northern Sweden'
- using a prefix: **nord-, syd-, öst-, väst-**, 'northern', etc.; **Sydeuropa** 'Southern Europe'
- using a noun: **i norr, i söder, i öster, i väster** 'in the North/South/East/West'
- **norr om, söder om, öster om, väster om** 'north of', etc.; **norr om Luleå** 'north of Luleå'
- **norrut, söderut, österut, västerut** 'northwards', etc.

Ordinal numbers

Once you can count in cardinal numbers ('one, two, three . . .') it is useful to learn ordinals ('first, second, third . . .').

	Cardinal numbers	*Ordinal numbers*
1	**ett**	**första**
2	**två**	**andra**
3	**tre**	**tredje**
4	**fyra**	**fjärde**
5	**fem**	**femte**
6	**sex**	**sjätte**
7	**sju**	**sjunde**
8	**åtta**	**åttonde**
9	**nio**	**nionde**
10	**tio**	**tionde**

11	**elva**	**elfte**
12	**tolv**	**tolfte**
***-de**, etc.*:		
13	**tretton**	**trettonde**
14	**fjorton**	**fjortonde**
15	**femton**	**femtonde**
***-nde**, etc.*:		
20	**tjugo**	**tjugonde**
30	**tretti(o)**	**trettionde**
100	**hundra**	**hundrade**

Months and dates

Notice the pronunciation:

> **januari, februari, mars, april, maj, juni, juli, augusti** (*pron.* agusti), **september, oktober, november, december**

written	*spoken*
måndag 6 maj	**måndagen den sjätte maj**

Dates are usually given in figures. If they are written out as words notice that the word **hundra** is necessary:

nittonhundraåtti(o)nio	nineteen (hundred and) eighty-nine

Exercise 6

To see how much you remember of what has been covered so far in Lesson 4, translate into Swedish:

1 This year the Forsbergs are visiting the town of Lund which is in Southern Sweden. 2 They usually serve smörgåsbord at the inn in the evening. 3 Joakim eats an enormous (**enorm**) hamburger at the hotel. 4 Only three hundred years ago the province was a part of Denmark. 5 After lunch they want to look at the cathedral. 6 It is just round the corner. 7 I must book two single rooms for tonight. 8 Can you please help me? 9 We have two big rooms on the fourth floor, with shower and toilet. 10 Will you please send a postcard to Olle? 11 Tonight we are intending to spend the night at a traditional Skåne inn. 12 Their son is not at all interested in good food.

Factual text 4

Lund

Lund är en gammal stad. Det är över 900 år sedan Knut den Store grundade den, och senare blev den Nordens första biskopssäte. Lunds domkyrka, med två höga fyrkantiga torn som dominerar staden, är från 1145. I domkyrkan kan man bl a se ett astronomiskt ur från 1300-talet. Kl 12 och 15 om vardagarna (söndag kl 13 och 15) kommer många besökare hit för att se när uret slår och olika figurer kommer fram – riddare och de tre vise männen.

I Lund finns det många museer, t ex Konstmuseet, Botaniska Trädgården och Kulturhistoriska Museet, eller 'Kulturen' som man brukar säga. Kulturen är ett mycket fint friluftsmuseum med en samling gamla byggnader – bondstugor och hus från stad och landsbygd i olika delar av södra Sverige och t o m en pittoresk gammal träkyrka.

Lunds universitet är från 1668. Det har många institutioner och idag läser ca 20 000 studenter där. Universitetsbiblioteket har mer än 3 miljoner böcker, allt från gamla handskrifter till dagens bestsellers.

Vocabulary

Knut den Store, King Canute
grunda/ -r -de, found
biskopssäte -t -n, bishopric
bl a, inter alia
ur -et -, clock
besökare -n -, visitor
hit, here
riddare -n -, knight
konst -en -er, art
t ex, for example
trädgård -en -ar, garden
friluftsmuseum, open air museum
samling -en -ar, collection
byggnad -en -er, building
bondstuga -n -or, peasant cottage,
landsbygd -en, country(side)
t o m, even
träkyrka -n -or, wooden church

Exercise 7

Svara på frågorna:

1 Vem grundade Lund? 2 Vad kan man se i domkyrkan? 3 Vilka museer finns det i Lund? 4 Vad är Kulturen? 5 När grundade man Lunds universitet? 6 Hur många studenter läser där? 7 Vad finns det i Universitetsbiblioteket?

The Centre of Lund

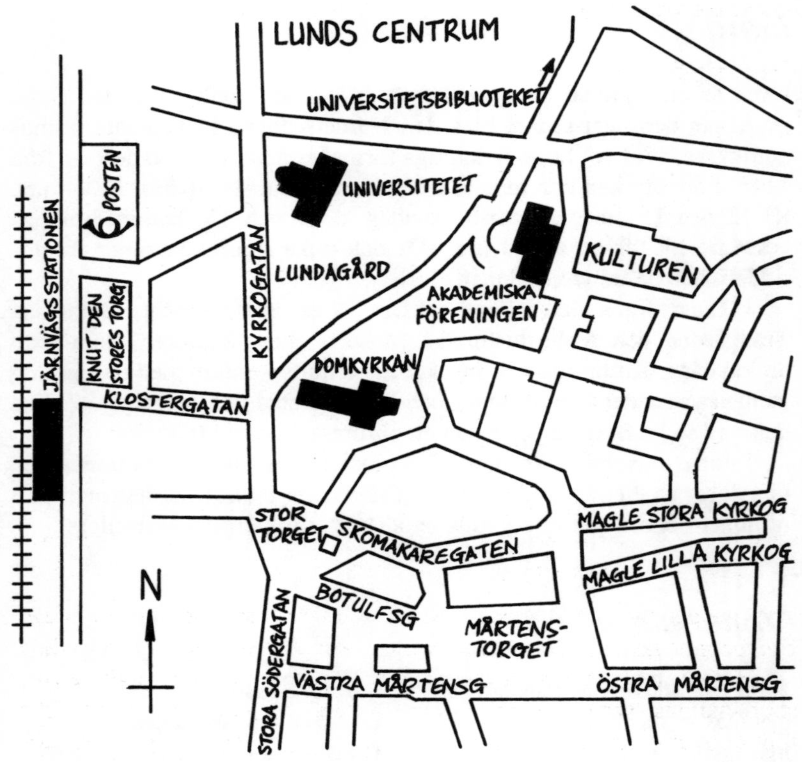

Centuries and decades

sixteenth century	= 1500s = **1500-talet**
eighteenth century	= 1700s = **1700-talet**
twentieth century	= 1900s = **1900-talet**
twenty-first century	= 2000s = **2000-talet** (*pron.* tjugohundratalet)

Compounds can be formed by placing date -s- before the second element:

1900-talskonst	twentieth-century art
en 1300-talskyrka	a fourteenth-century church

-tal is also used for decades and approximate numbers:

Han är född på 40-talet.	He was born in the 1940s.
en kyrka från 1250-talet	a church from the 1250s
ett trettital studenter	about thirty students

Exercise 8

What is the Swedish for:

1 the seventeenth century 2 the tenth century 3 the fifteenth century 4 the (19)70s 5 the (19)50s 6 the (19)80s 7 the 1990s 8 the 1820s

Compounding and abbreviation

These two tendencies in word formation seem to oppose one another; one makes words longer, the other shorter. Notice the following compounds in the factual text:

First element	*Last element*	*Noun compound*	
trä	**+ ett hus**	**> ett trähus**	
ett universitet	**+ ett bibliotek**	**> ett universitetsbibliotek**	(adds s)
en stad	**+ ett hus**	**> ett stadshus**	(adds s)
en bonde	**+ en stuga**	**> en bondstuga**	(drops e)

The gender of the compound is the gender of the last element. Compounds generally have two stresses: **ett trä + ett hus >ett trä | hus**

Factual texts, such as newspaper articles, often contain many abbreviations, something for which Swedish is infamous. Notice that full stops are omitted nowadays. In the text there are some common examples:

bl a	**bland annat**	inter alia
kl	**klockan**	o'clock
t ex	**till exempel**	e.g.
t o m	**till och med**	even, to, until
ca	**cirka**	approximately, circa

Some other important ones are:

osv	**och så vidare**	etc.	**nr**	**nummer**	number
dvs	**det vill säga**	i.e.	**p g a**	**på grund av**	because
el	**eller**	or	**t**	**timme (-ar)**	hour(s)
kr	**kronor**		**ung**	**ungefär**	approximately

Notice also: **en teve = en tv = en television**

5 Matlagning

Cooking

In this lesson we will look at:

- fronting
- difficult end articles
- predicting the plural forms of nouns
- how to cook 'Jansson's Temptation'
- imperatives
- how to pronounce **dj-, hj-, lj-, gj-**
- some useful telephone phrases
- object pronouns
- indefinite agreement of the adjective
- Stockholm

Text 5

Matlagning

Cooking

Rebecca äter fiskpinnar och pommes frites till lunch. På eftermiddagen dricker hon te med både socker och mjölk och äter några kex, och hon mumsar gärna på potatischips eller jordnötter framför teven. Det är fet och dålig mat, tycker Erik.

'Svenskarna äter också skräpmat', säger Rebecca. 'Kaffe dricker ni till exempel sex gånger om dagen och kakor eller bakelser äter ni jämt.'

'Du måste smaka riktig svensk mat', säger Erik. 'Kom så ska jag visa dig. Hämta två förkläden i garderoben och hjälp mig att laga Janssons frestelse! Vi behöver potatis, några lökar, en eller två burkar ansjovis, tjock grädde, lite skorpsmulor och smör. Snaps måste vi också ha. Ta och ställ brännvinet i kylskåpet! Janssons frestelse med en sup och ett glas öl är härlig svensk husmanskost. Läs receptet här i kokboken och titta på mig.'

'Tre deciliter vispgrädde och femti gram smör', muttrar Rebecca. 'Tala om fet mat!'

Vocabulary

matlagning -en, cooking
fiskpinne -n -ar, fish finger
pommes frites (*pron.* pomm fritt), (potato) chips
socker sockret, sugar
mjölk -en, milk
någon något några, some, any
kex -et -, biscuit
mumsa/ -r -de, nibble, chew
gärna, *here*: likes to
potatischips (*pron.* -tjipps), crisps
jordnöt -en -nötter, peanut
framför, in front of
fet -t -a, fat(ty)
dålig -t -a, bad; *here*: unhealthy
svenskarna, (the) Swedes
skräpmat -en, junk food
drick/a -er drack, drink
sex gånger om dagen, six times a day
bakelse -n -r, pastry, cake (often with filling or cream)
jämt, all the time
smaka/ -r -de, taste
riktig -t -a, real
visa/ -r -de, show
hämta/ -r -de, fetch
förkläde -t -n (*pron.* förrkle), apron
garderob -en -er, cupboard, wardrobe
hjälp/a -er -te, help
laga/ -r -de, mend (but **laga mat** = prepare food)
frestelse -n -r, temptation
behöv/a -er -de, need
potatis -en -ar, potato
lök -en -ar, onion
burk -en -ar, can
ansjovis, anchovies
tjock -t -a, thick
grädde -n, cream
skorpsmulor -na (*pl.*), breadcrumbs
smör -et, butter
snaps -en, akvavit, spirits, schnapps
brännvin -et, akvavit, spirits, schnapps
ställ/a -er -de, put
kylskåp -et -, refrigerator
sup -en -ar, dram, 'tot'
härlig -t -a, wonderful
husmanskost -en, plain (traditional) food
recept -et -, recipe; prescription
kokbok -en -böcker, cookbook
titta/ -r -de (på), look, watch
vispgrädde -n, whipping cream
muttra/ -r -de, mutter, mumble

Fronting

The subject is most often found at the beginning of the sentence, but a word or phrase (non-subject) can be moved to the beginning of a main clause sentence. This is known as 'fronting'. MPT-expressions are quite often fronted, and (rather less frequently) objects appear at the front:

Front	*Verb₁*	*(Subject)*	*Adverb*	*Verb₂*	*Obj/Comp*	*MPT*
Klockan 12 TIME	**kommer**	**många besökare**	—	—	—	**hit.**
Efter lunch TIME	**åker**	**de**	—	—	—	**över slätten.**
I domkyrkan PLACE	**kan**	**man**	**ju**	**se**	**ett astronomiskt ur.**	
I Lund PLACE	**finns**	**det**	**faktiskt**	—	**många museer.**	
Kakor OBJ	**äter**	**ni**	—	—	—	**jämt.**
Snaps OBJ	**måste**	**vi**	**också**	**ha.**		
Det OBJ	**tycker**	**jag**	**inte.**			

Notice that the subject always follows VERB$_1$ (inverted word order) when a non-subject is fronted. Normally the word(s) at the beginning of the sentence either:

(a) outline a situation: e.g. **I Lund . . .**, **I kväll . . .**, **När jag kommer hem . . .**

or:

(b) provide a link to a previous clause: e.g. **Sedan . . .**, **Efteråt . . .**, **Här . . .**, **Då . . .**

But fronted words may occasionally be used to point a contrast:

Kaffe dricker ni sex gånger om dagen och kakor äter ni jämt.

Exercise 1

Not all sentences begin with the subject! Re-write the piece below, placing the word(s) in italics first in the sentence and adjusting the word order.

Rebecca bor i Stockholm *just nu*. Hon läser svenska vid Stockholms universitet *i år*. Hon åker tunnelbana till universitetet *varje dag*. Hon börjar *ofta* klockan åtta på morgonen. Hon sitter *på biblioteket* och antecknar. Hon skriver en uppsats *ibland*. Rebecca går på föreläsningar *sju gånger i veckan*. Hon dricker kaffe *efteråt*. Hon tycker om *kaffe*. Hon åker tunnelbana hem *sedan*.

Difficult end articles

N-words ending in unstressed **-el**, **-er**, or **-or** take **-n** in the definite form (whereas other N-words ending in a consonant take **-en**, see p.33).

en bokhandel	**bokhandeln**	**en vinter**	**vintern**
en cykel	**cykeln**	**en motor**	**motorn**
en semester	**semestern**	**en doktor**	**doktorn**

Nouns ending in unstressed **-el** or **-er** also drop the last vowel before adding the plural ending:

en cykel	**två cyklar**	**en vinter**	**två vintrar**

T-words of this last kind drop the vowel in the stem before adding **-et**:

ett exempel	**exemplet**	**ett fönster**	**fönstret**

Exercise 2

Insert the correct form with end article of the noun provided.

1 (Elektriker) lagade tvättmaskinen. 2 Vi tyckte att (exempel, *neuter*) var svårt. 3 (Syster) heter Ulla. 4 Han har skurit sig i (finger, *neuter*). 5 Vi träffar (professor) i morgon.

Predicting noun plurals

Whilst it is advisable to learn the gender and plural with each new noun you come across, in most cases it is actually possible to predict the plural form if you are in possession of other information such as gender (N-word/T-word?) and pronunciation of the ending of the word (stressed/unstressed?). These clues can be expressed as a set of rules allowing you to work out the majority of noun plurals:

Rule 1 Both N-words with a stressed final syllable and T-words with a stressed final vowel add **-er**:

en affär	**två affär*er***
ett kafé	**två kafé*er***

Rule 2 N-words ending in unstressed **-a** drop the **-a** and add **-or**:

en kaka	**två kak*or***

Rule 3 N-words ending in unstressed **-e** drop the **-e** and add **-ar**:

en pojke	**två pojk*ar***

Rule 4 T-words ending in an unstressed vowel add **-n**:

ett äpple	**två äpple*n***

Rule 5 T-words ending in a consonant have no ending:

ett barn	**två barn**

Some endings tell you immediately what the plural is going to be. All N-words ending in:

-are add:	no ending	**en lärare** (a teacher)	**två lärare**
-er add:	no ending	**en indier** (an Indian)	**två indier**
-(n)ing add	**-ar**	**en tidning** (a newspaper)	**två tidning*ar***
-het add:	**-er**	**en nyhet** (a piece of news)	**två nyhet*er***

Some nouns, mostly single syllable N-words are, however, difficult to predict:

en dag	**två dagar**	**en burk**	**två burkar**
en kust	**två kuster**	**en plats**	**två platser**

There are still one or two groups we will look at later.

Exercise 3

Without looking these nouns up in the glossary, work out their plural endings from the clues given above. Notice where the stresses come:

en affär, en biljett, ett fjäll, en fabrik, en hamburgare, ett glas, ett hotell, en katolik, en invånare, en krona, en maskin, en bulle, en firma, en miljon, en människa, ett namn, en olycka, en portion, ett päron, en drottning, en skola, en skotte, en stuga, en timme, ett byte, en toalett, en kyrka, en turist, en vecka, ett ägg, en ökning.

Exercise 4

Preferably without looking the following nouns up in the glossary, predict their singular form with indefinite article (e.g. **en bil**):

två förkläden, två fiskpinnar, två kakor, två glas öl, två gånger, två dagar, två bondstugor, två museer, två hus, två vykort, två olyckor, två lärare, två timmar, två människor, två hotell, två väckarklockor.

The recipe Rebecca read in the cookbook was:

Janssons Frestelse

1 kg potatis	3 dl tjock grädde
2 stora gula lökar	1 msk skorpsmulor
1 burk ansjovis	50 g smör

Skala potatisen och skär den och löken i tunna skivor. Använd inte färsk potatis. Smörj generöst en eldfast form med raka kanter. Lägg i ett lager potatis och fortsätt sedan med lök och ansjovis. Upprepa och avsluta med ett lager potatis. Platta till ytan och häll över grädden. Späd med ansjovisspad. Strö skorpsmulor över och klicka ut smöret. Sätt formen i 250° varm ugn och grädda i en dryg timme.

Vocabulary

gul -t -a, yellow
msk = matsked, dessert spoon(ful)
skala/ -r -de, peel
skära skär skar, cut
tunn tunt tunna, thin
skiva -n -or, slice
färsk potatis, new potatoes
använd/a -er använde, use
smörj/a -er smorde, grease
generöst (*pron.* sjenneröst), generously
eldfast form, oven-proof dish

rak -t -a, straight
kant -en -er, edge
lägg/a -er lade lagt, lay, put,
lager lagret, layer
fortsätt/a -er -satte -satt, continue
upprepa/ -r -de, repeat
avsluta/ -r -de, finish off
platta /-r -de till, flatten off
häll/a -er -de, pour
späd/a -er -de, dilute; *here*: moisten
spad -et, juice, stock
strö/ -r -dde, sprinkle
sätt/a -er satte satt, place
klicka/r -de ut, dot with knobs of butter
grädda/r -de, bake
ugn -en -ar, oven
en dryg timme, a good hour

Imperatives

The recipe above contains a number of imperatives. Infinitives and present tense endings already appeared in Lesson 2, so a pattern for some verb endings can now be established:

Conjugation (verb group)	*Imperative (stem)*	*Infinitive*	*Present*
I	stem in **-a**	= stem	+ **-r**
	skala (peel)	**skala**	**skalar**
II, IV	stem in consonant	+ **-a**	+ **-er**
	ställ (put)	**ställa**	**ställer**
	skriv (write)	**skriva**	**skriver**
III	stem in vowel (not **-a**)	= stem	+**-r**
	strö (sprinkle)	**strö**	**strör**

The full pattern for verbs is given on p.116.

Onto the stem (= imperative) various endings are added to form tenses, usually **-a** and **-(e)r**, except for first conjugation verbs where the stem and infinitive both end in **-a**. Notice also the irregular verb 'to be':

var	**vara**	**är**

R-stem and **l**-stem verbs (those whose stem ends in **-r** or **-l**) are slightly different. They are Conjugation II verbs but add no ending in the present tense (cf. other II verbs which add **-er**):

skär	**skära**	**skär**
kör	**köra**	**kör**
mal	**mala**	**mal**

Imperatives are used in commands, wishes or advice. They are often found in instructions, recipes etc. When used in commands they may be made more palatable by the addition of some polite phrases meaning 'please':

Skala potatisen, är du bussig!	*lit.* Peel the potatoes and you are kind, i.e. Please peel . . .
Hjälp mig laga middag, är du snäll!	*lit.* Help me make dinner and you are nice, i.e. Please help me . . .

See also p.66.

Exercise 5

Change the following sentences into commands using the imperatives, as in the example, and omitting the subjects and modal verbs:

Example: **Han kör (fortare) > Kör fortare!**

1 Du kallar mig för Janne (är du snäll). 2 Du bör köpa en ny bil (till billigt pris). 3 Man serverar alltid vitt vin (till fisk). 4 Du talar bara svenska (i Sverige). 5 Du använder inte socker (om du inte vill bli tjock). 6 Du kan skala löken (om du är bussig). 7 Du kan läsa artikeln högt (så vi kan höra). 8 Ni kan skriva ett vykort till Eva (när ni kommer fram). 9 Ni måste resa till Grekland (i sommar). 10 Du kan ställa flaskan på bordet (är du snäll).

Exercise 6

What is the Swedish for:

1 Put the milk in the fridge please! 2 She is always nibbling at a biscuit. 3 We need some cans of beer. 4 Talk about junk food! 5 They eat three times a day. 6 Swedes always drink cold akvavit. 7 I do not use sugar in tea. 8 Do you always take cream in coffee? 9 You must taste real English beer. 10 They are eating fish fingers in front of the TV.

Pronunciation 5

Consonants dj-, hj-, lj-, gj-

Practise saying the following words. The initial letter is not pronounced and all of the groups are pronounced as Swedish **j-**:

dj-	place names:	**Djursholm Djäkneboda**
	others:	**djungel djup djävel djur**
hj-	place names:	**Hjo Hjortsberga Hjulsta Hjälmaren Hjåggböle**
	others:	**hjul hjortron hjälp hjärna hjärta**
lj-	place names:	**Ljungby Ljusnan Ljömsebo**
	others:	**ljud ljus ljuv**
gj-		**gjuta gjorde**

Dialogue 5

Telefonsamtal

Telephone calls

Erik is inviting people for dinner

LEIF: Leif Persson.
ERIK: Hej, det är Erik. Kan jag få tala med Bosse?
LEIF: Ett ögonblick så ska jag hämta honom.
ERIK: Tack.
LEIF: Han är inte inne tyvärr. Ska jag be honom ringa dig?
ERIK: Nej, det är inte så viktigt. Hej då.
PIA: 347592 (Trettifyra sjuttifem nittitvå).
ERIK: Hej, det är Erik. Har du mamma hemma?
PIA: Ja, ett ögonblick.
MALIN: Malin Nylén.
ERIK: Hej Malin, det är Erik.
MALIN: Nämen hej, hur har du det?
ERIK: Bra, och du själv?

MALIN: Jodå, bara fint.
ERIK: Är Jan-Åke hemma? Rebecca och jag vill bjuda er på middag ikväll. Vi har Janssons frestelse, snaps och några kalla öl här, men inga trevliga vänner. Vad säger du?
MALIN: Oh, vad synd! Vi har ingen barnvakt till Pia. Så det går nog inte.
ERIK: Jodå, vi lägger henne på soffan. Kom alla tre!
MALIN: Vilken god idé! Då kommer vi gärna. Hur dags?
ERIK: Vid sju-tiden. Välkomna.
MALIN: Då ses vi klockan sju. Hej så länge.
ERIK: Hej då.

Vocabulary

telefonsamtal -et -, telephone call, conversation
ögonblick -et -, moment
honom, him
tyvärr, unfortunately
be/ -r bad bett, ask (someone to do something)
viktig -t -a, important
mamma -n -or, mummy
inne, in
hemma, at home
Hur har du det?, How are things with you?
själv -t -a, (your)self
bjud/a -er bjöd, invite
middag -en -ar, dinner
trevlig -t -a, nice
vän -nen -ner, friends
Vad synd! (*pron.* synn), What a pity!
ingen inget inga, no, none
barnvakt -en -er, babysitter
Det går inte. It is not possible.
soffa -n -or, sofa
idé -n -er, idea
ses ses sågs setts, meet (**vi ses** = be seeing you)

Useful telephone phrases

(Anknytning) 123 tack.	Extension 123 please.
Jag söker Jan Forsberg.	I'm looking for Jan Forsberg.
Det gäller . . .	It's about . . .
Hur var namnet?	What is your name?
Vem är det jag talar med?	Who am I speaking to?
Ursäkta! Vad sa du?	Sorry! What did you say?
Kan du upprepa (ta om) det där?	Can you repeat that?
Det är upptaget.	The line is engaged.
Går det bra att vänta?	Do you mind holding?
Var god dröj! Dröj ett tag!	Just a moment.

Han har semester/är tjänstledig.	He's on holiday.
Jag ska koppla över.	I'm connecting you.
växel -n	switchboard
slå en signal	give (someone) a call
slå ett nummer	dial a number
telefonkiosk -en	telephone box
telefonnummer -numret	telephone number
telefonkatalog -en	telephone directory
telefontid -en -er	period when lines are open
svara i telefon	answer the phone
prata i telefon	speak on the phone
lyfta på/lägga på luren	pick up/put down the receiver
Tryck in SOS-knappen och slå 90 000.	Press the emergency button and dial 90 000.

Object pronouns

Subject pronouns		*Object pronouns*	
jag	I	**mig, mej***	me
du	you	**dig, dej***	you
ni	you (formal)	**er**	you (formal)
han	he	**honom**	him
hon	she	**henne**	her
den	it (N-words)	**den**	it
det	it (T-words)	**det** (*pron.* de)	it
vi	we	**oss**	us
ni	you (pl.)	**er**	you (pl.)
de	they	**dem, dom***	them

**Note*: Alternative informal spellings which reflect the pronunciation.

Exercise 7

Translate the sentences using the verbs **äta, träffa, tro, tala (med), titta (på), se, skicka, prata (med), läsa, bjuda, köpa, sälja, följa, hjälpa, beställa, hämta.**

Can you . . . eat it? . . . help us? . . . speak to her? . . . sell them? . . . fetch him? . . . buy it? . . . follow me? . . . meet him? . . . meet us?

Can we . . . believe her? . . . order them? . . . look at it? . . . follow you? . . . send him? . . . help you (pl.)? . . . read it? . . . meet you? . . . invite them? . . . talk to you (pl.)? . . . see it?

Adjectives, indefinite agreement

Adjectives usually agree with nouns wherever the noun comes in the sentence (see also p.62):

en pittoresk kyrka	**kyrkan är pittoresk**
***ett* pittoresk*t* slott**	**slott*et* är pittoresk*t***
pittoresk*a* by*ar*	**byarn*a* är pittoresk*a***

But this indefinite adjective + noun agreement also occurs after some other words:

någon stor pojke (a, some, any)	**någo*t* stor*t* hus**	**någr*a* stor*a* pojkar/hus**
ingen stor pojke (no)	**inge*t* stor*t* hus**	**ing*a* stor*a* pojkar/hus**
en annan stor pojke (another, a different)	**ett anna*t* stor*t* hus**	**andr*a* stor*a* pojkar/hus**
vilken stor pojke (what (a))	**vilke*t* stor*t* hus**	**vilk*a* stor*a* pojkar/hus**
all mat (all)	**all*t* smör**	**all*a* stor*a* pojkar/hus**

Notice the way that the 'gender/plural markers' **-t, -a** are echoed in the pronoun and the adjective.

Adjectives also agree with the pronoun **det**, i.e. add **-t**:

Det är varm*t* idag, men igår var det kall*t*.
It is hot today, but yesterday it was cold.

Det är rolig*t* att dansa.
It is fun dancing.

Det var tråkig*t* att behöva vänta.
It was boring to have to wait.

Adjectives agreeing with groups of words (not just one noun) usually add **-t**:

***Att dansa* är roligt.** Dancing is fun.

Here **roligt** agrees with an infinitive phrase. Swedish has no equivalent to '-ing' forms.

Någonting (something, anything) and **ingenting** (nothing) are also essentially T-words like **det**:

Ingenting är roligt längre. Nothing is fun any more.

Exercise 8

What is the Swedish for:

1 The food is bad. 2 The cream is thick. 3 The beer is cold. 4 Their cream cakes are wonderful. 5 Some yellow onions and some thin slices of potato. 6 A different cookbook with a different recipe. 7 No name and no address. 8 We have no biscuits and no cakes. 9 It's wonderful, it's fun, . . . it's expensive! 10 What a boring book! 11 What a big glass! 12 What big cakes! 13 What enormous portions! 14 Preparing food is fun. 15 Eating chips the whole time is boring. 16 We don't eat anything hot for lunch. 17 Nothing is boring.

Central Stockholm

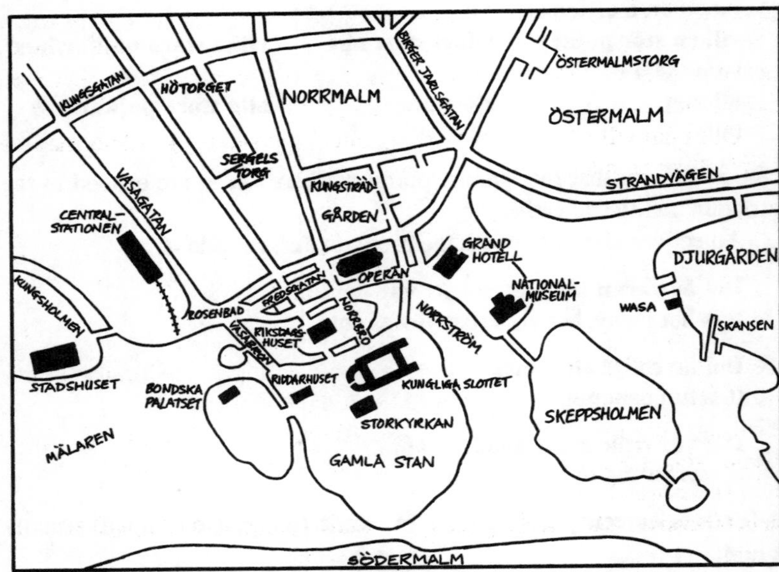

Factual text 5

Stockholm

På tre små öar mellan sjön Mälaren och Östersjön grundade Birger Jarl år 1252 Stockholm – staden som man med rätta har kallat 'Nordens Venedig'. Öarna kallar man nu för Gamla stan, och Stockholm har senare brett ut sig mot norr och söder: 'nya' stadsdelar är Norrmalm (affärscentrum), Södermalm (från början arbetarkvarter), Östermalm (de rikas stadsdel) och Kungsholmen (administrativa byggnader och bostadskvarter). Numera bor många stockholmare (det finns en miljon) i förorter långt från centrum. I Gamla stan kan man vandra i smala gränder mellan hus från 1500-talet. Här ligger Kungliga slottets väldiga fyrkant och Storkyrkan och andra fina kyrkor samt Riksdagshuset som nyligen renoverats. I Stockholm kan man besöka t ex ett av stadens många museer: Nationalmuseum innehåller en samling klassisk konst och Nordiska museet har intressanta historiska föremål.

Att gå på Skansen är ett populärt familjenöje. Skansen ligger på Djurgården och dit har gamla stugor och hus flyttats från hela Sverige. Där finns också ett zoo med huvudsakligen nordiska djur, t ex varg, lo och älg. Inte långt därifrån kan man besöka Wasa, krigsskeppet som sjönk i hamnen 1628 och som bärgades på 1950-talet.

Om man vill sitta och ta igen sig efter rundvandringen kan man gå in på ett av de många utekaféerna i sommarstockholm.

Vocabulary

ö -n -ar, island
Östersjön, the Baltic
med rätta, justifiably
Venedig, Venice
Gamla stan, the Old Town
bred/a -er bredde, spread
arbetarkvarter -et -, working class area
början, beginning
bostadskvarter -et -, residential area
förort -en -er, suburb
långt, far
gränd -en -er, alley
Kungliga slottet, the Royal Palace
väldig -t -a, mighty
fyrkant -en -er, rectangle
Storkyrkan, the Cathedral
samt = och
Riksdagshuset, the Parliament building
intressant - -a, interesting
föremål -et -, objects, artefacts
familjenöje -t -n, place of entertainment for the family

utflykt -en -er, excursion
bjud/a -er bjöd på, offer
huvudsakligen, mainly
djur -et -, animal
lo -n -ar (lodjur -et -), lynx
inte långt, not far
krigsskepp -et -, warship
bärga/ -r -de, salvage
ta igen sig, recover, rest
utekafé -et -er, pavement cafe

Exercise 9

Svara på frågorna:

1 Vad har man kallat Stockholm? 2 Vem grundade staden och när? 3 Vad är Gamla stan? 4 I vilken del av staden finner man . . . affärscentrum? . . . de rikas bostadskvarter? 5 Hur många stockholmare finns det? 6 Var ligger Kungliga slottet? 7 Var kan man hitta smala gränder och hus från 1500-talet? 8 Vad kan man se på Nationalmuseum? 9 Var kan man se gamla trähus från hela Sverige? 10 Vilka sorters djur ser man på Skansen? 11 Vad är Wasa? 12 Var kan man ta igen sig efter en rundvandring i Stockholm?

6 Nya möbler

New furniture

In this lesson we will look at:

- objects and complements
- adjectives – variations in the indefinite form
- some difficult noun plurals
- how to pronounce **-gn, gn-, kn-, -mn**
- how to agree and disagree with people
- demonstratives
- amplifiers
- spelling of words ending in **(m)m** and **(n)n**
- the seasons
- Norrland

Text 6

Nya möbler

New furniture

Eva och Jan Forsberg tänker köpa nya möbler till lägenheten. Deras möbler är gamla och fula. En lördag går de på ett stort möbelvaruhus utanför staden. Det blir en hel liten utflykt. Här tänker de leta efter en stor soffa till vardagsrummet och ett runt köksbord och några stolar till matvrån. Jan vill få tag på ett brett skrivbord till arbetsrummet eftersom hans skrivbord är för litet och smalt. 'Mina böcker och papper ramlar i golvet hela tiden', förklarar Jan. Eva vill skaffa några snygga små bordslampor, som de kan ha på nattduksborden bredvid sängen i sovrummet i stället för de väggfasta som de har nu.

På utställningen finns det många vackra möbler ofta till mycket hyggligt pris. De funderar på att köpa några djupa, bekväma fåtöljer samtidigt. 'Vi behöver nya eftersom våra är så slitna', säger Eva, men egentligen har de inte råd med allt. Jan tycker att de ska ha en tavla som kan hänga på väggen i Joakims rum i stället för hans popaffischer, men det tycker inte Joakim. 'Popgrupperna eller ingenting', säger han. 'Ingenting', tycker Jan.

Vocabulary

möbel -n möbler, (a piece of) furniture
ful -t -a, ugly
varuhus -et -, department (or large) store
utflykt -en -er, excursion, trip out
vardagsrum -met -, living room
rund runt runda, round
köksbord -et -, kitchen table
stol -en -ar, (ordinary) chair
matvrå -n -r, dining area
få/ -r fick fått tag på, get hold of
bred brett breda, broad, wide
skrivbord -et -, desk
arbetsrum -met, study
papper -et -, (sheet of) paper
ramla/ -r -de, fall
golv -et -, floor
hela tiden, the whole time
förklara/ -r -de, explain
skaffa/ -r -de, get, acquire
snygg -t -a, attractive, pretty
bordslampa -n -or, table lamp
sovrum -met -, bedroom
bredvid, beside
säng -en -ar, bed
i stället för, instead of
de väggfasta, the wall-mounted ones
utställning -en -ar, display, exhibition
hygglig -t -a, reasonable
pris -et -, price
fundera/ -r -de, think, ponder
djup -t -a, deep
bekväm -t -a, comfortable
fåtölj -en -er, armchair
samtidigt, at the same time
sliten slitet slitna, worn
ha råd (med), afford (to)
tavla -n -or, picture
häng/a -er -de, hang
vägg -en -ar, wall
affisch -en -er (*pron.* afi<u>sj</u>), poster
popgrupp -en -er, pop group
ingenting, nothing

Other useful words describing housing:

badrum -met -	bathroom
hall -en -ar	hall
källare -n	basement
garage -t - (*pron.* gar<u>a</u>sj)	garage

tak -et -	ceiling, roof
skåp -et -	cupboard

Exercise 1

Translate into Swedish:

1 Their flat is big and old. 2 The posters are beautiful. 3 They cannot afford to buy a deep comfortable armchair. 4 He is lying reading on the sofa. 5 Eva wants a big table lamp for the living room. 6 He falls on the floor all the time because his bed is so narrow. 7 We want to get a picture at a reasonable price. 8 Eva doesn't like the desk at all. 9 They need some wide round chairs for the study.

Objects and complements

Direct objects (DO) are often a noun phrase or pronoun:

Nils äter kakan.
DO

Hon gillar honom.
(likes) DO

Indirect objects (IO) are often people for whose sake an action is undertaken:

Jag gav Nils boken.
IO DO

Jag gav boken till Nils.
DO IO

The order of objects in Swedish is much the same as in English. The distinction between verbs that take a direct object (transitive verbs, like **äta, gilla**) and verbs that do not (intransitive verbs like **sova** 'sleep') will later be seen to be an important one in Swedish. The complement is found in sentences with verbs like **vara, bli, heta** which are 'empty verbs' needing a complement to fill out their meaning. Complements are either nouns or adjectives:

Han heter Erik.
COMP

Det är vackert här.
COMP

Hon är lärare.
COMP

These are subject complements (SC) and agree with the subject – nouns are singular/plural, adjectives agree with N-words, T-words and plural nouns, or with pronouns:

De är student*er*.	**Vi blir gaml*a*.**	**Det är rolig*t*.**
SUBJ SC	SUBJ SC	SUBJ SC

Object complements agree with the object:

Det gjorde dem arg*a*. It made them angry.
OBJ OC

Adjectives, indefinite variations

Most adjectives in the indefinite simply add either **-t** or **-a** (see p.62) with T-words or plurals respectively, but one or two show slight variations on this pattern:

Adjectives ending in a stressed vowel add **-tt** with T-words:

en ny soffa	**ett ny*tt* bord**	**ny*a* soffor** **ny*a* bord**

Also: **blå** (blue), **grå** (grey)

Adjectives ending in vowel +**-d** drop the **-d** and add **-tt** with T-words:

en bred säng	**ett bre*tt* skrivbord**	**breda sängar** **breda skrivbord**

Also: **god** (good), **glad** (happy), **röd** (red)

Adjectives ending in a consonant +**-d** drop the **-d** before adding **-t** with T-words:

en hård säng	**ett hårt bord**	**hårda sängar** **hårda bord**

Also: **mild** (mild), **vild** (wild), **ond** (evil)

Adjectives ending in **-er**, **-el** drop the **e** before adding **-a** with plural nouns:

en vacker soffa	**ett vackert bord**	**vackra soffor** **vackra bord**

Also: **mager** (thin), **nykter** (sober), **säker** (sure)

en enkel fåtölj	**ett enkelt skrivbord**	**enkla fåtöljer** **enkla skrivbord**

Also: **acceptabel** (acceptable), **flexibel** (flexible)

Adjectives ending in **-en** are like those in **-er** but also drop the **-n** in the neuter form:

en öppen dörr	**ett öppet fönster**	**öppna dörrar** **öppna fönster**

Also: **egen** (own), **ledsen** (sad)

Liten and **gammal** are irregular and should be learned individually:

en liten soffa	**ett litet bord**	**små soffor** **små bord**
en gammal säng	**ett gammalt bord**	**gamla sängar** **gamla bord**

Exercise 2

Insert the correct form of the adjective provided.

1 På tavlan ser man flera (naken) flickor. 2 Jag vill bara köpa (enkel) möbler. 3 Golvet var (röd). 4 De ville ha ett (rund) bord. 5 De hade ett mycket (bred) rum. 6 Lars ville köpa ett (ny) skrivbord. 7 Lars skrivbord är (gammal). 8 Deras möbler är mycket (sliten). 9 Klimatet i norr är (hård). 10 Vädret i söder är (mild). 11 Det är (vacker) på landet. 12 Svenska kyrkor är (vacker). 13 Deras fåtöljer är ganska (liten) och kaffebordet är också (liten). 14 Är vinet (god)? 15 Är dina möbler (gammal)? 16 Är våra studenter (nykter)? 17 Nej och imorgon blir de (ledsen).

Some difficult noun plurals

(a) A small group of nouns change their root vowel and add **-er:**

en hand (hand)	**två händer**	**en strand** (beach)	**två stränder**
ett land (country)	**två länder**	**en stad** (town)	**två städer**
en natt (night)	**två nätter**	**en rand** (stripe)	**två ränder**
en son (son)	**två söner**	**en bok** (book)	**två böcker**
en fot (foot)	**två fötter**	**en rot** (root)	**två rötter**

(b) A small group of nouns of both genders ending in a vowel add **-r**:

en bakelse (gateau)	**två bakelser**	**ett fängelse** (prison)	**två fängelser**
en sko (shoe)	**två skor**	**en tå** (toe)	**två tår**

(c) Many nouns ending in a vowel **+-n/l/r** drop their final vowel before adding the plural ending:

en fågel (bird)	**två fåglar**	**en sommar** (summer)	**två somrar**
en möbel (piece of furniture)	**två möbler**	**en regel** (rule)	**två regler**

(d) Some loanwords ending in **-ium**, **-eum** drop **-um** before adding **-er**:

ett museum (museum)	**två museer**
ett laboratorium (laboratory)	**två laboratorier**

(e) Some loanwords ending in **-um** have alternative plural forms:

ett centrum (centre)	**två centrum or centrer or centra**
ett faktum (fact)	**två faktum or fakta**

(f) A few nouns are highly irregular:

ett öga (eye)	**två ögon**	**ett huvud** (head)	**två huvuden**
ett öra (ear)	**två öron**		

(g) Some nouns, mostly recent English loanwords, retain a plural in **-s**:

två thrillers, två blinkers, två designers, chips (crisps)

Exercise 3

Fill in the missing forms:

(a)	en . . .	två tänder	(tooth)
	en bokstav	två . . .	(letter of the alphabet)
	en bonde	två . . .	(farmer, peasant)
	en . . .	två böcker	(book)
(b)	en ko	två . . .	(cow)
	en stadsbo	två . . .	(city dweller)
	en . . .	två hustrur	(wife)
	en . . .	två bastur	(sauna bath)
	en . . .	två aktier	(share in a company)
(c)	en vinter	två . . .	(winter)
	en afton	två . . .	(evening)
	en . . .	två muskler	(muscle)
	ett . . .	två fingrar	(finger)

Pronunciation 6

Consonants -gn, gn-, kn-, -mn

Practise saying the following words. Remember that -ng (Pronunciation 4) is pronounced as one sound. Do not worry about the meanings of the words.

-gn (Swedish **ng** + **n**) **Ragnar regn vagnen ugn dygn**

gn- (Swedish **g** + **n**) **Gnosjö gnaga gnissel gnällig gnola**

In the following groups both consonants are pronounced, *unlike* English 'knife', 'salmon', 'hymn':

kn- (Swedish **k** + **n**) **Knut knivar knä knyta knott**

-mn (Swedish **m** + **n**) **namnet jämn somna Köpenhamn**

Dialogue 6

Den där vill jag ha

I want that one

Jan and Eva are trying to decide which sofa to buy

JAN: Ska vi titta på sofforna först? En skön soffa behöver vi.
EVA: Tycker du verkligen det? De här är så förskräckligt dyra.
JAN: Ja men vår gamla är förfärligt sliten. Vad tycker du om den där?
EVA: Jag vet inte. Den är grönrandig. Är den inte hemskt gräll i färgerna?
JAN: Inte alls! Jag tycker den är väldigt snygg och vi behöver något som lyser upp rummet.
EVA: Ja, det har du rätt i, men är den inte lite väl knallgrön?
JAN: Jo, kanske.
EVA: Och vi har ju rödrutiga gardiner . . .
JAN: Ja, just det. Därborta står en ganska billig soffa. Den är väl inte så dum?
EVA: Nej, den är riktigt hyfsad. Men vi kan väl titta på köksborden.
JAN: Javisst. Här har du ett rejält furubord.
EVA: Det bordet står i alla kök. Jag vill ha något ovanligt.
JAN: På det här varuhuset hittar du inga ovanliga möbler. Här handlar alla svenskar.

Vocabulary

först, first
skön -t -a, beautiful, comfortable
verkligen, really
förfärligt, terribly
den där, that one
vet/a vet visste vetat, know
grönrandig -t -a, green striped
hemskt, awfully
gräll -t -a, loud, garish
färg -en -er, colour
lys/a -er -te upp, brighten up
ha rätt i, be right
knallgrön -t -a, vivid green
kanske, perhaps
rödrutig -t -a, red checked
gardin -en -er, curtain
därborta, over there
billig -t -a, cheap, inexpensive
inte så dum -t -ma, not bad
riktigt hyfsad, quite nice
rejäl -t -a, solid
furu, pine
kök -et -, kitchen
hitta/ -r -de, find

ovanlig -t -a, unusual

handla/ -r -de, shop

Exercise 4

Always be on the look out for the sign **Rea** where there may be goods at **nedsatt pris**. A real **fynd** perhaps! You may go to a large **varuhus** or a small **affär** or **butik**. Once inside a big store you may wish to go up from the **gatuplan** to **övre plan** or down to **nedre plan**, so use the **hiss** or the **rulltrappa**. Remember when ascending or descending to **stå till höger, gå till vänster**. When you have finished your shopping go to the **utgång**.

Can you guess what these are in English?

Agreeing and disagreeing with people

In the dialogue find phrases meaning: 'Of course'; 'Not at all'; 'Well, perhaps you're right'; 'Maybe'; 'Yes, quite'. Here are some other useful phrases:

Agreement		*Disagreement*	
Det tycker jag.	I think so.	**Det tycker jag inte.**	I don't think so.
Det tror jag.	I believe so.	**Det tror jag inte.**	I don't believe so.
Det är sant.	That's true.	**Det är inte sant.**	That's not true.
Det är rätt.	That's right.	**Det är inte rätt.**	That's not right.
Det är riktigt.	That's correct.	**Det är inte riktigt.**	That's not right.
Det stämmer.	That's right.	**Det stämmer inte.**	That's not right.

Det håller jag med om.	I agree with you (about that).
Det håller jag inte med om.	I don't agree with you (about that).

Doubt may be expressed by using **kanske** (perhaps), **möjligen** (possibly), a question (**Tycker du det?**) or **Det vet jag inte** (I don't know). The word **tyvärr** (unfortunately) ameliorates disagreement: **Tyvärr tycker jag inte det.**

Demonstratives

After the demonstratives **den här** *etc.*, **den där** *etc.*, ˈ**den** *etc.* the noun adds the end article:

Non-neuter	*Neuter*	*Plural*
den här soffan (this, these)	**det här bordet**	**de här sofforna/borden**
den där soffan (that, those)	**det där bordet**	**de där sofforna/borden**
ˈden tiden (this/that, these/those)	**ˈdet året**	**ˈde frågorna**

Note: **ˈden** *etc.* (stressed **den**) is often used with abstract nouns. **Den här, den där, ˈden** *etc.* can also be used on their own:

Vad tycker du om den där?	What do you think of *that one?*
Det där är väl fint!	*That one is* nice!

See also p.169.

Amplifiers

These are adverbs qualifying an adjective or an adverb, e.g. **mycket** (very); **helt, alldeles, fullständigt** (completely); **ganska** (rather, quite), **lite** (a little); **inte alls** (not at all):

Han var mycket trevlig. He was very nice.
AMP + ADJ

De går mycket långsamt. They walk very slowly.
AMP + ADV

Notice that in terms of the sentence structure:

AMP + ADJ = Complement
AMP + ADV = MPT-expression (manner)

Note:		
very	**mycket**	**Han var mycket trevlig.**
not very	**inte särskilt**	**Han var inte särskilt trevlig.**
not much	**inte mycket**	**Han var inte mycket trevligare än Sven.** (nicer than Sven)

mycket on its own can mean 'a lot':

Han dricker mycket.	He drinks a lot.
Han dricker inte mycket.	He doesn't drink much (a lot).

Adverbs formed from adjectives (i.e. adjective + **-t**) are often used as amplifiers:

De är förskräckligt dyra	They are terribly expensive.
De är hemskt dyra	They are awfully expensive.

De är väldigt	**dyra**	They are very expensive.
De är otroligt	**dyra**	They are unbelievably expensive.

Spelling of words ending in m and n

In the section on Pronunciation at the beginning of the book a useful rule was given, namely that – generally speaking – in stressed syllables a single consonant follows a long vowel and two consonants follow a short vowel:

mat **matt** **makt** **mast**

Words ending in **-m** and **-n** are a prominent exception to this rule, however, as most of them have a short vowel followed by a single consonant, this consonant therefore acting as if it were already a long or doubled consonant:

dum hem rum program

man den din en han hon vän in igen kan min män än

But between two vowels the **m** or **n** is also doubled in the spelling:

rum	**rummet**
dum	**dumma**
man	**mannen**
vän	**vännen**

Exceptions: words with a long vowel:

fin	**fina**
bekväm	**bekväma**

Conversely, one **m** or **n** is dropped when a consonant is added in an inflected form:

gammal gamla **sommar somrar** **ett nummer numret**

Exercise 5

(a) What is the plural form of these adjectives: **gammal, långsam, tunn, dum** (stupid)?

(b) Give the form without end article of the following nouns: **programmet, mannen, hemmet** (the home), **numret, timret** (the timber)
(c) Give the singular form of the following nouns: **vänner, somrar, munnar** (mouths), **trädstammar** (tree trunks)

Factual text 6

Norrland

Man brukar dela in Sverige i tre delar – Götaland, dvs. södra landsdelen, Svealand, dvs. centrala Sverige kring Mälaren, och Norrland, resten av landet. Norrland är mycket stort men glesbefolkat. Det omfattar mer än hälften av Sveriges areal men har bara 1,2 miljoner invånare. Av dessa är 50 000 finsktalande Tornedalsbor och 15 000 är samer. Samerna talar ett eget språk, samiska, och bara 3 000 av dem är numera renskötare. I norra Norrland ser man inte solen på åtta veckor under midvintern och temperaturen kan sjunka till arktiskt låga siffror, men på sommaren är midnattssolen en stor turistattraktion. Norrland har väldiga ödemarker: myrar, mossmarker, glaciärer och höga kala fjäll över trädgränsen, och mycket folk kommer hit för att vandra i Europas sista vildmark. Men här finns också viktiga naturtillgångar: skog, mineraler och vattenkraft. För att kunna utnyttja järnmalmsfyndigheterna i Norrbotten byggde man i seklets början en järnväg mellan Luleå vid Bottniska viken och Narvik på Norges isfria atlantkust, och på 1980-talet blev en ny bilväg färdig over fjällen mellan de båda länderna.

Vocabulary

dela/ -r -de, divide
glesbefolka/d -t -de, sparsely populated
hälft -en, half
finsktalande, Finnish-speaking
språk -et, language
renskötare -n -, reindeer farmers
samiska -n, Sami, Lappish
siffra -n -or, figure
ödemark -en -er, wilderness
kal -t -a, treeless
naturtillgång -en -ar, natural resource
utnyttja/ -r -de, exploit
vattenkraft -en, hydroelectric power

järnmalmsfyndighet -en -er, iron ore find
bygg/a -er -de, build
sekel seklet sekler, century
färdig -t -a, complete, ready

The seasons

vår -en -ar	spring
sommar -en somrar	summer (note the plural)
höst -en -ar	autumn
vinter -n vintrar	winter (note the plural)
försommar	early summer
senhöst	late autumn
midvinter	midwinter
på vintern *etc.*	in the winter *etc.*

Exercise 6

(a) Fill in the missing words:

Sverige består av Norrland, Svealand och . . .
Centrala Sverige heter . . .
Norrland omfattar . . . av Sveriges areal.
Norrland har bara . . . invånare.
I Tornedalen bor 50 000 människor som talar . . .
. . . talar ett eget språk, nämligen samiska.
Bara 3000 samer är . . .
På . . . varje vinter ser man inte solen i Norrland.
Turister kommer till Norrland varje sommar för att se . . .
Långt i norr kan man . . . i Europas sista vildmark.
Omkring 1900 byggde man en . . . mellan Luleå och Narvik.
Nu kan man åka . . . på en ny väg mellan Sverige och . . .

(b) Place the words in italics first in the sentence and adjust the word order:

I norra Norrland ser *man* inte solen på åtta veckor.
På sommaren är *midnattssolen* en stor turistattraktion.
Här finns också *viktiga naturtillgångar.*
För att kunna utnyttja järnmalmsfyndigheterna byggde *man* en järnväg.
För ett par år sedan blev *en ny bilväg* färdig.

7 På stan

In town

In this lesson we will look at:

- how to link main clauses together
- the end article plural on nouns
- possessive pronouns
- how to express future time
- prepositions of place
- adverbs of location and direction
- how to translate 'where' into Swedish
- how to pronounce some difficult words
- how to understand and give directions
- money
- energy and environmental protection in Sweden

Text 7

På stan

In town

Bill Morris ska till Göteborg i affärer. Han kommer dit med tåg från Oslo. Göteborg ligger omkring 50 mil sydväst om Stockholm, på Sveriges västkust, och 30 mil söder om Oslo. På morgonen är han på möten på olika kontor och fabriker i stan. Sedan tar hans affärsvänner ut honom på lunch. Nu på eftermiddagen tänker han gå och handla. Han vill köpa några presenter, men han har inga pengar. Först går han in på en bank för att växla några resecheckar. När han kommer ut ur banken med pengarna går han längs Kungsportsavenyn för att titta i affärerna och varuhusen där. Efter alla inköp vill han dricka kaffe så han går genom parken till ett konditori vid kanalen där han vet att han kommer att få goda bakelser. När han går därifrån en halvtimme senare vill han gå på lite sightseeing. Göteborg har ett stort konstmuseum, men Bill tar spårvagnen ut till Liseberg, en stor nöjespark där det finns underhållning på kvällen.

Vocabulary

(resa) i affärer, (travel) on business
dit, there
omkring, about
mil, unit of distance (= 10 km or 6.2 English miles)
möte -t -n, meeting
pengar -na, money
affärsvän -nen -ner, business contact
present -en -er, present
bank -en -er, bank
växla/ -r -de, change (money)
in på/ut ur, into/out of
för att, to (+ intention, see p.172)
resecheck -en -ar (-er) (*pron.* - tjekk), traveller's cheque
inköp -et -, purchases
genom, through
park -en -er, park
konditori -et -er, coffee shop
vid, by, next to
kanal -en -er, canal
halvtimme -n, half hour
konstmuseum -museet -museer, art gallery
nöjespark -en -er, amusement park
underhållning -en, entertainment

Linking main clauses together

We can link together things that are of the same kind, e.g. subjects, objects, verbs or clauses. We accomplish this by placing a link word (a *coordinating conjunction* such as **och** (and)) between the words we want to link:

Erik	***och***	**Sven dricker öl.**	2 subjects are linked
De sitter	***och***	**dricker.**	2 verbs are linked
Jag gillar öl	***och***	**det gör Erik också.**	2 clauses are linked
Jag gillar öl	***men***	**Erik tycker om vin.**	2 clauses are linked
Eva dricker	***antingen***	**öl *eller* vin.**	2 objects are linked

Other link words are: **eller** (or), **men** (but), **utan** ('but' in negating clauses), **för** (as, because). Notice also: **antingen . . . eller** (either . . . or), **varken . . . eller** (neither . . . nor). Notice that they do *not* affect the word order in the main clauses they join.

Exercise 1

Insert either **och, eller, men** or **för**:

1 Joakim spelar popmusik . . . skriver brev. 2 Bill måste ha pengar . . . han ska köpa presenter. 3 Bill kan antingen ta en kopp te . . . en kopp kaffe. 4 Sofforna var mycket vackra . . . de var också dyra. 5 Han åker till Liseberg . . . där finns det underhållning.

Nouns, end article plural

How to add the end article singular to nouns is dealt with on p.33 and p.75, and how to predict the plural endings of nouns on p.75. Adding the end article plural is relatively simple. It goes on the end of the plural form. Its form can be determined by only three rules:

Type of noun	*Ending*	*Plural indefinite*	*Plural with end article*
Rule 1			
Plurals ending in a vowel + **-r**:	add **-na**	**flickor** (girls)	**flickorna** (the girls)
Note: nouns in **-are** drop **-e**:		**lärare** (teachers)	**lärarna** (the teachers)
Rule 2			
Plurals ending in other consonants (both N-words and T-words):	add **-en**	**barn** (children)	**barnen** (the children)
Note: stems in **-el, -en, -er** drop **-e**:		**lager** (layers)	**lagren** (the layers)
Rule 3			
Plurals of T-word ending in a vowel + - **n**:	add **-a**	**yrken** (occupations)	**yrkena** (the occupations)

Exercise 2

Provide the forms of these nouns in the plural and plural with end article:

ett år; en vinter; ett rum; en vecka; en timme; en skiva; en sko; en passagerare; ett landskap; ett land; ett hotell; en hamburgare; ett förkläde; en besökare; en biljett.

Possessive pronouns

These are of two types – possessives ending in **-s** we have already seen (in Lesson 4) do not add endings, but the other type have to agree with T-nouns and plurals. Here are both types:

Personal pronoun	*Possessive pronoun*		
	N-words	*T-words*	*Plurals*
jag	min son	mitt hem	mina söner/hem
du	din son	ditt hem	dina söner/hem
han	hans son	hans hem	hans söner/hem
hon	hennes son	hennes hem	hennes söner/hem
den	dess pris	dess pris	dess priser
det	dess pris	dess pris	dess priser
vi	vår son	vårt hem	våra söner/hem
ni	er son	ert hem	era söner/hem
de	deras son	deras hem	deras söner/hem

Exercise 3

What is the Swedish for:

1 Their house is very unusual. 2 Our hotel is small and simple. 3 My office is in London. 4 Where are your shoes? 5 I must change my traveller's cheques. 6 Her husband is fat but he is very pleasant. 7 His wife is beautiful but she is awfully boring. 8 Bill walks along Kungsportsavenyn with its expensive shops.

Future time

There are three ways of expressing future time in Swedish, *none* of which involves adding any special ending to the verb:

1 The present tense (often with a time marker):

Jag åker imorgon. I'll be leaving tomorrow.

Notice two verbs especially, **bli** (be, become), **tänka** (intend, think):

Det blir mörkt snart.	It'll be dark soon.
Erik tänker studera engelska.	Erik is thinking of studying English.

2 **Kommer att** + infinitive. This denotes an action independent of the speaker's hopes or wishes. An impersonal subject is often used:

Det kommer att regna ikväll.	It is going to rain tonight.

3 **Ska(ll) (skulle)** + infinitive. This usually indicates intention, warning or threat and is often used with a personal subject:

Ska du gå på bio på lördag.	Will you be going to the cinema on Saturday?
Det här ska du få ångra!	You will regret this!

Prepositions of place

In translating 'in, on, at' etc. there is a rule of thumb for distinguishing **i** from **på**:

på + surface	**i** + volume
duken på bordet the cloth on the table	**duken i skåpet** the cloth in the cupboard
Han sitter på stolen. He is sitting on the chair.	**Han sitter i stolen.** He is sitting in the (arm)chair.
Hon bor på landet. She lives in the country(side).	**Hon bor i landet.** She lives in the country (= state).

Note: **Han har ett rum i ett hus på Götgatan i Stockholm (i Sverige).**

There are unfortunately a number of common exceptions to this rule of thumb:

(a) **på** is used with public buildings, places of work or study and places of entertainment:

Vi träffas på kontoret!	See you at the office!

Han arbetar på Ericssons/ ett varuhus.	He works at Ericssons/ a department store.
Vi träffades på bio.	We met at the cinema.

Note: **i skolan, i affären (butiken), i kyrkan** (at school, in the shop, at church).

(b) **hos** is used with the names of people or professions (like French 'chez', German 'bei'):

Vi var hos Olssons igår.	We were at the Olsson's yesterday.
Han är hos tandläkaren.	He is at the dentist's.

(c) **vid** is used with things that extend lengthways:

De bor vid kusten/floden.	They live on (at) the coast/on (by) the river.

Prepositions indicating movement are:

från/till:

Bill åker från Oslo till Göteborg.	Bill is travelling from Oslo to Gothenburg.

genom, längs, över:

Han går genom parken, längs ån och över bron.	He walks through the park, along the river and over the bridge.

mot:

Spårvagnen åker mot Liseberg.	The tram travels to(wards) Liseberg.

in i (på) / ut ur:

Han gick in i huset (på kontoret), men en minut senare kom han ut ur huset igen.	He went into the building (office), but a minute later he came out of the building again.

Exercise 4

Insert a suitable preposition of place:

1 Han satt . . . en soffa . . . vardagsrummet. 2 Jag arbetar . . . ett kontor . . . Eriksgatan. 3 Förr bodde vi . . . landet, men nu har vi ett hus . . . staden. 4 Nils går . . . skolan och hans syster Eva arbetar . . . ett

varuhus. 5 Bill åkte . . . Oslo . . . Göteborg . . . tåg. 6 Igår åt vi middag . . . . Olssons och ikväll tänker vi gå . . . bio. 7 Han gick . . . parken och . . . ån. 8 Det fanns ett konditori . . . kanalen. 9 Bill gick . . . konditoriet. 10 När han hade kommit . . . banken, tog han spårvagnen . . . Liseberg.

Adverbs of location, direction and origin

Swedish adverbs of place (which are MPT-expressions) often have three different forms to indicate location at a place, movement towards a place or movement from a place:

Location (no movement)		*Direction (movement towards)*		*Origin (movement away from)*	
Bill sitter *där*. Bill is sitting there.		**Han åker *dit*.** He is going there.		**Han går *därifrån*.** He is leaving there.	
Notice also:					
här	here	**hit**		**härifrån**	from here
var	where	**vart**		**varifrån**	where . . . from
hemma	at home	**hem**	(to) home	**hemifrån**	
borta	away	**bort**		**bortifrån**	
inne	in	**in**		**inifrån**	
ute	out	**ut**		**utifrån**	
uppe	up	**upp**		**uppifrån**	
nere	down	**ner**		**nerifrån**	
framme	in front, there	**fram**		**framifrån**	from the front

The adverb alone or MPT-expression (see p.59) may indicate movement and the verb of motion may be omitted when a modal verb is present:

Han ska till Lund imorgon.	He is going to Lund tomorrow.
Jag ska hem.	I'm off home.

Adverbs of the same kind can be compounded: **därnere** (down there), **därborta** (over there), **ditin** (in there) (movement), etc.

Where

When it is a v-word in a question the word 'where' may (as we have seen above) be **var** if it implies location or **vart** if it implies motion, but as a relative pronoun it is **där** if it implies location or **dit** if it implies motion:

ett bra konditori där han kommer att få bakelser	a good café where he will get cakes
en stor nöjespark där det finns underhållning	a large amusement park where there is entertainment
ett konditori dit vi kan gå	a café where we can go
en nöjespark dit vi kan åka	an entertainment park where we can go

där is also used for 'there' (of place):

det ligger många affärer där	there are a lot of shops there

Exercise 5

What is the Swedish for:

1 Where are you going? 2 I'm off out shortly. 3 Where are you now? 4 I am here at home. 5 Can you get in here immediately as I am going out soon? 6 Is there a bank there? 7 Where is the bank? 8 It's over there by the canal. 9 I know a bank where you can change your traveller's cheques.

Pronunciation 7

Some difficult words

(a) Silent letters:

-g: **jag** (I), **dag** (day), **dagen** (the day), **någon** (someone), **morgon** (morning), **i söndags** (last Sunday)
Notice shortening of the vowel, in (*pron.*) nån

-d: **med** (with), **vad** (what), **staden** (the town), **sådan** (such), **sedan** (then), **bredvid** (beside)
Notice shortening of the vowel, in:(*pron.*) va, sån, sen

-k: **hemskt** (awfully), **kritiskt** (critically)

-l:	**karl** (chap), **världen** (the world)
-t:	**det** (it), **mycket** (very), **litet** (little), **konsert** (concert), **skjuts** (lift)

(b) Words not spelled as they are pronounced:

de (they)	*pron.* dom	**att** (to)	*pron.* å, att
dem (them)	*pron.* dom	(cf. **att** (that)	*pron.* att)
lade (laid)	*pron.* la	**mig** (me)	*pron.* mej,
sa(de) (said)	*pron.* sa	**dig** (you),	*pron.* dej
och (and)	*pron.* å, ock	**sig** (himself)	*pron.* sej

(c) Loan words:

Notice these *exceptions* to the rules in Pronunciation 2 and 4 for **g-**, **j-**, **sk-**, and that the final **-e** is not pronounced in these words:

As Swedish **sj**: **gara*g*e** (garage), **baga*g*e** (luggage), **bei*g*e** (beige), **reporta*g*e** (report)

***g*eni** (genius), ***g*enerad** (embarrassed), ***g*enre** (genre)

***sh*erry**, ***sh*orts**

***j*ournalist** (reporter), ***j*alusi** (jealousy), ***j*ustera**, (adjust)

männi*sk*a (human being)

Dialogue 7

Att hitta rätt

Finding your way

Bill gets talking in the bank

BILL MORRIS:	Jo, jag skulle vilja växla några resecheckar. Går det bra här?
BANKTJÄNSTEMANNEN:	Ja, det går fint. Finns det legitimation?
BILL MORRIS:	Jag har mitt pass, men det duger kanske inte?

BANKTJÄNSTEMANNEN:	Jodå. Det är svenskarna som inte får använda passet. Hur vill du ha pengarna? Hundralappar?
BILL MORRIS:	Två femhundrakronorssedlar och resten i hundralappar, tack.
BANKTJÄNSTEMANNEN:	Varsågod.
BILL MORRIS:	Hur kommer jag förresten härifrån till Wahlströms konditori?
BANKTJÄNSTEMANNEN:	Vi ska se. Gå den här gatan rakt fram tills du kommer till trafikljusen vid gatukorsningen. Ta till vänster där och gå rakt igenom parken på andra sidan, så kommer du till kanalen och där ligger det.
BILL MORRIS:	Är det långt?
BANKTJÄNSTEMANNEN:	Inte särskilt. Tio minuter högst.
BILL MORRIS:	Tack för hjälpen!
BANKTJÄNSTEMANNEN:	Prova deras Napoleonbakelser. De är särskilt goda.
BILL MORRIS:	Det ska jag komma ihåg.

Vocabulary

banktjänsteman -nen -män, bank clerk
Går det bra?, Is that all right?
legitimation -en, identification
pass -et -, passport
dug/a -er dög, be acceptable, good enough
hundralappar (see 'Money' below)
härifrån, from here
trafikljus -et -, traffic lights
höger, vänster, right, left
rakt fram (see 'Directions' below)
gatukorsning- en -ar, junction
högst, at most
prova/ -r -de, try, test
Napoleonbakelse -n -r, puff pastry and cream cake with pink icing
komma ihåg, remember

Directions

In the dialogue find phrases meaning: 'turn left', 'then you come to the canal', 'go straight down the street', 'on the other side', 'is it far?' Here are some other useful phrases:

ta till vänster (höger)	turn left (right)
på vänster (höger) hand	on the left (right) hand side
rakt igenom/tvärs över	straight through/across

du följer den gatan förbi kyrkan	you follow that street past the church
innan du kommer till	before you come to
nära/i närheten av/intill	close to, in the vicinity of
(i riktning) mot	in the direction of/towards
runt	round

Exercise 6

What is the Swedish for:

1 The stores are in the centre – go straight on and they are on your right. 2 His office is on this side of the park, past the art gallery. 3 Go over the canal and then turn left. 4 Then take tram number 7. 5 Go along the river, and it's near the church, before you come to the station. 6 It's not very far from here, three minutes at most.

Money

Remember **100 öre = 1 krona (pl. kronor)**. Swedish currency has the following denominations:

Coins **(mynt)**: 50 öre, 1 krona, 5 kronor, 10 kronor.
Notes **(sedlar)**: 50 kronor, 100 kronor, 500 kronor, 1000 kronor, 10 000 kronor

Notice the names of coins and notes:

femti(o)öring -en -ar	50 öre coin
enkrona -n -or	1 krona coin
femkrona -n vor	5 kronor coin
tjuga -n -or	20 kronor note
femtilapp -en -ar	50 kronor note
hundralapp -en -ar	100 kronor note

Prices are expressed as follows:

Written	*Spoken*
1,50 or 1 50	enåfemti
8,90 or 8 90	åttaånitti

Other phrases:

växel/småpengar	change
Kan du växla en femma i enkronor?	Can you change a five kronor (coin) into one krona coins?

The 20-kronor note or 'tjuga'

Shown is the Nobel Prize-winning author Selma Lagerlöf; this note is sometimes called 'en selma'.

The 100-kronor note

Shown is the Swedish botanist Carl von Linné. See also Factual text 16.

Factual text 7

Energi och miljövård

Energy and environmental protection

Enligt en folkomröstning den 23 mars 1980 blir det en ändring i Sveriges energipolitik. I framtiden kommer man inte att använda så mycket olja, för man vill spara energi. Man ämnar sluta med kärnkraft före år 2010, och Sveriges 12 kärnkraftverk ska avvecklas successivt. Det är emellertid osäkert om detta går att verkställa inom utsatt tid, men de flesta politiker är ense om att man bör försöka. Det är inte särskilt billigt med kärnkraft och det är farligt. Tjernobylolyckan bevisar detta. P g a. olyckan kommer renarna i Norrland att förbli radioaktiva i många år och samernas kultur är hotad. Avfallsfrågan är inte heller löst. Man tänker undersöka alternativa kraftkällor som sol, vind och torv. Man kommer också att pumpa mer värme direkt ur marken. Sverige har inget eget kol och ingen olja. Det finns mycket vattenkraft i landet, och den kan man naturligtvis bygga ut för att få mer el, men då blir det säkert konflikt med miljövännerna. De är rädda för att nya vattenkraftverk vid norrlandsälvarna kommer att förstöra miljön.

Vocabulary

folkomröstning -en -ar, referendum
ändring -en -ar, change
sluta/ -r -de (med), finish, stop
kärnkraft -en, nuclear power
avveckla/s - -des, be phased out
verkställ/a -er -de, carry out
ense, agreed
farlig -t -a, dangerous
bevisa/ -r -de, prove
p g a = på grund av, because of
ren -en -ar, reindeer
hota/d -t -de, threatened
lös/a -er -te, solve
spara/ -r -de, save
undersök/a -er -te, investigate
avfall -et, waste
bygg/a -er -de ut, develop, expand
i framtiden, in future
källa -n -or, source, spring
torv -en, peat
mark -en, ground
el = elektricitet -en, electricity
miljövän -nen -ner, environmentalist
förstör/a -de, destroy
miljö -n -er, environment

Exercise 7

Svara på svenska:

1 När blev det en folkomröstning om energipolitik? 2 Hur många kärnkraftverk har Sverige nu? 3 Hur många kärnkraftverk blir det efter år 2010? 4 Vad bevisar Tjernobylolyckan? 5 Varför är samernas kultur hotad? 6 Vilka andra kraftkällor finns det förutom olja? 7 Har Sverige kol och olja? 8 Har Sverige vattenkraft? 9 Vad är miljövännerna rädda för?

8 På universitetet

At the university

In this lesson we will look at:

- verb patterns
- the perfect and pluperfect tenses
- postponing the subject
- subordinate clauses
- link words
- indeclinable adjectives
- how to pronounce voiced consonants with **s, t**
- more phrases for agreeing and disagreeing with people
- how to use the particles **ju, nog, väl** and **nämligen**
- Midsummer

Text 8

På universitetet

At the university

Nu har universitetskurserna börjat, och Rebecca ska studera svensk litteratur. Hon har anmält sig till en fempoängskurs i Strindbergs dramatik. Hon har köpt ett kollegieblock och en pärm i Akademibokhandeln och har tagit med sig en svensk–engelsk ordbok ifall hon behöver slå upp några svåra ord. Det sitter ett trettiotal studenter i föreläsningssalen. De pratar om vad de har gjort på sommaren. För det mesta har de badat och solat sig. Rebecca har inte lärt känna någon av de andra studenterna ännu. Fastän hon har jobbat hårt med språket hela sommaren har hon ändå svårt att förstå stockholmarna. Eftersom hon inte har fått arbetstillstånd, har hon inte kunnat arbeta i Sverige, och därför har hon inte haft så mycket pengar heller. Nu har läraren kommit in. Föreläsningen har börjat och alla antecknar flitigt. Rebecca tycker att det är ganska lätt att följa med, eftersom hon har läst 'Mäster Olof' tidigare. Mot slutet vågar hon ställa en fråga. Läraren blir imponerad av hennes kunskaper och frågar varifrån hon kommer. De andra studenterna börjar titta intresserat på henne. På rasten, när hon har ställt sig i kaffekön, kommer ett par av dem fram till henne och börjar prata.

Vocabulary

kurs -en -er, course
litteratur -en -er, literature
anmäl/a -er -de sig, register, enrol oneself
fempoängskurs, five week course
dramatik -en, drama
kollegieblock -et -, note pad
pärm -en -ar, folder
Akademibokhandel -n, the university bookshop
ordbok -en -böcker, dictionary
ifall, if, in case
slå/ -r slog upp, look up
svår -t -a, difficult
ord -et -, word
ett trettiotal, about thirty
föreläsningssal -en -ar, lecture room
bada/ -r -de, swim
sola/ -r -de sig, sunbathe
lär/a - -de känna, get to know
ännu, yet
fastän, although
jobba/ -r -de, work
ändå, nevertheless
språk -et -, language
stockholmare -n -, Stockholmer
arbetstillstånd -et -, work permit
därför, this is why
heller, either
anteckna/ -r -de, take notes
flitigt, assiduously
följ/a -er -de med, follow
'Mäster Olof', *Master Olof* (play by Strindberg)
tidigare, earlier
lätt - -a, easy
slut -et, end
våga/ -r -de, dare
ställ/a -er -de en fråga, ask a question
imponerad -t -de, impressed
kunskap -en -er, knowledge
rast -en -er, break
ställ/a -er -de sig, *lit.* place oneself; *here*: join
kö -n -er, queue
komm/a -er kom fram till, go up to
par -et -, couple

Verb patterns

Some verb patterns are found on p.78. The complete pattern of regular tense endings for conjugations I–IV is as follows:

	Imperative (= stem)	Infinitive	Present	Past	Supine
I	**-a/** **parkera** (park)	**-a/** **parkera**	**-a/r** **parkerar**	**-a/de** **parkerade**	**-a/t** **parkerat**
IIa	-consonant/ **bygg** (build)	**-/a** **bygga**	**-/er** **bygger**	**-/de** **byggde**	**-/t** **byggt**
IIb	-consonant/ **hjälp** (help)	**-/a** **hjälpa**	**-/er** **hjälper**	**-/te** **hjälpte**	**-/t** **hjälpt**
III	-vowel/ (not-**a**) **sy** (sew)	-vowel/ (not-**a**) **sy**	**-/r** **syr**	**-/dde** **sydde**	**-/tt** **sytt**
IV	-consonant/ **skriv** (write)	**-/a** **skriva**	**-/er** **skriver**	Change of stem vowel. No ending. **skrev**	**-/it** **skrivit**

Conjugations I, II and III are sometimes called 'weak' verbs – they form their past tense by adding an ending: **parkera** – **parkera*de*** (cf. park – park*ed*), whilst Conjugation IV verbs are 'strong' verbs they form their past tense by changing the stem vowel: **dr*i*cka** – **dr*a*ck** (cf. dr*i*nk – dr*a*nk). As you can see from the examples, this is a distinction also found in English. Conjugation IIa verbs have stems ending in a voiced consonant, IIb verbs have stems ending in an unvoiced consonant (**-k**, **-p**, **-s**, **-t**).

Perfect and pluperfect tenses

The perfect tense is formed by the verb **har** + the supine (i.e. **har** is VERB$_1$ and the supine is VERB$_2$). The supine is an unchanging form which corresponds to the past participle in most European languages. Swedish supines always end in **-t** but vary slightly in form according to conjugation:

	Imperative (*= stem*)	*Perfect* (**har** + *supine*)	*Supine ending*
I	**Parkera bilen!**	**Vi har parkera/*t* bilen.**	**-t**
IIa	**Bygg en stuga!**	**De har bygg/*t* en stuga.**	**-t**
IIb	**Hjälp dem!**	**Jag har hjälp/*t* dem.**	**-t**
III	**Sy gardiner!**	**Hon har sy/*tt* gardinerna.**	**-tt**
IV	**Skriv brevet!**	**Har du inte skriv/*it* brevet?**	**-it**

The pluperfect tense is formed by using **hade** + supine:

Vi hade parker*at* bilen.
De hade bygg*t* en stuga.
Jag hade hjälp*t* dem.
De sy*tt* gardiner.
Hon hade skriv*it* ett brev.

These tenses are employed in much the same way as in English.

Exercise 1

Change the verb into the past tense:

1 Rebecca har anmält sig till en kurs. 2 Hon har köpt ett kollegieblock. 3 Hon har lärt känna några studenter. 4 De har börjat titta på henne. 5 Det har varit lätt. 6 Hon har ställt sig i kön.

Exercise 2

Change the verb into the perfect tense:

1 Studenterna pratar om semestern. 2 De antecknar flitigt. 3 Rebecca vågar ställa en fråga. 4 Hon behöver slå upp några ord. 5 Hon ställer en fråga. 6 Han frågar henne om Strindberg. 7 Hon tycker att det är svårt. 8 Hon skriver brev.

Exercise 3

Give the form with end article plural of the following nouns:

ett kraftverk; en miljövän; ett kollegieblock; en ordbok; ett ord; en sommar; ett språk; en kurs; en stockholmare; en fråga, en föreläsning.

Postponing the subject

When a completely new idea is introduced this idea is usually postponed, i.e. moved towards the end of the sentence, but it has then to be replaced as subject with a *formal subject* (FS). This happens in both English and Swedish. In Swedish the formal subject is always **det**. In English it is 'there' or 'it' depending on the type of postponed or *real subject* (RS).

Någon **sitter i köket.** RS	**Det sitter** ***någon*** **i köket.** FS RS
Someone is sitting in the kitchen.	There is someone sitting in the kitchen.
Att lära sig svenska **är lätt.** RS	**Det är lätt** ***att lära sig svenska.*** FS RS
Learning Swedish is easy.	It is easy to learn Swedish.

Notice that in Swedish the real subject is always moved to the right of the verb, where the complement or object might go.

Det sitter ofta *studenter* på biblioteket.
FS VERB ADV RS PLACE

The major difference between Swedish and English is that any intransitive verb may be used in Swedish constructions of this kind, whilst English only permits the verb 'to be':

Det bor 8 miljoner människor i Sverige.	There are 8 million people living in Sweden.

One of the most frequent verbs used is **finnas** (be, exist):

Det finns bröd i skåpet.	There is bread in the cupboard.

Notice that this construction is very frequent in questions, when the formal subject comes immediately before the real subject:

Finns det *inget öl* hemma? Is there no beer in the house?
VERB FS RS

Exercise 4

It is unusual to begin a sentence with an indefinite noun phrase, so make sentences of the following groups, inserting a formal subject:

1 ett konditori/ ligger/ vid kanalen 2 ett tåg/ till Göteborg/ går/ kl åtta 3 en lärare/ kommer/ hit till Rebecca 4 många studenter/ står/ i kön 5 en miljon böcker/ finns/ på universitetsbiblioteket

Sub(ordinate) clauses

Subordinate clauses or sub clauses are groups of words which include a verb and form part of a main clause sentence, i.e. they are: MPT-expression, subject or object.

	Verb	*Adverb*	*Object*	*MPT-expression*
Vi	**äter**	**ju**	**middag**	***kl 8.***
Vi	**äter**	**ju**	**middag**	***när Erik kommer.***

The words in italics are both MPT-expressions but **kl 8** is a noun phrase (NP), and **när Erik kommer** is a clause.

Sentences containing a clause of this kind are:

Rebecca har lätt för det, *eftersom hon har läst boken.*
Hon har tagit med en ordbok *ifall hon behöver slå upp några ord.*

Clauses like this can be moved to the front just like other MPT-expressions, but then the subject and verb in the main clause must be inverted:

När hon har ställt sig i kön,	**kommer**	**ett par studenter fram.**
	VERB	SUBJ
Fastän hon har jobbat hårt,	**har**	**hon svårt att förstå.**
	VERB	SUBJ

Link words

Sub clauses usually begin with a link word (*subordinating conjunction*, cf. p.101) which is part of the clause. The most frequent of these are:

att (that) which introduces indirect speech:

Rebecca sa *att hon hade läst boken.*

om (whether) which introduces indirect yes/no questions:

De frågade henne *om hon hade läst boken tidigare.*

Link words introducing clauses which are MPT-expressions:

With clauses denoting time:

när/då/sedan	when, after
medan	while
innan	before

Vi fikar *innan vi går på föreläsningen.*

With clauses denoting cause:

för att	because
eftersom	because
därför att	because

Hon har inte kunnat arbeta *eftersom hon inte har fått arbetstillstånd.*

With clauses denoting condition:

ifall	if
om	if

Hon kunde ha solat sig *om hon hade haft pengar.*

With clauses denoting concession:

fast(än)	although

***Fastän hon har jobbat hårt* har hon svårt att förstå.**

Sub clauses are often placed either at the beginning or end of the sentence, and the link word may therefore introduce the sentence:

Du får glass *ifall du är snäll.* ***Ifall du är snäll* får du glass.**
SUB CLAUSE SUB CLAUSE

Hon kan förstå läraren *eftersom hon har studerat svenska tidigare.*
***Eftersom hon har studerat svenska tidigare* kan hon förstå läraren.**

Exercise 5

Form one sentence from the words below, beginning with the link word in italics.

1 *när*	Rebecca kommer in i salen. Ett trettital studenter sitter där.
2 *ifall*	Du behöver slå upp några ord. Du måste ha en ordbok.
3 *eftersom*	Hon ställer en fråga. Några kommer fram och pratar med henne.
4 *om*	Vi jobbar hårt. Vi kommer att kunna förstå stockholmarna.
5 *fastän*	Jag har läst boken tidigare. Jag har svårt att följa med.

Som/att

Both **som** and **att** translate English 'that'. Both introduce a new clause, but notice:

Att immediately follows a verb – it is a link word (subordinating conjunction, = 'that'):

Jag sa att hon talade bra svenska.	I said that she spoke good Swedish.

Som usually follows a noun – it is a relative pronoun (= who, which):

Kön som hon ställde sig i var lång.	The queue that she joined was long.

Som is also used in emphatic constructions (see p.135, = 'who, which'):

Det var en bok som hon hade lånat mig förra veckan.	It was a book that she had lent me last week

However, as with 'that' or 'which' in English, **som** is often omitted when it is not the subject and **att** is often omitted in speech after verbs of saying, thinking, perceiving:

Den svenska (som) hon talade hade hon lärt sig i England.	The Swedish (that) she spoke she had learnt in England.
Hon sa (att) det inte var roligt.	She said (that) it was not funny.

Indeclinable adjectives

Adjectives usually agree with the noun they qualify (see also p.62):

ett stor*t* hus	**rolig*a* historier**
huset är stor*t*	**historierna var rolig*a***

But a small group of adjectives add no endings. These are of four kinds:

1 Adjectives ending in **-s**:

gammaldags möbler	old-fashioned furniture
ett medelålders biträde	a middle-aged assistant

Exception: those in **-ös**:

ett nervös*t* barn	a nervous child

2 Adjectives ending in **-e**:

ett öde hus	a deserted house
ett främmande språk	a foreign language

This group includes all present participles in **-(a)nde** or **-ende** (often used as adjectives, see p.186):

ett växande intresse	a growing interest

3 Adjectives ending in **-a**:

ett bra tag	a good while
ett medeltida slott	a medieval castle

4 Others:

Arbetet var slut för dagen.	Work was over for the day.
Jag slog fel nummer.	I dialled the wrong number.
Fönstret är sönder.	The window is broken.

Exercise 6

Give the correct indefinite form of the adjective:

1 På posten får man ett (gratis = 'free') vykort. 2 Man får (god) bakelser på konditoriet. 3 Det är ett (bra) konditori. 4 De studerar ett (samtida = 'contemporary') drama. 5 Hon har köpt ett (stor)

kollegieblock. 6 De tittade på henne med (äkta = 'genuine') intresse. 7 Det är ett (främmande) ord. 8 Göteborg har ett (fin) konstmuseum.

Pronunciation 8

s, t and voiced consonants

Before or after **s** the pronunciation of some consonants often changes from voiced to voiceless. Notice the following cases:

d > t:	**onsdag**	*pron.*	onsta	
g > k:	**hur dags?**	*pron.*	hur daks	(what time?)
	vilken slags?		slaks	(what kind?)
v > f:	**livstid**	*pron.*	lifstid	(lifetime)
	till havs		till hafs	(to sea)
b > p:	**substantiv**	*pron.*	suppstantiv	(noun)
	asbest	*pron.*	aspest	(asbestos)

This also happens before **t**:

g > k:	**högt**	*pron.*	hökt	(high(ly))
	sagt		sakt	(said)
b > p:	**snabbt**	*pron.*	snappt	(quickly)

Dialogue 8

Ja, det stämmer

Yes, that's right

Rebecca is talking to two new friends at Stockholm University

PERNILLA: Ska vi slå oss ner här?

HENRIK: Nej, helst inte. Här får man ju inte röka. Vi sätter oss därborta där det är tillåtet. Gör det något om jag röker, Rebecca?

REBECCA: Nej, för all del.

HENRIK: Så du kommer från England.

REBECCA: Ja, det stämmer.

HENRIK: Vad tycker du om Stockholms universitet då?
REBECCA: Jag vet inte. Det är hemskt stort och anonymt. Jag föredrar nog England.
HENRIK: Ja, jag håller med dig, men det är inte så farligt som det verkar här. Studenterna har nämligen mycket kontakt med varandra.
PERNILLA: Du pratar jättebra svenska. Visst gör hon, Henrik! Och Strindberg har du redan läst. Hur länge har du pluggat svenska?
REBECCA: Två år.
PERNILLA: Men då hade du väl studerat lite svenska innan du började.
REBECCA: Nej, inte en rad. Jag hade aldrig hört eller läst svenska, men jag hade träffat en svensk kille. Han lurade mig att läsa svenska.
HENRIK: Ångrar du dig då?
REBECCA: Nej, inte ett dugg.
PERNILLA: Nej, och det bästa sättet att lära sig svenska är att bli kär i en svensk, inte sant Henrik?
HENRIK: Jo, precis.

Vocabulary

slå/ -r slog sig ner, sit down
sätt/a -er satte sig, sit down
tillåtet, allowed
Gör det något?, Does it matter?
för all del, by all means
anonym -t -a, anonymous
föredra/ -r -drog något, prefer something to
framför något annat, something else
håll/a -er höll med någon, agree with someone
Det är inte så farligt, It's not so bad.
verka/ -r -de, seem
varandra, each other
jättebra, terrific
Visst gör hon?, Doesn't she though?
plugga/ -r -de (*colloquial*), study = **studera**
rad -en -er, line
hör/a hör -de, hear
kille -n -ar (*colloquial*), boy = **pojke**
lura/ -r -de, fool someone
ångra/ -r -de sig, regret
inte ett dugg, not a bit
bli kär i någon, fall in love with someone
sätt -et -, way

More phrases for agreeing and disagreeing with people

See also p.95. In the dialogue find phrases meaning roughly: 'Yes, exactly', 'No, not a bit', 'Isn't that right Henrik?', 'No, not at all', 'Yes, that's correct', 'I agree (with you).' Here are some other useful phrases:

agreement:	**Det stämmer.**	That's right.
	Jag håller med dig.	I agree (with you).
	Precis.	Exactly.
	Absolut!	Absolutely!
	Just det!	Quite!
	Det har du rätt i.	You are quite right.
	Inte jag heller.	Nor me.
	Inte sant?	Isn't that so?
	Nej, för all del.	No, of course not.
doubt:	**Nja . . .**	Well . . .
	Möjligen/Kanske.	Possibly/Perhaps.
	Ja, . . . men . . .	Yes . . . but . . .
disagreement:	**Inte alls.**	Not at all.
	Visst inte.	Of course not.
	Det tycker jag inte.	I don't think so.
	Det är fel.	That's wrong.
	Jag håller inte med dig om detta.	I don't agree with you (about that).

Ju, nog, väl, nämligen

These are unstressed adverbs which indicate the attitude of the speaker to the listener:

ju = 'you know, of course'. You expect the listener to agree or be familiar with what you are saying:

Där kommer ju Pelle!

nog = 'presumably, probably, I expect, I daresay'. You inject a note of doubt:

Det går nog bra, ska du se.

väl = 'surely, I hope, I suppose'. You hope the listener will agree:

Du är väl inte sjuk?

nämligen = 'you understand, you see'. You are saying something new. Compare:

Du måste komma idag. Imorgon är jag nämligen borta.
You must come today. As you know, I am away tomorrow.

Du måste komma idag. Imorgon är jag ju i Uppsala.
You must comes today as I shall be in Uppsala tomorrow, you see.

Exercise 7

To see what you have learned from Lesson 8 so far, translate into Swedish:

1 All summer the others have been sunning themselves, but Rebecca has been working hard. 2 She had brought to the lecture a pad that she bought at the bookshop. 3 Afterwards a couple of the students ask where she comes from and how long she has studied Swedish. 4 Swedish teachers are awfully difficult to understand, aren't they Rebecca? 5 Yes, that's right. 6 But, if you have read a bit before you come to Sweden you can understand the Swedes. 7 Is it as bad as it seems in Stockholm? 8 No, not at all. 9 I agree with you that it's anonymous and I really prefer Bradford. 10 Falling in love with a Swedish boy is the best way of getting to know the country.

Factual text 8

Midsommar

Midsummer

Kring midsommar har man korta ljusa nätter och i norra Sverige kan man se midnattssolen. Midsommar firar man en fredag i juni. På midsommarafton pryder folk huset, bilen och kyrkan med blommor och löv. Flickorna binder blomsterkransar som de bär på huvudet. Många flyr staden den helgen och åker ut på landet. Dalarna är särskilt populärt. På eftermiddagen reser man majstången mitt i byn. Sedan blir det dans kring stången, och på kvällen och natten fortsätter man att dansa på en loge eller en brygga. På midsommarafton äter man ofta traditionella rätter: sill och färskpotatis med dill, och till efterrätt nyplockade jordgubbar. Om en ung flicka vill veta vem hon ska gifta sig med ska hon gå ut på en äng på midsommarnatten, plocka sju sorters blommor och stoppa dem under kudden. Då drömmer hon alltid om den blivande brudgummen. En annan säker metod är att äta en saltsill (den s.k. 'drömsillen').

Vocabulary

kort - -a, short
ljus -t -a, light
fira/ -r -de, celebrate
pryd/a -er -de, decorate
blomsterkrans -en -ar, flower garland
helg -en -er, weekend, holiday
majstång -en -stänger, maypole
bär/a - bar, carry; *here*: wear
loge -n -ar, barn
brygga -n -or, jetty
sill -en, herring
efterrätt -en -er, sweet course
jordgubbe -n -ar, strawberry
äng -en -ar, meadow
kudde -n -ar, pillow
den blivande brudgummen, her bridegroom-to-be

Exercise 8

Sätt ett kryss i rutan: (Place a cross in the box)	**rätt** (*right*)	**fel** (*wrong*)
I hela Sverige ser man midnattssolen kring midsommar.	☐	☐
Midsommarafton firas alltid på en fredag.	☐	☐
Man arbetar inte på midsommarafton.	☐	☐
Många åker ut på landsbygden över midsommar.	☐	☐
Man brukar resa majstången på en loge eller brygga.	☐	☐
Kring stången dansar man.	☐	☐
Om en flicka vill veta vem hon ska gifta sig med plockar hon jordgubbar och stoppar dem under kudden.	☐	☐
Saltsill är en traditionell rätt vid midsommar.	☐	☐

Flickor sätter kransar på huvudet.	☐	☐
Om man äter saltsill drömmer man om den blivande brudgummen.	☐	☐

9 Sven mådde illa

Sven felt sick

In this lesson we will look at:

- weak conjugations (I, II, III) of verbs and the past tense
- definite adjective forms
- emphatic constructions
- expressions of time
- avoiding intrusive r in pronunciation
- how to express likes and dislikes
- the pronouns **sådan, någon, ingen,** etc.
- Gustav Vasa – the founder of Sweden

Text 9

Sven mådde illa

Sven felt sick

En lördagskväll ordnade några av studenterna en fest. Det var Pernilla som kom på idén och som samlade in pengar av dem som skulle vara med. Men det var Erik och Sven som åkte ner på staden för att handla. De köpte olika sorters ostar, hårt bröd, franskbröd och smör, ett par burkar sill och lite korv. Sedan valde de bland frukten. De gröna äpplena passade till äppelkaka, de saftiga persikorna var billiga och de blåa druvorna behövde de till osten. De hittade inga bananer.

Öl och sprit skaffade de på Systemet. Skulle de servera danskt brännvin och svenskt öl eller tvärtom? Erik ville ha dansk snaps, men Sven föredrog renat. Till slut köpte de 'Skåne', en kompromiss. De glömde köpa pappersservetter och stearinljus, så de stannade vid ett näröppet på hemvägen. Eftersom de betalade med kreditkort märkte de inte hur dyrt det blev.

Hemma hos Sven dukade de på det stora bordet i köket. De prydde glasen med de lila servetterna och tände de små stearinljusen. Klockan halv nio började gästerna anlända och klockan tio hade alla kommit. De pratade och dansade, lyssnade på musik och smakade på den goda maten.

Nästa morgon mådde Sven förskräckligt illa. Han måste gå på toaletten och där spydde han. Hans huvud dunkade och han lovade att han aldrig skulle dricka någon alkohol mer så länge han levde.

Vocabulary

må/ -r -dde illa, feel ill
ordna/ -r -de, organise
fest -en -er, party
kom på idén, had the idea
samla/ -r -de in, collect
franskbröd -et, French bread
hårt bröd, crispbread
korv -en -ar, sausage
välj/a -er valde, choose
frukt -en, fruit
passa/ -r -de (till), be suitable (for)
saftig -t -a, juicy
persika -n -or, peach
druva -n -or, grapes
banan -en -er, banana
sprit -en, spirits
skaffa/ -r -de, get, obtain
Systemet = Systembolaget, state-run liquor store
servera/ -r -de, serve
dansk -t -a, Danish
svensk -t -a, Swedish
tvärtom, vice versa
renat, unflavoured schnapps
'Skåne', schnapps flavoured with aniseed
kompromiss -en -er, compromise
glömm/a -er glömde, forget
pappersservett -en -er, paper napkins
stearinljus -et -, candle
(ett) näröppet, corner shop (often open late)
kreditkort -et -, credit card
märk/a -er -te, notice
duka/ -r -de, set the table
lila (*indeclinable*), mauve
tänd/a -er -e, light
gäst -en -er, guest
anländ/a -er -e, arrive (of people)
lyssna/ -r -de, listen
musik -en, music
spy/ -r -dde, be sick
dunka/ -r -de, pound
lova/ -r -de, promise
alkohol -en, alcohol
lev/a -er -de, live

Verbs – weak conjugations (I, II, III), past tense

The pattern for verbs given on p.115 included weak verbs whose past tense (sometimes called *imperfect* or *preterite)* endings, as in English (call/*ed*, ask/*ed*), always include a **-d** or **-t**:

	Infinitive	*Present*	*Past*	*Supine*	
I	**fråga/**	**fråga/r**	**fråga/de**	**fråga/t**	ask
IIa	**bygg/a**	**bygg/er**	**bygg/de**	**bygg/t**	build
IIb	**läs/a**	**läs/er**	**läs/te**	**läs/t**	read
III	**tro/**	**tro/r**	**tro/dde**	**tro/tt**	believe

Conjugation I

This group with a stem ending in **-a** contains two-thirds of all Swedish verbs in the dictionary and a quarter of all verbs in common use as well as all verbs in **-era** and all new verbs, e.g. loan words: **jobba** (work), **lifta** (hitch a lift), **parkera** (park a car), **nationalisera** (nationalise), **studera** (study).

Conjugation II

As we can see above, Conjugation II verbs are divided into two subgroups according to the form of the past tense ending – IIa verbs have **-de**, IIb verbs have **-te**.

Conjugation IIb verbs all have stems ending in the unvoiced consonants **-k**, **-p**, **-s**, **-t** or **-x**:

tyck/*te*, köp/*te*, läs/*te*, möt/*te*, väx/*te*

One or two types of Conjugation II verbs have patterns varying slightly from the main pattern (see also **r**-stem verbs on p.78):

Verbs whose stems end in a consonant + **-d** only add **-e** in the past tense, and drop the **-d** in the supine:

använd/a	**använd/er**	**använd/e**	**använt**	use

Verbs whose stems end in **-mm** and **-nn** drop an **-m** or **-n** before adding **-de** in the past tense (see p.97) and **-t** in the supine:

glömm/a	**glömm/er**	**glöm/de**	**glöm/t**	forget
känn/a	**känn/er**	**kän/de**	**kän/t**	feel

Verbs whose stems end in a consonant + **-t** only add **-e** in the past tense and drop the **-t** in the supine:

gift/a	**gift/er**	**gift/e**	**gift/**	marry

Conjugation III

This is a very small group of verbs whose stems end in a long stressed vowel other than **-a**. This vowel is shortened before the past tense ending **-dde** and supine ending **-tt**:

- **-e**: **ske** (occur)
- **-o**: **tro** (believe), **bero** (depend)
- **-y**: **avsky** (detest), **bry** (care)
- **-ö**: **strö** (sprinkle)
- **-ä**: **klä** (dress)
- **-å**: **rå** (be able, manage)

Irregular weak verbs

These verbs do not fit in exactly with any of the patterns seen so far, and they should be learned individually. Some have alternative forms, others have one or more deviations from the main pattern:

	Infinitive	*Present*	*Past*	*Supine*	
I irr.	**betala**	**betalar**	**betalade/ betalte**	**betalt**	pay
	koka	**kokar**	**kokade/ kokte**	**kokt**	boil
II irr.	**göra**	**gör**	**gjorde**	**gjort**	do, make
	ha	**har**	**hade**	**haft**	have
	heta	**heter**	**hette**	**hetat**	be called
	kunna	**kan**	**kunde**	**kunnat**	can, be able

	lägga	**lägger**	**la(de)**	**lagt**	lay, place
		måste	**måste**	**måst**	have to, must
	skola	**ska(ll)**	**skulle**	**skolat**	shall, will
	säga	**säger**	**sa(de)**	**sagt**	say
	sälja	**säljer**	**sålde**	**sålt**	sell
	sätta	**sätter**	**satte**	**satt**	put, place
	veta	**vet**	**visste**	**vetat**	know
	vilja	**vill**	**ville**	**velat**	want
III irr.	**be**	**ber**	**bad**	**bett**	ask
	dö	**dör**	**dog**	**dött**	die
	få	**får**	**fick**	**fått**	get
	ge	**ger**	**gav**	**gett**	give
	gå	**går**	**gick**	**gått**	go
	le	**ler**	**log**	**lett**	smile
	se	**ser**	**såg**	**sett**	see
	stå	**står**	**stod**	**stått**	stand

Exercise 1

Change the verbs into the present tense:

1 Vi ordnade en fest. 2 De åkte ner på staden. 3 Vi behövde druvor till osten. 4 Erik ville ha någon dansk ost. 5 Skulle de köpa brännvin? 6 Sedan tände de ljusen. 7 Det kostade mycket. 8 Det blev dyrt. 9 Gästerna anlände. 10 Sven mådde illa. 11 Han levde länge. 12 Gästerna använde inte servetterna.

Exercise 2

Change the verbs into the past tense:

1 Vi stannar vid Systemet. 2 Jag ska köpa brännvin. 3 Erik väljer dricka. 4 De handlar mat. 5 De glömmer servetterna. 6 Sven köper osten. 7 Vad tycker du om Sverige? 8 Röker du? 9 Det stämmer faktiskt! 10 Jag avskyr persikor. 11 Hör du musiken? 12 Jag lär mig svenska. 13 Gör du det? 14 De sätter sig därborta. 15 Säger du det? 16 Rebecca ställer sig i kaffekon.

Definite adjective forms

It is advisable at this stage to revise indefinite adjective forms (-, +t, +a) and how to use these after certain words (see pp.62, 83 and 90):

en/någon/ingen/en annan	**stor bil**
e*tt*/någo*t*/inge*t*/e*tt* anna*t*	**stor*t* hus**
två/någr*a*/ing*a*/andr*a*/all*a*	**stor*a* bilar/stor*a* hus** *etc.*

Revise also the Swedish end article (= 'the') in singular and plural:

bil/en	the car	**bilar/na**	the cars
hus/et	the house	**hus/en**	the houses

When the noun with end article is combined with an adjective, Swedish has a special construction:

the big car	**den stor/a bil/en**	the big cars	**de stor/a bilar/na**
the big house	**det stor/a hus/et**	the big houses	**de stor/a hus/en**

Firstly, a new article is added – **den, det** or **de** – known as the *front (or adjectival) article* because it always comes at the front (unlike the end article) and because it is only used with adjectives. It is identical to the pronoun 'it' and the demonstrative 'that'. Next, the adjective nearly always takes the definite ending **-a**, a form learned already for plural indefinite. Finally, the noun takes the familiar *end article.* In effect what happens is that the phrase is marked in three different ways as definite:

Def (front article)	*Adj + Def (definite ending)*	*Noun + Def (end article)*
den	**god*a***	**mat*en***
det	**god*a***	**öl*et***
de	**god*a***	**druvor*na***

This basic pattern is varied somewhat for different kinds of definite declension. For the present it is enough to learn this main pattern and just one exception: when this construction is used with a *masculine singular* noun, i.e. with one male person, the **-a** ending on the adjective is usually changed to **-e**:

the big boy **den stor/e pojken**
the tall man **den lång/e mannen**

In all other cases the -a ending is used

de stor/a pojkarna, de lång/a männen (masculine plural)
den stor/a flickan (feminine)
det stor/a slottet (neuter)

Exercise 3

Change the indefinite phrase into a definite one:

Example: en stor bil > den stora bilen

1 en trevlig fest 2 en saftig persika 3 ett stort bord 4 god mat 5 ett danskt brännvin 6 en fin äppelkaka 7 svenskt öl 8 hårt bröd 9 en ung pojke 10 ett grönt äpple

Emphatic constructions

In order to emphasise a particular phrase equally with other phrases, that phrase (X) may be taken out of the sentence and put into the construction: **Det är (var) X som . . .** just as in the English 'It is (was) X who (that) . . .'. Note, however: 'that' = **som**:

Det var ˈ*Erik och Sven* som åkte ner på staden (och inte Malin).

Det var en ˈ*dansk* snaps (som)* Erik ville ha (och inte en svensk).

These constructions are common in questions:

Var det ˈ*Erik och Sven* som åkte ner på staden (och inte Malin)?

Var det en ˈ*dansk* snaps (som)* Erik ville ha (och inte en svensk)?

* See p.121.

Exercise 4

Make emphatic constructions, stressing the word(s) in italics:

1 *Pernilla* är kär i Henrik. 2 *Han* lurade henne att läsa svenska. 3 *Hon* kommer från England. 4 Pratar *du* så bra svenska? 5 Har han ställt sig i *kaffekön*? 6 Får man röka *här*? 7 Jag föredrar *Bradford*. 8 Läraren blir imponerad av *hennes kunskaper*.

Expressions of time (I)

Expressions of time are difficult because of the different kind of prepositional constructions used. Patterns for constructing them should emerge from the table:

Past	*Habitual*	*Present*	*Future*
Seasons, festivals			
Förra våren/i våras	**på våren**	**i vår**	**i vår/nästa vår**
last spring	in the spring	this spring	next spring
i julas	**på julen/ jularna**	**i jul**	**i jul/nästa jul**
last Xmas	at Xmas	this Xmas	next Xmas
Days			
i söndags	**på söndagarna**		**på söndag**
last Sunday	on Sundays		next Sunday
igår, i förrgår		**idag**	**imorgon, i övermorgon**
yesterday, the day before yesterday		today	tomorrow, the day after tomorrow
Parts of the day			
i morse	**på morgonen**	**nu på morgonen**	**imorgon bitti**
(earlier) this morning	in the morning(s)	this morning	tomorrow morning

i eftermiddags	**på eftermid-dagen**	**nu på eftermid-dagen**	**i eftermiddag**
(earlier) this afternoon	in the afternoons	this afternoon	(later) this afternoon
igår kväll	**på kvällen/ kvällarna**	**ikväll**	**imorgon kväll**
yesterday evening	in the evening(s)	this evening	tomorrow evening
i natt	**på natten/ nätterna**	**i natt**	**i natt**
last night	at night	tonight	(later) tonight
Years, months			
i fjol, förra året		**i år**	**i år, nästa år**
last year		this year	(later) this year next year
i januari	**i januari**	**i januari**	**i januari**
last January	in January	this January	next January

Exercise 5

What is the Swedish for:

1 Tomorrow I shall read Strindberg. 2 Yesterday we bought food for the party. 3 Next spring they are going to England. 4 In the evening we usually watch TV. 5 On Tuesday I shall start a new course. 6 Next June you can see the Midnight Sun. 7 Last Christmas I was at home.

Pronunciation 9

Vowel hiatus

English speakers often insert an unnecessary -r- between two vowels in adjacent words: *Africa(r) and Asia; an area(r) of disagreement; drama(r) and music*. This extra -r- sounds ugly in Swedish and must be avoided. Practise saying the following *without* an intrusive -r-, simply gliding from one vowel to another:

inte alls	not at all
lite extra	a little extra
lite av varje	a little of everything
De kunde unna sig lite extra lyx.	They could allow themselves a little extra luxury.
De bor på ett litet hotell.	They live at a small hotel.
De försöker hitta en taxi.	They are trying to find a taxi.
Några av dem ville tala om det för oss.	Some of them want to tell us it.
De sitter på en buss.	They are sitting on a bus.
Det var ofta en fredag.	It was often on a Friday.
Man kan ju läsa en bok.	One can read a book, of course.
Det måste du komma ihåg.	You must remember that.

Dialogue 9

Tjänare!

Hi there!

Erik and Sven are planning a party

ERIK: Tjänare Sven!
SVEN: Tjänare. Hur är läget?
ERIK: Jodå hyfsat. Det ska bli kul ikväll.
SVEN: Ja, vad ska vi handla för käk då?
ERIK: Ost, bröd, frukt. Lite av varje. Det är väl inte så noga.
SVEN: Sådana där gröna äpplen är goda. Tjejerna kan göra äppelkaka.
ERIK: De är rätt dyra.
SVEN: Äpplena eller tjejerna?
ERIK: Det var äpplena jag tänkte på.
SVEN: Det struntar jag i. Sådana ska vi ha. Och en klase vindruvor. Jag älskar druvor.
ERIK: Gillar du persikor?
SVEN: Nej, jag avskyr det luddiga skalet. Vi tar druvorna.

ERIK: Det är inte du som bestämmer. Vi köper några persikor eftersom jag råkar tycka om dem. Frukt, ost, bröd. Var det allt?
SVEN: Det var det nog.
ERIK: Har du något kaffe hemma?
SVEN: Nej, det har jag inte, och inga melittafilter. Och jag har ingen mandel till äppelkakan.
ERIK: Gissa vad det har kostat!
SVEN: Nej. Det spelar ingen roll. Är det fest så är det.

Vocabulary

tjänare!, hi !
Hur är läget? How are things?
hyfsat, not so bad
kul = roligt, fun
käk -et (*colloquial*) = **mat**, food
lite av varje, a bit of everything
tjej -en -er (*colloquial*) = **flicka**, girl
klase -n -ar, bunch
luddig -t -a, fluffy, downy
skal -et, shell; *here*: skin
bestämm/a -er -de, decide
råka/ -r -de, happen
melittafilter, coffee filter
mandel -n mandlar, almond
gissa/ -r -de, guess
Är det fest . . . = Om det är fest . . .

See also 'Expressing likes and dislikes' below.

Expressing likes and dislikes

In the dialogue find three phrases expressing indifference, meaning roughly: 'It doesn't really matter', 'I'm not bothered about that.' Here are some phrases for expressing likes and dislikes:

Likes		*Dislikes*	
tyck/a -er -te om	like	**tyck/a -er -te inte om**	dislike
gilla/ -r -de	like	**ogilla/ -r -de**	dislike
älska/ -r -de	love	**hata/ -r -de**	hate
		avsky/ -r -dde	detest

Sådan, sådant, sådana

Notice the different word order in:

Jag har aldrig sett en sådan röra!	I have never seen such a mess.

Det var en sådan vacker dag!	It was such a beautiful day.

Sådan + här/där = 'this/that kind of, one like that' *etc.*:

En sådan här klase druvor vill jag ha.	I want a bunch of grapes like this.

Pronunciation is often: sån, sånt, såna.

Någon, något, några

Någon *etc.* can go with a noun, and is often used in questions:

Har du något öl hemma?	Have you got any beer in the house?
Finns det någon skola i byn?	Is there a school in the village?
Har hon någon bror?	Has she got a brother?
Erik ville ha någon dansk sort.	Erik wanted a Danish sort.

Någon *etc.* can also be used with a negative or by itself:

Vi har inte någon ost hemma.	We haven't any cheese in the house.
Har du någon?	Do you have any?

Någon can mean 'someone/anyone' when used by itself:

Någon har glömt sina handskar.	Someone has forgotten their gloves.
Kan någon säga vad som har hänt?	Can anyone say what has happened?

Något can mean 'something/anything' when used by itself:

Hörde du något?	Did you hear anything?

Pronunciation is often: nån, nåt, nåra.

Ingen, inget, inga

Ingen *etc.* can go with a noun:

Det var ingen dum idé.	That's not a bad idea.
De hittade inga bananer.	They didn't find any bananas.

Jag har inget kaffe hemma.	I have no coffee in the house.

Ingen *etc.* can also be used by itself:

Kan jag få ett glas vin?	Can I have a glass of wine?
Vi har inget.	We have none.
Han ville låna pengar, men jag hade inga.	He wanted to borrow money, but I had none.

Ingen can mean 'no one, none' when used by itself:

Jag känner ingen med det namnet.	I know no one by that name.
Jag ville träffa studenterna, men det var inga där.	I wanted to meet the students, but none were there.

Inget/ingenting means 'nothing':

Jag letade men fann inget/ ingenting.	I looked but found nothing.

Exercise 6

What is the Swedish for:

1 I like grapes like those. 2 Have you any apples? 3 Yes, but we don't have any peaches. 4 She tried to buy some cheese, but they didn't have any. 5 Shall we buy some beer? 6 We don't have any in the house. 7 Someone has forgotten the napkins. 8 But you are not drinking anything! 9 It was such a nice party!

Exercise 7

When you are in the supermarket you may need to visit the following parts of the store to buy some things for the evening meal: **bröd**, **frukt**, **grönsaker**, **kött**, **drycker** and **konserver**. On your way out you might get things that don't keep so well from the section marked **mejerivaror**, perhaps some **smör**, **mjölk** or **filmjölk** and something from the section marked **djupfryst**, some **fiskpinnar** perhaps for the children? If you have only a few items you can go through the **snabbkassa (högst 5 varor)**.

Can you guess what these are in English?

Factual text 9

Gustav Vasa – Sveriges grundläggare

Gustav Vasa – founder of Sweden

Under perioden 1389 till 1521 var Sverige förenat med Danmark och Norge i en union (den s.k. unionstiden). Men svenskarna ville befria sig från dansk dominans. År 1520 startade Gustav Vasa ett befrielsekrig i Dalarna och när han till slut jagat danskarna ur landet, blev han vald till konung år 1523.

Under en lång regeringstid skapade Gustav Vasa en stark kungamakt. Med hjälp av Olaus Petri genomförde han reformationen i Sverige, introducerade Luthers idéer och berövade den katolska kyrkan dess makt och dess enorma rikedomar. År 1541 kunde folk läsa hela Bibeln på svenska för första gången. Men både bönder och adelsmän var missnöjda med Gustav Vasa. De tyckte inte om den nya religionen, de höga skatterna och de grymma fogdarna. De gjorde flera uppror, men de kunde inte störta kungen. Gustav Vasa byggde ut handeln med de andra västeuropeiska länderna och den svenska ekonomin blomstrade. Han enade Sverige till en modern nationalstat med stark central byråkrati, och när han dog 1560 blev hans söner kungar i Sverige efter honom.

Vocabulary

förenad -t -de, united
rike -t -n, kingdom
när han till slut = när han till slut hade, when he had finally (this ellipsis is common in written Swedish, see p.247)
jaga/ -r -de ut, chase out
regeringstid -en -er, reign
skapa/ -r -de, create
makt -en -er, power
genomför/a -för -de, carry through
beröva/ -r -de, deprive
adelsman -nen -män, noble(man)
missnöjd -t -a, displeased
skatt -en -er, tax
grym -t -ma, cruel
fogde -n -ar, sheriff
uppror -et -, revolt
störta/ -r -de, overthrow
handel -n, trade
ena/ -r -de, unite

Exercise 8

Välj ord ur Facktext (*Factual text)* 9:

1 En förening mellan två länder kallas . . . 2 Den period när de nordiska länderna var förenade kallas . . . 3 Ett krig för att befria ett land från främmande dominans heter . . . 4 Pengar som betalas till en kung eller till staten kallas . . . 5 En period då en kung regerar heter . . . 6 Den tid då Luthers idéer introducerades i Västeuropa heter . . . 7 Ett försök att störta en kung med våld kallas . . . 8 Ett land i Västeuropa är ett . . . land.

10 Familjen Forsberg

The Forsberg family

In this lesson we will look at:

- strong verbs (Conjugation IV) and how to form their past tense
- word order in subordinate clauses
- SIV (subject-**inte**-verb order in subordinate clauses)
- **ingen** and **inte någon**
- expressions of time
- how to express opinions on people and things
- Queen Christina and the Swedish Empire

Text 10

Familjen Forsberg

The Forsberg family

Forsbergs är en ganska vanlig svensk familj, som består av pappa Jan, 40 år, mamma Eva, 37 år och sonen Joakim, 15 år.

Jans pappa, Joakims farfar, var byggnadsarbetare i Härnösand och hans mor var dotter till en bonde i trakten. Jan kom till Stockholm och blev så småningom ingenjör. Han såg Eva i en busskö och blev genast förälskad i henne. De fick Joakim när de ännu var ganska unga. Eva njöt av att vara hemma hos Joakim som nästan aldrig skrek. Han satt, kröp, stod, gick och sprang, och när han var två år fick han en dagisplats. Jan och Eva skaffade sig inte fler barn, utan Eva började då utbilda sig till lärare i matematik och fysik. Nu undervisar hon på högstadiet. Jans föräldrar dog för några år sedan, men han har fortfarande släktingar i Norrland bl.a. systern Kerstin och hennes familj. Evas mamma, Karin, lever ännu – hon är pensionär och bor i närheten. Det gör också Evas två bröder som båda är gifta och har barn. Joakim, som alltså inte har några syskon, träffar ofta sina kusiner och morbröder, och mormor pratar han med i telefon nästan varje dag. Faster Kerstin brukade han besöka på sommarloven när han var liten, men nu när han är tonåring vill han stanna i Stockholm eller tågluffa.

Vocabulary

vanlig -t -a, normal, ordinary
bestå/ -r bestod, consist
pappa -n -or, dad
mamma -n -or, mum
farfar farfadern -fäder, (paternal) grandfather
mor modern mödrar, mother
dotter -n döttrar, daughter
byggnadsarbetare -n -, building worker
trakt -en -er, area
så småningom, eventually
ingenjör -en -er (*pron.* insjenjör), engineer
busskö -n -er, bus queue
bli förälskad i, fall in love with
njut/a -er njöt av, enjoy
skrik/a -er skrek, cry, yell
kryp/a -er kröp, crawl
spring/a -er sprang, run
dagis -et = daghem -met, nursery school
fler, more
utbilda/ -r -de sig, train, get an education
matematik -en, maths
fysik -en, physics
undervisa/ -r -de, teach
högstadi/um -iet, upper classes of secondary school
förälder -n föräldrar, parent
dö/ -r dog, die
släkting- en -ar, relative
syster -n systrar, sister
pensionär -en -er (*pron.* pansjonär), pensioner
bro(de)r -n bröder, brother
båda, both
gift -a, married
alltså, therefore
syskon -et -, brother or sister, sibling
kusin -en -er, cousin
morbror (-brodern), (maternal) uncle
mormor (-modern), (maternal) grandmother
i telefon, on the telephone
faster -n fastrar, (paternal) aunt
sommarlov -et -, summer holidays
tonåring -en -ar, teenager
tågluffa/ -r -de, go interrailing

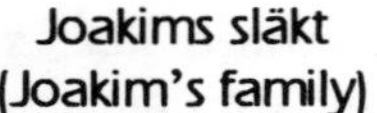

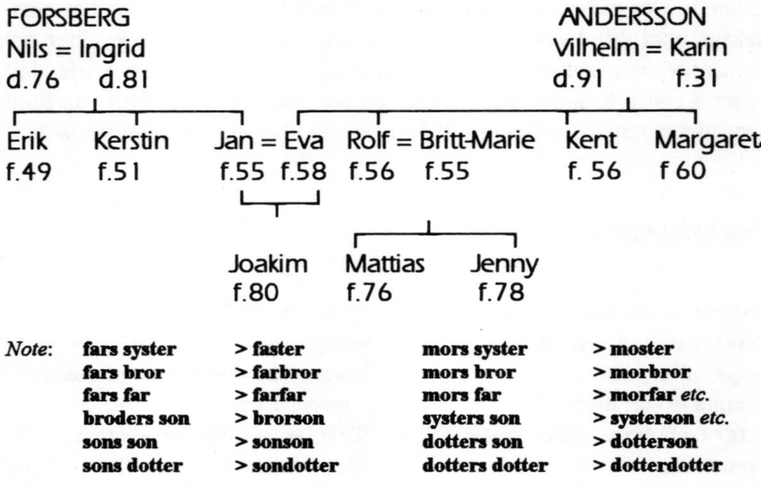

Note:

fars syster	**> faster**	**mors syster**	**> moster**
fars bror	**> farbror**	**mors bror**	**> morbror**
fars far	**> farfar**	**mors far**	**> morfar** *etc.*
broders son	**> brorson**	**systers son**	**> systerson** *etc.*
sons son	**> sonson**	**dotters son**	**> dotterson**
sons dotter	**> sondotter**	**dotters dotter**	**> dotterdotter**

Exercise 1

1 Joakim är Karins . . .?
2 Joakim är Kerstins . . .?
3 Joakim är Rolfs . . .?
4 Joakim är Mattias' . . .?
5 Vilhelm var Joakims . . .?
6 Erik är Joakims . . .?
7 Kent är Joakims . . .?
8 Margareta är Joakims . . .?
9 När är Jan född?
10 När dog Joakims morfar?
11 När är Kent född?
12 När dog Joakims farmor?

Verbs – strong conjugation (IV), past tense

Strong verbs are those that form their past tense by changing the stem vowel. This vowel is often changed again for the supine:

infinitive	*present*	*past*	*supine*	*past participle*
drick/a	**(dricker)**	**drack**	**druck/it**	**(drucken)**

You may, of course, learn the 100 or so strong verbs individually as you come to them, but it may well be a help to learn the vowel change patterns (e.g. **i-a-u** for the verb **dricka**), as a whole group changes in the same way (like **dricka** go: **hinna, slippa, spricka** *etc.*). The vowel is usually the same for both the infinitive and present, and for the supine and past participle (see p.216), as in the case of **dricka** above. Most strong verbs have present tenses in **-er**, supines in **-it**.

Vowel change patterns
(in order of importance – some examples only)

Infinitive	*Present*	*Past*	*Supine*	
i - e - i				
skriva	**skriver**	**skrev**	**skrivit**	write
skrika	**skriker**	**skrek**	**skrikit**	yell
bli	**blir**	**blev**	**blivit**	be, become
y - ö - u				
flyga	**flyger**	**flög**	**flugit**	fly
frysa	**fryser**	**frös**	**frusit**	freeze, feel cold
krypa	**kryper**	**kröp**	**krupit**	creep
ju - ö - u				
bjuda	**bjuder**	**bjöd**	**bjudit**	invite
sjunga	**sjunger**	**sjöng**	**sjungit**	sing
njuta	**njuter**	**njöt**	**njutit**	enjoy
i- a -u				
sitta	**sitter**	**satt**	**suttit**	sit
springa	**springer**	**sprang**	**sprungit**	run
finnas	**finns**	**fanns**	**funnits**	be, exist
Some other patterns:				
dra	**drar**	**drog**	**dragit**	pull
bära	**bär**	**bar**	**burit**	carry
komma	**kommer**	**kom**	**kommit**	come
äta	**äter**	**åt**	**ätit**	eat
vara	**är**	**var**	**varit**	be

Notice also irregular Conjugation III verbs that change their vowels like strong verbs. See p.131.

Exercise 2

By studying the vowel change patterns on p.146 above try to predict the changes. Change the strong verb from present to past.

1 Mormor lider (*suffers*) av reumatism. 2 De springer för livet. 3 Karin skryter (*boasts*) om sin familj. 4 De sjunger (*sing*) hela kvällen. 5 Sven sitter på soffan. 6 Joakim sticker (*goes off*) på semester. 7 Han hinner inte med (*misses*) tåget. 8 Han kommer inte till stationen i tid.

Exercise 3

By studying the vowel change patterns on pp.131 (III irregular) and 146 try to predict the changes. Change the strong verb from past to present.

1 Många dog av alkoholism. 2 Pojkarna gav ut (*spent*) för mycket pengar. 3 Sven sov länge dagen efter festen. 4 Åt gästerna upp druvorna? 5 Eva fick inga fler barn. 6 Han såg henne i en busskö.
7 Han teg (*was silent*) om festen. 8 De satt i köket.

Word order in sub(ordinate) clauses

A sub clause is a group of words containing a verb that is usually the subject, object or MPT-expression in a larger main clause sentence (see pp.119–20) and usually begins with a link word (subordinating conjunction) e.g., **att**, **om**, **som** etc. Consider the sub clauses in the following main clause sentences:

De gifte sig *när de ännu var unga.*

Hon älskade barnet *som aldrig skrek.*

De sa *att det inte var varmt i sjön.*

Vi frågade *om det aldrig hade regnat i öknen.*

If the internal pattern of these sub clauses is analysed, it becomes immediately obvious that the beginning of the sub clause is different from that of the main clause (see pp.59 and 74), while the end of both clause types is the same:

Link (Conjunction)	*Subject*	*Adverb*	*Verb₁*	*Verb₂*	*Obj/ Comp*	*MPT-expression*
... när	**de**	**ännu**	**var**	—	**unga.**	
... som	—	**aldrig**	**skrek.**			
... att	**det**	**inte**	**var**	—	**varmt**	**i sjön.**
... om	**det**	**aldrig**	**hade**	**regnat**	—	**i öknen.**

Distinguishing features of the sub clause:

1 The sub clause begins with a link word (conjunction). Compare the main clause, which can begin with any part of the sentence.
2 The sub clause nearly always has straight word order: subject – verb. Compare the main clause which even in statements often has inverted word order.

The part of the main clause sentence that is not the sub clause is called the *context*:

De gifte sig **när de ännu var ganska unga**
CONTEXT SUB CLAUSE

När de ännu var unga, ***gifte de sig.***
SUB CLAUSE CONTEXT

SIV (subject, inte, verb)

Adverbs in the main clause were discussed on pp.45 and 59. They always come immediately *after* VERB₁. As can be seen in the examples in 2 above, the adverb in the sub clause always comes immediately *before* VERB₁ and this is, in fact, a distinguishing feature of the sub clause. This is very hard to remember for learners, who must be aware the whole time of what kind of clause they are dealing with. One rather simplified way of remembering the order is the mnemonic: SIV (actually a Swedish girl's name), i.e. subject – **inte** – verb, where **inte** represents all adverbs of this kind (**aldrig, alltid, ju, egentligen** *etc.*) and verb = VERB₁.
Compare the following sentences:

Main clause:		*Sub clause:*		
Bill tar	**aldrig taxi.**	**Bill säger, att han**	**aldrig**	**tar taxi.**
Bill kan	**aldrig ta taxi.**	**Bill säger, att han**	**aldrig**	**kan ta taxi.**
VERB1	ADV		ADV	VERB1
		Remember: S	I	V

Exercise 4

Insert the adverb provided in the sub clause.

1 *inte*	Han sa, att Jans pappa var stockholmare.
2 *aldrig*	Han sa, att han drack sprit.
3 *alltid*	Hon undrade, om han hade varit förälskad i henne.
4 *äntligen*	När han fick dagisplats, kunde Eva börja utbilda sig.
5 *också*	Han undrar, om hon träffar sina kusiner.

Exercise 5

Make the two phrases into one sentence, adjusting the word order.

1 Sven säger att . . .	Han är inte sjuk.
2 Jan förklarar (*explains*) att . . .	Han blev genast förälskad i henne.
3 Vi undrar om (*wonder whether*) . . .	Jan har fortfarande släktingar i Norrland.
4 Jag frågar om . . .	Hans gamla mor lever ännu.
5 Eva förklarar att . . .	Joakim har alltså flera kusiner.

Ingen/inte någon

With simple tenses (present or past) **ingen (inget, inga)** and **inte någon (inte något, inte några)** are alternatives as subject or object:

> **De fick ingen middag. = De fick inte någon middag.**
> **Ingen sa något.**

But **inte någon** *etc.* rather than **ingen** *etc.* must be used:

1 in a main clause with a complex tense (perfect, pluperfect or with an auxiliary verb or particle verb)
2 as the object of a sub clause.

Compare these sentences with those above:

De har inte fått någon middag.	main clause, complex verb
De ska inte få någon middag.	main clause, complex verb
Han säger, att de inte har fått någon middag.	sub clause. *Note*: position of inte accords with SIV!

Note: see similar use of:
ingenting and **inte någonting** (nothing)
ingenstans and **inte någonstans** (nowhere)
Någonting and **någonstans** are often pronounced: **nånting, nånstans.**

Exercise 6

First revise the supines of strong verbs on p.146 above and the forms of irregular verbs on p.131. Then change the tense of the verbs below to perfect.

1 De åt inga persikor. 2 De fick inga fler barn. 3 De drack inget kaffe. 4 Det blev ingen fest. 5 Vi gjorde ingenting. 6 Hon skrev inga brev.7 De bjöd inga flickor. 8 Han såg inga älgar.

Exercise 7

Make the two phrases into one sentence, but keep to the same tense.

1 Jag förklarade att . . .	Det finns inga älgar i Stockholm.
2 Olle undrar om . . .	Han drack ingen sprit igår.
3 Joakim säger, att . . .	Han har inga syskon.
4 Biträdet sa, att . . .	De hade inga bananer.
5 Olle undrar om . . .	Det finns inget kaffe hemma.

Expressions of time (2)

Prepositions used in time expressions denoting duration and frequency are confusing for English-speakers. Notice the following expressions and compare with English:

Han slutade *för* ett halvår *sedan*.	He left six months ago.
tre gånger *i* minuten/*i* veckan	three times a minute/a week
tre gånger *om* dagen/*om* året	three times a day/a year
tre gånger *per* år	three times per year
De reser dit *om* en timme.	They will be going there in an hour('s time).

De reser dit *på* en timme.	They will take an hour to get there.
De reser *i* en timme.	They will be travelling for an hour.
Han har bott där *i* ett år.	He has lived there for a year.
Han har *inte* bott där *på* ett år.	He hasn't lived there for a year.

Dialogue 10

Det var väldigt trevligt

It was really nice

Eva's mother phones up

MORMOR: Hej Joakim. Hur står det till med dig?
JOAKIM: Skapligt.
MORMOR: Jag hörde att du var på bio igår. Var det en bra film?
JOAKIM: Nej, den var urdålig.
MORMOR: Så synd! Jag hade hört att den var så skojig.
JOAKIM: Den var barnslig och långtråkig. Botten faktiskt.
MORMOR: Jaha, ja, det var ju tråkigt. Får jag tala med mamma ett tag?
JOAKIM: Jadå, ett ögonblick. Morsan, mormor i telefon!
EVA: Hallå ja. Hej mamma. Hur har du det?
MORMOR: Tack bra. Och du själv? Hur var det på festen häromkvällen?
EVA: Det var väldigt trevligt. Fantastiskt god mat, intressanta människor. Det var enormt mycket folk där. Vi hade verkligen roligt.
MORMOR: Så trevligt! I övermorgon ska jag förresten träffa Britt-Marie.
EVA: Vilken Britt-Marie?
MORMOR: Din svägerska så klart.
EVA: Ja, naturligtvis. Så dum jag är! Du får hälsa henne så mycket. Vi måste bjuda hem dem snart. Det var evigheter sedan. Och de som jämt har varit så hyggliga mot Joakim.
MORMOR: Bry dig inte om det! Britt-Marie vet att du har mycket om dig och kring dig.
EVA: Margareta däremot var rätt snorkig, när jag pratade med henne i morse. Hon tycker uppenbarligen att jag är självsäker och mallig.

MORMOR: Hon är bara avundsjuk. Det har ju gått så bra för dig. Nej, nu ska jag se på Aktuellt. Sköt om dig och hälsa Jan!

EVA: Hej då mamma. Tack för att du ringde. Grundskolelärare i matte, är det så avundsvärt?

Vocabulary

Hur står det till . . .? How are things . . .?
skapligt, not so bad
urdålig -t -a, really bad
bio -n, cinema
skojig -t -a, fun
barnslig -t -a, childish
långtråkig -t -a, boring
botten, awful
tråkigt, a shame
jadå, sure (thing)
morsa = mor
häromkvällen, the other night
intressant - -a, interesting
ha roligt, have fun, enjoy oneself
svägerska -n -or, sister-in-law
i övermorgon, the day after tomorrow
så klart, of course, obviously
hälsa/ -r -de någon, give someone your regards
evighet -en -er, eternity, ages
bry/ -r -dde sig om, worry/care about
ha mycket om sig och kring sig, be very busy, have a lot on your plate
däremot, on the other hand
snorkig -t -a, superior (*negative*)
uppenbarligen, clearly
självsäker -t självsäkra, self-confident
mallig -t -a, stuck-up
avundsjuk -t -a, envious
Aktuellt, TV news
sköt/a -er -te om sig, look after oneself
grundskolelärare -n -, teacher at comprehensive school
matte = matematik
avundsvär/d -t -da, enviable

Opinions on people and things

In the dialogue find phrases meaning: 'that's a shame,' 'really nice', 'how nice!', 'of course', 'don't worry about it', 'give my love to Jan', 'how are you?', 'we had great fun', 'thanks for ringing'. In the dialogue there are a number of adjectives describing opinions: **urdålig, långtråkig** *etc.* In colloquial, often somewhat slangy, Swedish it is usual to modify adjectives by using a strengthening prefix (cf. also amplifiers p.96). These usually just mean 'to a very high degree':

jätte-: **jättebra, jättefin, jättekul, jättestor** (usually positive)
toppen-: **en toppenbil, en toppenkille** (always positive)
ur-: **urdålig, urdum, urfånig** (usually negative)
skit-: **skitbillig, skitdålig, skitbra, skitbussig** (both positive and negative)

This last prefix is not nearly as strong in Swedish as in English.

Some other less slangy words for expressing opinions on people are: **snäll** (nice, kind, decent, well-behaved); **elak** (spiteful, malicious, nasty); **snygg** (pretty, handsome); **ful** (plain, ugly, bad); **vacker** (beautiful, pretty); **vänlig** (kind(ly), friendly, amiable); **pålitlig** (reliable, dependable); **jobbig** (difficult, wearing); **livlig** (lively, vivacious); **ytlig** (superficial, shallow); **blyg** (shy, diffident); **öppen** (open, frank); **kylig** (cool, distant); **stel** (formal, reserved, wooden); **varm** (warm, hearty, cordial); **flitig** (diligent, industrious); **lat** (lazy, idle).

Factual text 10 🕮

Kristina och Stormaktstiden

Queen Christina and the Swedish Empire

Kung Gustav II Adolf (1611–32) hade gjort Sverige till en stormakt, och landet hade under trettioåriga kriget vunnit stora landområden i Nordtyskland och Baltikum. Hemma i Sverige grundade Gustav Adolf ett 30-tal nya städer bl.a Göteborg och Sundsvall, skapade högre skolor (gymnasier) och förnyade landets armé och ekonomi. Men Gustav Adolfs plötsliga död i slaget vid Lützen lämnade landet utan någon regent. Hans dotter Kristina var bara barnet och blev drottning först år 1644. Kristina ville inte gifta sig – hon hittade ingen som var hennes intellektuella like. Hon ägde ett imponerande bibliotek och brevväxlade med den tidens främsta filosofer och vetenskapsmän. Drottningen bjöd den franska filosofen Descartes till Stockholm är 1649 – och förde långa samtal med honom på det kalla och dragiga slottet till följd av kylan dog han av lunginflammation! På 1600-talet var Sverige ett manssamhälle där intellektuella kvinnor betraktades med misstänksamhet. Efter några år avsade sig Kristina den svenska tronen

(1654) och lämnade omedelbart landet. På väg ner till Rom efter abdikationen övergick hon till katolicismen. I Rom levde hon i ytterligare 34 år.

Karl X Gustavs djärva tåg över isen mot Köpenhamn resulterade i att Sverige vann Skåne, Blekinge och Halland från Danmark år 1658. En annan krigarkung, Karl XII, förde krig mot Polen och Rysslands tsar, Peter den Store. Svenska armén led ett stort nederlag vid Poltava och efter 18 års krig blev kungen ihjälskjuten i Norge 1718. Det stora nordiska kriget slutade med att Sverige förlorade en stor del av Östersjöprovinserna. Den svenska stormaktstiden var slut.

Vocabulary

krig -et -, war
Tyskland, Germany
Baltikum, the Baltic area
stormakt -en -er, great power
plötslig -t -a, sudden
död -en, death
slag -et -, battle
regent -en -er, monarch
like, equal
äg/a -er -de, own
imponerande, impressive
främst -a, leading, foremost
vetenskapsman -nen -män, scientist
för/a för -de samtal, have a conversation
dragig -t -a, draughty
till följd av, as a result of
manssamhälle -t, male-dominated society
misstänksamhet -en -er, suspicion
avsäg/a -er -sade sig, renounce
ytterligare, further
djärv -t -a, daring
tåg -et, march
för/a för -de krig, wage war
lid/a -er led ett nederlag, suffer a defeat
ihjälskjuten, shot and killed
förlora/ -r -de, lost

Exercise 8

1 How long did the Swedish Empire last? 2 Who won the Empire and who lost it? 3 Apart from his military conquests, what did Gustavus Adolphus accomplish? 4 What were Kristina's interests? 5 Why was she not appreciated in seventeenth-century Sweden? 6 How did Charles X beat Denmark? 7 What did he gain for Sweden? 8 Who was Charles XII's opponent in the Great Northern War? 9 How did Charles XII die? 10 What did Sweden lose at the end of the Great Northern War?

11 Jockes kompisar

Jocke's friends

In this lesson we will look at:

- the definite declension of the adjective in outline and Type 1
- adjectival nouns
- s-verbs: reciprocal deponent and passive
- names like **Olle, Kalle** and **Maggan**
- **vem** and **vem som**
- how to express indifference
- slang expressions
- sport and leisure in Sweden

Text 11

Jockes kompisar

Jocke's friends

Joakim, eller Jocke, som han brukar kallas, är ganska skoltrött och lyckas ofta smita från läxläsning och annat betungande skolarbete. Han och hans kompisar brukar träffas på eftermiddagarna för att spela fotboll. Det är ett ganska högljutt och stökigt gäng som samlas. Många tycker att de här ungdomarna ser likadana ut i täckjackor, jeans, sportskor och med freestyle i öronen, men egentligen är de mycket olika. Jocke är lång och blond och ser inte alls ut som den korte, mörke José. Ludvigs rufsiga lugg liknar inte precis Oskars korta snagg. Oskar är en mycket öppen och livlig kille och helt olik Mårten som är den tystlåtne och allvarlige i gänget. Så nog ser man vem som är vem. De här killarna trivs ihop. De brukar dra ner på stan på lördagarna för att 'kolla läget', och flera eftermiddagar i veckan tränar de som sagt fotboll.

Josés föräldrar är politiska flyktingar från Uruguay. De kan nu återvända dit, men José som inte minns särskilt mycket av sitt hemland, vill ogärna lämna kompisarna. Hans kompisar hoppas förstås att han ska stanna i Sverige, men de vet att det i alla fall finns ett jättebra fotbollslag i Uruguay.

Vocabulary

kompis -en -ar, friend
kallas kallas kallades, be called
skoltrött - -a, tired of school
lyckas lyckas lyckades, succeed
smit/a -er smet från, get out of
läxläsning -en, doing homework (**läxa -n -or,** homework)
betungande, burdensome
arbete -t -n, work
spela/ -r -de, play
träffas träffas träffades, meet
högljudd -ljutt -ljudda, noisy
stökig/ -t -a, untidy
gäng -et -, gang
samla/s -s -des, gather
ungdom -en -ar, youth, youngster
se/ -r såg likadan ut, look similar
täckjacka -n -or, quilted jacket
sportskor -na, trainers
freestyle -n -s, personal stereo, 'Walkman'
olik/ -t -a, different, unlike
rufsig/ -t -a, unkempt, scruffy
lugg -en -ar, fringe
likna/ -r -de (see p.193), be like, similar to
snagg -en, crew cut
livlig -t -a, lively
tystlåt/en -et -na, quiet
allvarlig/ -t -a, serious
triv/as -s -des, get on well,
ihop, together
dra/ -r drog, *here*: go off
'kolla läget', check out the scene
träna/ -r -de, practise, train
flykting -en -ar, refugee
återvänd/a -er -e, return
minn/as minnas -des, remember
sitt, his (see p.205)
hemland -et -länder, home country
ogärna, (be) reluctant (to)
lämna/ -r -de, leave
hoppa/s hoppas -des, hope
förstås, of course
i alla fall, anyway
fotbollslag -et -, football team

Definite adjective declension in outline and Type I

The basic pattern for the definite declension of the adjective is shown on p.134 **den stora bilen, det stora huset, de stora bilarna** *etc.* This pattern in which the adjective always has a definite ending (**-a** or **-e**) forms the basis for other types of construction, which for ease we will call Types 1–4:

Type 1 Front article/Demonstrative (**den här** *etc.*) + end article:

den	**stor/a**	**bil/en**	the big car
det	**stor/a**	**hus/et**	the big house
de	**stor/a**	**bilar/na (hus/en)**	the big cars (houses)
den här (där)	**stor/a**	**bil/en**	this (that) big car
det här (där)	**stor/a**	**hus/et**	this (that) big house
de här (där)	**stor/a**	**bilar/na (hus/en)**	these (those) big cars (houses)

Type 2 Genitive or possessive or demonstrative (**denna** *etc.)* – no end article:

Olles	**ny/a**	**bil/**	Olle's new car
firmans	**ny/a**	**bil/**	the firm's new car
min	**ny/a**	**bil/**	my new car
denna	**ny/a**	**bil/**	this/that new car

Type 3 No front article + end article

—	**svensk/a**	**språk/et**	the Swedish language
—	**hel/a**	**dag/en**	the whole day

Type 4 No front article or end article:

—	**lill/a**	**vän/**	little friend
—	**först/a**	**klass/**	first class

Exercise 1

Revise definite adjective forms on p.134, then make the expressions definite as in the example:

Example: **en svensk familj > den svenska familjen**

1 en dålig film 2 ett vanligt barn 3 en trevlig bok 4 god mat 5 intressanta människor 6 en snäll pojke 7 en vacker syster 8 små sportskor 9 ett litet ljus 10 dansk ost 11 ett växande intresse

Exercise 2

Make the expressions definite as in the example:

Example: **en svensk flicka > den där svenska flickan**

1 en ung kille 2 ett stort bord 3 nya glas 4 en gammal täckjacka 5 milt väder 6 gröna äpplen 7 andra studenter 8 ett nytt kollegieblock 9 en medelålders dam 10 ett bra fotbollslag 11 saftiga persikor

Adjectival nouns

Adjectival nouns are definite adjective + noun phrases in which the noun is obvious and is therefore omitted. This is a variation on Type 1 above. As in English a noun (here: **människorna**) is often omitted in the plural definite:

the young	**de unga**
the poor	**de fattiga**
the old	**de gamla**

But Swedish goes further than English in that adjectival nouns may occur in the following cases:

The indefinite:	**en blind**	a blind person
	en död	a dead person
The N-form singular definite:	**den gamle**	the old man (cf. p.134)
	den gamla	the old woman
The T-form singular definite:	**det nya**	the new thing
	det enda	the only thing
	det sista	the last thing
Participles:	**de närvarande**	those present
	den inneboende	the lodger

Swedish adjectival nouns often correspond to English constructions like 'a big one', 'the white one':

Jag har ett gammalt hus och ska köpa ett nytt.	I have an old house and am going to buy a new one.
Vi har en röd bil och en grå.	We have a red car and a grey one.
Jag tar den röda.	I'll have the red one.

Exercise 3

(a) If you were describing a woman, what is the Swedish for: the short one, the lively one, the blonde one, the dark one, the pretty one, the intelligent one?

(b) If you were describing a man, what is the Swedish for: the tall one, the quiet one, the small one, the boring one, the handsome one, the ugly one?

S-verbs: reciprocal, deponent and passive

Some Swedish verbs have forms ending in **-s**. In most tenses the **-s** is added to the existing tense ending for the relevant conjugation, but notice how the present tense forms have been altered:

	Infinitive	*Present*	*Past*	*Supine*	
I	**laga/s**	**laga/s**	**lagade/s**	**lagat/s**	be mended
IIa	**behöva/s**	**behöv/s**	**behövde/s**	**behövt/s**	be needed
IIb	**söka/s**	**sök/s**	**sökte/s**	**sökt/s**	be sought
III	**bebo/s**	**bebo/s**	**bebodde/s**	**bebott/s**	be inhabited
IV	**skriva/s**	**skriv/s**	**skrev/s**	**skrivit/s**	be written

To construct the present tense forms:

laga/r	delete **-r** and add **s** to the stem	> **lagas**
behöv/er	delete **-er** and add **s** to the stem	> **behövs**
skriv/er	delete **-er** and add **s** to the stem	> **skrivs**

Conjugation II verbs retains the **-e** in formal Swedish:

Bär köpes! Berries bought.

Verbs with stems in **-s** also retain the **-e:**

De kysses. They are kissing.

S-verbs are of three main kinds:

The passive:	**Bilen lagas.**	The car is being mended.
The reciprocal:	**Vi träffäs kl 2.**	We'll meet at 2 o'clock.
The deponent:	**Det finns inga bananer.**	There are no bananas.

The passive will be discussed in Lesson 17.

It takes two to reciprocate! So the reciprocal form has a plural subject which carries out the action and is at the same time the object of the action. Notice the equivalent with a reciprocal pronoun:

Vi kramades. = **Vi kramade varandra.** = We hugged (each other).

Other reciprocal verbs are: **enas** (I) (agree); **ses** (III irr.) (meet); **slåss** (IV) (fight); **höras** (IIa) (be in touch); **följas åt** (IIa) (accompany); **hjälpas åt** (IIb) (help each other); **skiljas åt** (IIa) (part); **talas vid** (I) (talk).

Deponent verbs are active in meaning and do not normally possess a form without **-s:**

Jag hoppas att de lyckas. I hope they succeed.

Other deponents are: **finnas** (IV) (be, exist); **umgås** (IV) (be friendly with); **minnas** (IIa) (remember); **låtsas** (I) (pretend); **tyckas** (IIb) (seem); **envisas** (I) (persist); **trängas** (IIa) (push); **andas** (I) (breathe); **hoppas** (I) (hope)

Exercise 4

Insert the correct form of the s-verb provided:

(*tyckas*)	Det . . . inte bli någon lektion idag.
(*talas vid*)	Igår . . . vi . . . om detta.
(*ses*)	Imorgon . . . vi vid kaféet.
(*följas åt*)	Senare den dagen . . . de . . . neråt staden.
(*finnas*)	Har det någonsin . . . så förfärliga vapen?
(*trängas*)	Igår. . . folk så förskräckligt i kaffekön.
(*lyckas*)	Nu har han äntligen . . . med sin uppgift.
(*umgås*)	För några år sedan . . . de med familjen.

Olle, Kalle and Maggan

The name that Jocke has on his birth certificate is Joakim. Jocke is a pet-name like Bill instead of William. Similar pet-names are:

pojkar:		**flickor**:	
Janne (*Jan*)	Stickan (*Stig*)	Kicki (*Kristina*)	Kajsa (*Karin*)
Nisse (*Nils*)	Gurra (*Gustav*)	Bettan (*Elisabeth*)	Gittan (*Birgitta*)
Kalle (*Karl*)	Berra (*Bertil*)	Lotta (*Charlotta*)	Bibbi (*Birgitta*)
Pelle (*Per*)	Bosse (*Bo*)	Maggan (*Margareta*)	
Roffe (*Rolf*)	Olle (*Olof*)		

Vem/vem som

When **vem**, **vad** or **vilken** begins the sub clause (i.e. is the subject of an indirect question) it must be followed by the subject marker **som**, which has no equivalent in English:

Sub clause:

Cf. **Jag undrar** ***vem hon*** **älskar.**
OBJ SUBJ
(I wonder who she loves.)

and: **Jag undrar** ***vem som*** **kysser** ***henne*** **nu.**
SUBJ OBJ
(I wonder who's kissing her now.)

Cf. **Jag undrar** ***vad han*** **gör.**
OBJ SUBJ
(I wonder what he is doing.)

and: **Jag undrar** ***vad som*** **händer.**
SUBJ
(I wonder what is happening.)

Exercise 5

What is the Swedish for:

I wonder . . . who the short one is; . . . what Jocke is doing; . . . who is going down town; . . . what they are buying; . . . who has got my red sweater; . . . what has happened to it; . . . who is playing football; . . . who she is meeting tonight; . . . what Jose likes; . . . who he is talking to?

Dialogue 11

Det gör detsamma

That doesn't matter

Joakim must find his red sweater

JOCKE: Var är min röda tröja?
EVA: I tvätten. Den var praktiskt taget svart.
JOCKE: Det gör detsamma. Jag måste ha den idag.
EVA: Du får allt ta en av de andra. Jag ska tvätta i eftermiddag.
JOCKE: Jag sa ju att jag skiter i om den är skitig. Jag måste ha den röda. Jag ska spela fotboll.
EVA: För all del. Skyll dig själv om den stinker. Men varför måste du ha just den röda?
JOCKE: Lagfärgen. Har inte du en som jag kan låna?
EVA: Jo, om du vill ha den där tjusiga med axelvaddar och 'Tjejgympan' tvärs över bröstet. Men ta pappas gamla!
JOCKE: Schysst! Hej då! Jag sticker.
JAN: Du Eva, den där gamla träningsoverallen, minns du var jag lade den? Jag hittar bara byxorna.
EVA: Nej, dina kläder får du hålla reda på själv.

Vocabulary

tröja -n -or, sweater
tvätt -en, wash(ing)
praktiskt taget, almost, practically
svart - -a, black
tvätta/ -r -de, wash
skit/a -er sket i, do not care
skitig -t -a, dirty, mucky
skyll/a -er -de sig själv, have only oneself to blame
stink/a -er stank, smell
lagfärg -en -er, team colour
låna/ -r -de, borrow
tjusig -t -a, gorgeous
axelvadd -en -ar, shoulder pad(ding)
'Tjejgympan', Girls' Gym(nastics)
tvärs över bröstet, right across the chest
schysst = juste, *lit.* fair; *here*: fair enough
stick/a -er stack, leave, be off
träningsoverall -en -er, tracksuit
byxor -na, trousers, bottoms
håll/a -er höll reda på, look after

Expressing indifference

Find phrases in the dialogue meaning: 'that doesn't matter', 'I don't care if it's . . .', 'It's not my fault if . . .', 'You'll just have to take one of the others.' Here are some more phrases expressing indifference:

Det spelar ingen roll.	That doesn't matter.
Det gör inget.	That doesn't matter.
Sak samma.	That doesn't matter.
Det struntar jag i.	I am not bothered about that.
Det bryr jag mig inte om.	I am not bothered about that.

Slang (I)

Here are some frequent slang words to describe friends and relations, with their standard Swedish equivalents:

kille -n -ar (*pron.* with 'hard' **k**)	**pojke, pojkvän**
tjej -en -er	**flicka, flickvän**
kompis -en -ar	**kamrat, vän**
polare -n -	**kamrat, vän**
grabb -en -ar	**pojke**
tös -en -er	**flicka**
brorsa -n -or	**bror**
farsa -n -or	**far, pappa**
morsa -n -or	**mor, modern, mamma**
syrra -n -or	**syster**
gubbe -n -ar	**pappa, man, gammal man**
gumma -n -or	**fru, gammal kvinna**
fruga -n -or	**fru**
kärring -en -ar (*derogatory*)	**fru, kvinna**
unge -n -ar	**barn**

Exercise 6

Translate into Swedish:

1 These young boys get on very well together. 2 José and his friends usually get together on Saturdays. 3 Do you have to have the new one? 4 The only thing he likes is playing football. 5 Kristoffer is the tall dark one in training shoes. 6 Jocke is completely different from the serious

Mårten. 7 He doesn't look at all like Jocke. 8 Do the young boys look alike? 9 It's your own fault if you can't look after your clothes.

Factual text 11 📖

Idrott och fritid

Sport and leisure

Svensk idrott är känd över hela världen genom stjärnor som tennisspelaren Björn Borg och slalomåkaren Ingemar Stenmark. Men den är mycket mer än så. Inte mindre än 2 miljoner svenskar är medlemmar i Sveriges Riksidrottsförbund, dvs en tredjedel av alla vuxna i landet, och de flesta barn sportar också.

Fotboll lockar många sportintresserade – alla fotbollsspelare är amatörer och det finns 30 000 klubbanslutna spelare. Under de senaste åren har antalet kvinnliga fotbollsspelare ökat kraftigt. På vintern är skidåkning i skog och mark en populär familjesport och de som tycker om utförsåkning åker till fjällen. Många åker skridskor på isbanor och på de frusna sjöarna.

Tusentals svenskar joggar, springer eller vandrar i skogen eller i fjällen. Motionsgymnastik har också blivit populärt i alla åldrar. Landets kommuner lägger ned mycket pengar årligen på sporthallar, simbassänger (inomhus och utomhus), fotbollsplaner, skridskobanor och upplysta motionsspår för löpning och skidåkning.

Sverige har tusentals sjöar och en lång kust, och många svenskar har tillgång till båt – roddbåt, segelbåt eller motorbåt. Segling och fiske är därför mycket populärt – man fiskar t o m. på vintern genom att borra hål i isen och släppa ner en lina.

Vocabulary

värld -en -ar, world
slalomåkare -n -, slalom skier
inte mindre än, no less than
Riksidrottsförbund, National Sports Federation
vuxna, adults
de flesta, most
klubbansluten, members of clubs
utforsåkning -en, downhill skiing
skridsko -n -r, skate
motionsgymnastik -en, keep fit
ålder -n åldrar, age
lägg/a -er lade lagt ned, spend
upplyst, illuminated

motionsspår -et -, jogging/skiing track
tillgång till, access to
släpp/a, -er, -te ner, let down

Exercise 7

Hitta ord i texten som betyder detsamma som:

sport; gå i skogen; åka skidor nedför backen (*downhill*); swimmingpool; toppspelare; bergen; ge ut pengar; varje år; sport för hela familjen; gillar; folk som är intresserade av sport; spelare som är medlemmar av en klubb; spår där man kan åka när det är mörkt; springa lugnt.

12 Bills krångliga bilresa

Bill's difficult car journey

In this lesson we will look at:

- the definite declension of the adjective Type 2
- modal verbs
- uses of the infinitive
- how to apologise and respond to apologies
- **själv**
- duplicates and 'heavy' expressions
- Swedish food traditions

Text 12

Bills krångliga bilresa

Bill's difficult car journey

När Bill fick lite tid över mellan affärssamtalen, beslöt han sig för att hälsa på några gamla vänner djupt inne i Värmlands mörka skogar. Han fick låna en väns ganska risiga bil och fick också reda på allt han borde tänka på när han körde: treans växel var trög, vindrutetorkarna kunde haka upp sig, och ibland tog bromsarna dåligt. Han fick förstås inte glömma att ha lyktorna tända och att akta sig för polisens hastighetskontroller.

Vägarna ut ur Göteborg var breda och fina, men han undvek som alltid de stora vägarna.

Efter några timmar visade bensinmätaren att han måste tanka, och han körde in på en bensinstation. Han tankade själv och lyckades efter några svordomar få hundralappen att passa in i sedelautomaten. Sedan lyfte han på motorhuven och kollade olja och vatten. Luften i däcken brydde han sig däremot inte om. När han satt och tittade på kartan, såg han att han kunde svänga av på nästa avtagsväg.

Det var en smal och gropig grusväg, och Bill körde förbi röda stugor, hagar och skog. Men var det samma röda stugor hela tiden? Hade han kört vilse? Det hade han varit med om förut, och då hade han dessutom fått punktering och stått mitt i ödemarken utan reservhjul. Dunk, dunk, dunk . . . Inte nu igen! Bill bet ihop tänderna och öppnade bagageluckan, där reservhjulet brukade ligga. Det gjorde det också, men domkraften, var fanns den?

Vocabulary

krånglig -t -a, difficult, complicated
över, *here*: (to) spare
affärssamtal -et -, business meeting
beslut/a -er beslöt sig för, decide to
hälsa/ -r -de på, visit
djupt inne i, in the middle of
risig -t -a, tatty, battered
få/ -r fick reda på, learn, find out; *here*: was told
treans växel, third gear
trög -t -a, stiff
vindrutetorkare -n -, windscreen wiper
haka/ -r -de upp sig, stick
broms -en -ar, brake
lykta -n -or, headlight
akta/ -r -de sig för, watch out for
polis -en -er, police(man)
hastighetskontroll -en -er, speed trap
undvik/a -er undvek, avoid
bensinmätare -n -, fuel gauge
tanka/ -r -de, fill up
bensinstation -en -er, filling station
svordom -en -ar, oath, swearword
passa/ -r -de in i, fit into
sedelautomat -en -er, automatic pump – takes banknotes
lyft/a -er , lift
motorhuv -en -ar, car bonnet
kolla/ -r -de, check
olja -n -or, oil
luft -en, air
däck -et -, tyre
däremot, on the other hand
karta -n -or, map
sväng/a -er -de av, turn off
avtagsväg -en -ar, side road
gropig -t -a, potholed
grusväg -en -ar, dirt road
stuga -n -or, cottage
hage -n -ar, meadow
kör/a kör -de vilse, get lost
förut, previously
vara med om, experience
dessutom, also
punktering -en -ar, puncture
reservhjul -et, spare wheel

bit/a -er bet ihop, clench
bagagelucka -n -or, (car) boot
domkraft -en -er, jack

Definite declension of the adjective, Type 2

Remember (see p.157) that after certain types of words the adjective takes the definite ending **-a** (sometimes **-e**) but the noun has no ending. There are several different constructions to learn:

1 After the genitive: **Svens ny*a* båt, faderns ny*a* hus, skolans ny*a* studenter, mannen vars gaml*a* mor har dött.**

2 After the possessive: **hans risig*a* bil, hennes lång*a* samtal, deras rolig*a* vänner.**

3 After the demonstrative: **denna**, etc: **denna gropig*a* grusväg, detta slitn*a* däck, dessa röd*a* stugor.**

4 After some other words: **samma** (the same); **nästa** (the next); **följande** (the following); **föregående** (the previous): **samma mörk*a* skog, nästa vackr*a* helg.**

There are two minor exceptions to this:

1 After the genitive of measurement the adjective takes the indefinite form (+ **-t**/+ **-a**), agreeing with the noun that follows it:

en sorts/ett slags dyrbar båt	a kind of expensive boat
en sorts/ett slags rutig*t* tyg	a kind of checked material

2 After both the genitive and possessive the word **egen** takes the indefinite form (+ **-t**/+ **-a**):

pappas egen lilla Eva	daddy's own little Eva
deras ege*t* lilla hus	their own little house

Notice that **denna** *etc.* is most frequent in written Swedish and takes no end article, while **den här** *etc.* is most frequent in spoken and informal written Swedish and is always followed by an end article:

denna nya bil – den här nya bilen

Exercise 1

Translate into Swedish:

1 Bill's old friend Gunnar 2 Bill's Swedish car 3 the next small sideroad 4 the same beautiful cottage 5 Jocke's red sweater 6 dad's own red tracksuit 7 Värmland's large forests 8 the men's long business discussion 9 their little village 10 that difficult journey (use **denna**)

Modal verbs

The most frequent modal auxiliary verbs are inflected as follows:

Infinitive	*Present*	*Past*	*Supine*	
kunna	**kan**	**kunde**	**kunnat**	be able, can
skola	**ska(ll)**	**skulle**	**skolat**	shall, will
vilja	**vill**	**ville**	**velat**	will, want to
	måste	**måste**	**måst**	must, have to
böra	**bör**	**borde**	**bort**	should, ought to
få	**får**	**fick**	**fått**	may, be allowed to, must, have to

There are some 'false friends' here:

(a) shall/will:
ska sometimes = 'will':

Ska du följa med på bio? — Will you be coming to the cinema?

vill = 'want to':

Nej, jag vill inte! — No, I don't want to.
Vill du ha ett glas vin? — Would you like (Do you want) a glass of wine?

(b) must/must not:
måste = **får** = 'have to' (*compulsion*) only in positive expressions:

Jag måste/får tyvärr gå nu. — I have to go now unfortunately.

måste inte = do not have (*need*) to:

Du måste inte röka så mycket! — You don't need to smoke so much!

Cf. **får inte** = must not:

Du får inte röka så mycket! You must not smoke so much!

(c) ought/should:

bör, borde = ought to, should:

Du borde jogga mer. You ought to (*should*) jog more.

Cf. **skulle** = should, would (often conditional, i.e. when accompanied by an **om/ifall** clause):

Jag skulle jogga om jag inte skadat benet. I would go jogging if I hadn't hurt my leg.

Exercise 2

Translate into Swedish:

1 Rebecca should read this book. 2 She would read the book if she could find it. 3 But will she read it? 4 And does she want to read it? 5 Sven must not drink so much beer. 6 He doesn't have to drink so much. 7 Do you want a cup of coffee? 8 I have to drink coffee in the mornings.

Uses of the infinitive

(a) The infinitive without **att**:

The infinitive is used with modal verbs (see pp.53 and 59) and with modal equivalents in two-verb constructions, just as in English:

Ska du åka bort över jul? Will you be going away over Christmas?

Du brukar åka bort. You usually go away.

Some of the most frequent modal equivalents used in this way are:

tänker (think, intend); **behöver** (need); **börjar** (begin); **fortsätter** (continue); **försöker** (try to); **hoppas** (hope to); **lyckas** (succeed in); **orkar** (manage to); **slipper** (avoid); **slutar** (stop); **vägrar** (refuse).

Another use is the 'object + infinitive' construction after **se** (see), **höra** (hear), **låta** (allow), **tillåta** (allow) and **anse** (consider):

Jag såg honom gå. I saw him leave.

Vi hörde dem sjunga. We heard them singing.

(b) The infinitive with **att** is used in the following cases:

as subject:

Att köra bil kan vara krångligt.	Driving can be difficult.

as object:

Han älskar att köra fort.	He loves driving fast.

after a preposition:

Efter att ha stannat motorn tankade han bilen.	After turning off the engine he filled up.
Han gick hem utan att säga adjö.	He went home without saying goodbye.
Han tycker om att vara på landet.	He likes being in the country.

Notice that in the above examples English '-ing' form often corresponds to the Swedish infinitive.

Note: in expressions indicating an intention **för att** is used before the infinitive:

Han åkte dit för att hälsa på Gunnar och Ulla.	He went there (in order) to visit Gunnar and Ulla.

after a noun:

Har du tid att göra det?	Have you got time to do it?

Dialogue 12

Förlåt!

Sorry!

Bill apologises for being late

GUNNAR: Välkommen!
BILL: Förlåt att jag kommer så sent!
GUNNAR: Det gör ingenting. Var det svårt att hitta hit?
ULLA: Du körde väl inte på någon älg?
BILL: Nej, jag fick punktering och så hade jag ingen domkraft.
ULLA: Jösses! Hur i allsin dar klarade du det?

BILL: Jag har dolda talanger. Nej, jag fick gå till en bondgård och be om hjälp. Det var därför det tog sån tid. Jag är hemskt ledsen.

GUNNAR: Ingen fara. Vi håller på och fixar den här gamla pumpen. Vi har ju inte rinnande vatten i stugan, och när vi kom ut så fungerade inte pumpen heller.

ULLA: Stig in så länge! Ska du packa ur bilen, så bär vi in dina grejer.

BILL: Vad mysigt det är här! Tack för att ni bjöd hit mig. Jag hoppas att jag inte ställer till för mycket besvär.

ULLA: Inte alls. Du får ta det som vi har det. Du stannar väl ett tag nu, förresten?

BILL: Nej, tyvärr, jag måste tillbaks i övermorgon.

ULLA: Så synd! Ska det vara alldeles nödvändigt, det? Och vi som hoppades få rå om dig ordentligt.

BILL: Du får gärna rå om mig ändå. Särskilt om Gunnar lagar pumpen hela tiden.

ULLA: Du är dig lik!

BILL: Jag tog med mig marmelad och kex från England. Och lite skotsk whisky. Var så god.

GUNNAR: Samma gamla Bill! Tusen tack! Hoppas att du inte blir alltför besviken när jag säger att pumpen är lagad.

Vocabulary

förlåt, sorry
välkomm/en -et -na, welcome
hitta/-r -de hit, find (your) way here
hur i allsin dar?, how on earth?
klara/r -de något, manage (to do) something
dolda talanger, hidden talents
bondgård -en -ar, farm
ingen fara, no matter
håller på och fixar, is (in the process of) fixing
pump -en -ar, pump
rinnande, running
fungera/ -r -de, work
stig/a -er steg in, come inside
packa/ -r -de ur, unpack
grej -en -er, thing
ställ/a -er -de till, cause
ta det som vi har det, take us as you find us
besvär -et, trouble, bother
(ett) tag, while
tillbaks = tillbaka, back
nödvändig -t -a, necessary
rå/ -r -dde om någon, have someone to oneself
ordentligt, properly
Du är dig lik!, You haven't changed!
marmelad -en, jam, marmalade
kex -et -, biscuit
besvik/en -et -na, disappointed
alltför = för, too

Road signs Bill may see on his drive to Värmland

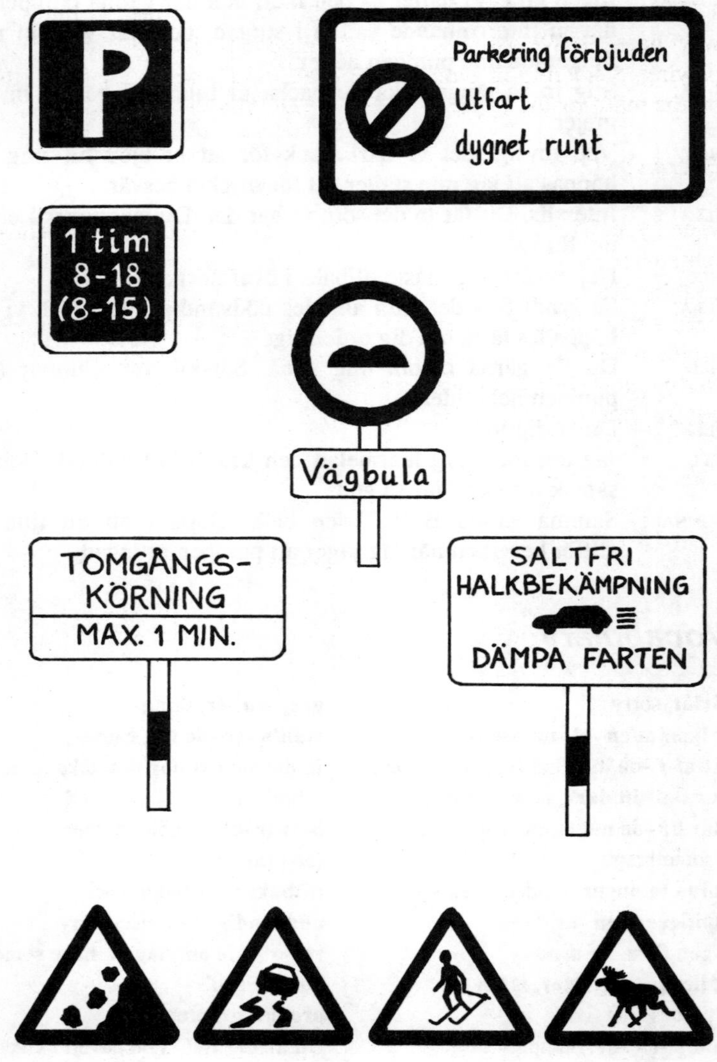

Exercise 3

Translate into Swedish:

1 He is thinking of having a party. 2 They succeeded in finding their way here. 3 We stopped (**sluta/**) smoking. 4 You can hear them playing. 5 Jogging is good for the health (***hälsan***). 6 We avoid driving on the main roads.

Exercise 4

When you drive into the **bensinmack** and stop next to the **bensinpump** remember to **stanna motorn!** Now look around. Over there is the **snabbtvätt** so you don't have to drive home with a dirty car. If you need **reservdelar** for the car you can get them here or if you have a problem with the car there is the **verkstad** where you can also get a routine **smörjning**. Before you leave do not ignore the signs **luft** and **vatten**. Stop and check these otherwise you may end up like Bill!

Can you guess what these are in English?

Apologies and responding to thanks and apologies

In the dialogue find phrases meaning: 'That doesn't matter', 'Not to worry', 'What a shame!', 'I'm awfully sorry!', 'I hope I am not being too much trouble to you', 'Thanks a lot!' Here are a few additional phrases:

Ursäkta!	Excuse me! Sorry!
Varsågod!	Not at all! Don't mention it.
För all del!	By all means!
Ingen orsak!	It's quite all right!

Själv

This is used for emphasis, but is not itself a reflexive (see p.184):

Kan du göra det själv?	Can you do it yourself?
Poliserna tvättar bilarna själva.	The policemen themselves wash the cars.

Duplicates and 'heavy' expressions

It is common in spoken Swedish to duplicate subjects, objects or adverbs:

Ska det vara nödvändigt, *det*?	*Lit.* Is that necessary, that?
Min röda tröja, vet du var *den* är?	My red sweater, do you know where it is?
***Jocke*, han är aldrig hemma, *han*.**	Jocke, he's never at home (he isn't).
Det är inte så dumt, *inte*.	It is not so bad.

These duplicates often go outside the clause proper, at either end. The words **så** and **då** often duplicate within the clause the phrase that is outside it:

När vi kom ut, så (då) fungerade inte pumpen.
When we came out the pump wasn't working.

Long or 'heavy' expressions such as infinitive phrases or object clauses also go at the extreme end of the clause, after any MPT-expressions:

Front	*Verb₁*	*(Subject)*	*Adverb*	*Verb₂*	*Obj/Comp*	*MPT*	*'Heavy'*
Det	**är**	—	—	—	**roligt**	**ibland**	**att spela tennis.**
Han	**sa**	—	**inte**	—	—	**då**	**att han tänkte sluta.**

Factual text 12

Svenska mattraditioner

Swedish food traditions

Nuförtiden kan man äta turkisk kebab, italiensk pizza eller amerikanska hamburgare i Sverige, men det finns också äkta svensk mat. Den har en lång tradition.

På 1400-talet började man använda salt för att konservera kött och det var vanligt förr att man åt stekt salt sill och potatis. Till fest brukade man lägga in sillen i t ex ättika och lök, dvs dagens inlagda sill. Till den salta maten drack man mycket öl, och på 1700-talet blev det vanligt att bränna brännvin som man gjorde av potatis. Innan salt blev vanligt torkade man fisk – lutfisk vid jul är ett minne från den tiden. Ett annat sätt att konservera fisk var att syra eller grava den. Surströmming, ursprungligen en norrländsk rätt, äter man vid fester på hösten. Gravad lax är också festmat. Att ha kräftskiva är mycket vanligt i augusti.

Knäckebrödet eller tunnbrödet bakade man för att det skulle hålla länge. De stora runda brödkakorna hade hål i mitten så att man kunde hänga dem på stänger under taket. Svamp växte i alla skogar men det var först för 100 år sedan som folk på landsbygden började äta denna mat som de kunde plocka helt gratis. I skogen plockar man också bär på hösten. På 1700-talet började rika svenska familjer dricka kaffe och det blev snabbt populärt över hela norden att 'fika'. De nordiska folken är idag världens mest kaffedrickande folk.

Vocabulary

nuförtiden, nowadays
kött -et, meat
stek/a -er -te, fry
lägg/a -er lade in, pickle
ättika -n, vinegar
bränn/a -er -de, burn; *here*: distil
torka/ -r -de, dry
lutfisk -en, stockfish
syra, grava, method of preparing fish or meat by rubbing with salt, spices and keeping it for some days
surströmming -en -ar, fermented herring
ursprungligen, originally
lax -en -ar, salmon
kräfta -n -or, crayfish
kräftskiva -n -or, crayfish party
knäckebröd -et -, crispbread
håll/a -er höll, *here*: keep
stång -en stänger, peg, pole
svamp -en -ar, mushroom, fungi
fika/ -r -de, drink coffee

Exercise 5

Fill in the missing words:

1 Man drack så mycket öl eftersom det fanns . . . i maten. 2 Ofta åt man . . . sill och . . . 3 För att konservera fisk kunde man . . . den eller . . . den. 4 Att . . . blev vanligt för 200 år sedan. 5 . . . åt man ursprungligen i Norrland. 6 I augusti brukar man äta . . . vid fester. 7 Brödkakorna var . . . och . . . 8 Man hängde de . . . 9 I skogen plockar man mycket . . . och . . . på hösten. 10 Svenskarna dricker förfärligt mycket starkt . . .

13 Skogsvandring

A walk in the forest

In this lesson we will look at:

- article use
- the definite declension of the adjective Type 3
- adjectives and adverbs
- how to express permission and prohibition
- reflexive pronouns and verbs
- present participles
- the spring

Text 13

Skogsvandring

A walk in the forest

I Sverige får man plocka svamp och bär i stort sett överallt. Allemansrätten ger alla människor rätt att vistas i och njuta av skog och mark hela året. Man får t o m tälta och göra upp eld på privat område, bara man inte stör ägarna eller förstör naturen. Om man vill tälta mer än ett dygn, måste man be markägaren om lov, och det är inte tillåtet att bryta av levande kvistar på träd eller att plocka fridlysta blommor. Men alla kan vandra fritt i skogarna, bada i sjöarna och duka fram picknick på ängen. Det är viktigt för svenskarna som älskar naturen, kanske särskilt på sommaren.

Innan Bill åker tillbaka till staden följer han därför med Gunnar och Ulla på bärutflykt. Gunnar och Ulla fyller snabbt och effektivt jättelika korgar, medan några ensamma blåbär ligger och skramlar i Bills lilla hink. Svamp vågar han inte plocka eftersom många sorter är giftiga eller i varje fall inte särskilt välsmakande.

När Bill för första gången får se en älg komma gående är dagen räddad. Höstens stora älgjakt har inte börjat, så både han och älgen kan vara trygga. Tyvärr försvinner älgkon genast trots att det enligt jaktlagen är förbjudet att skjuta älg så här års. Men det kanske är bäst att inte lita på en engelsman.

Vocabulary

i stort sett, in the main; *here*: virtually
överallt, anywhere
allemansrätten, the right of common access
plocka/ -r -de, pick
rätt -en -er, right
vista/s vistas -des i, stay; *here*: be
njut/a -er njöt av, enjoy
t o m = till och med, even
tälta/ -r -de, put up a tent
privat -a, private
område -t -n, area
ägare -n, owner
eld -en -ar, fire
bara man inte = så länge man inte, as long as one does not
stör/a stör -de, disturb
dygn -et, day, i.e. 24 hours
markägare -n -, landowner
be någon om lov, ask someone's permission
natur -en, environment, countryside
bryt/a -er bröt, break
levande, live
kvist -en -ar, branch
träd -et -, tree
fridlyst - -a, protected
fritt, freely
bärutflykt -en -er, berry-picking expedition
effektivt, efficiently,
jättelik -t -a, gigantic
korg -en -ar, basket
ensam -t -ma, lonely
blåbär -et -, bilberry, blueberry
skramla/ -r -de, rattle
fyll/a -er -de, fill
hink -en -ar, bucket
giftig -t -a, poisonous
särskilt, especially
välsmakande, pleasant tasting
komma gående, coming along
Dagen är räddad. That made his day.
älgjakt -en -er, elk hunt
trygg -t -a, safe, secure
försvinn/a -er försvann, vanish, disappear
älgko -n -r, elk cow
genast, immediately
enligt, according to
höst -en -ar, autumn
jaktlag -en -ar, hunting regulation
förbjud/en -et -na, prohibited
skjut/a -er sköt, shoot
så här års, at this time of year
lita/ -r -de på, trust

Article use (I)

Use of indefinite and definite (end) articles in Swedish is often the same as in English, but notice the following differences:

(a) End article in Swedish – no article in English

Abstract nouns in a general sense:

Svenskarna älskar naturen.	Swedes love nature.
Priserna stiger.	Prices are rising.
Sådant är livet.	Such is life.
Tiden går.	Time flies.

Locations:

Fredrik går i kyrkan/skolan.	Fredrik goes to church/school.
Eva åker till staden/är i staden.	Eva is going to/is in town.

Days, seasons and festivals:

På fredagarna åker de ut på landet.	On Fridays they go out to the country.
På vintern kan man åka skridskor.	In (the) winter you can skate.

(b) No article in Swedish – indefinite article in English

There is no article before nouns of nationality, profession, religious and political belief (**Han är svensk.** See p.33). There are two further cases of this kind:

Count nouns in a general sense:

Man får göra upp eld.	One may light a fire.
De väntar barn och söker lägenhet.	They are expecting a child and are looking for a flat.
Hon har inte bil/körkort.	She does not have a car/driving licence.

Nouns after **vilken, mången**:

Vilken vacker dag!	What a beautiful day!

Exercise 1

Fill in the articles where necessary:

1 Bill brukar åka till . . . stad . . . på . . . måndagar . . . 2 Han får inte skjuta . . . älg . . . i Sverige. 3 Svenskar . . . vill hålla . . . natur . . . ren. 4 Får man göra upp . . . eld . . . här? 5 Får man plocka . . . svamp . . .? 6 På . . . höst . . . kan man plocka . . . bär . . . i . . . skog . . .

Definite declension of the adjective, Type 3

Remember (see p.157) that on occasion the front article is omitted, the adjective takes the definite ending (**-a**, sometimes **-e**) and the noun has an end article:

Svenska akademien	**Röda korset**	**Förenta staterna**
(the Swedish Academy)	(the Red Cross)	(the United States)

This happens generally when the expression becomes a set phrase, as in the above examples, when the adjective loses its stress.

Compare:	**det vi̲ta hu̲set**	the white house
and:	**Vita hu̲set**	the White House

But the construction *always* occurs:

- with **hela** (the whole), **halva** (half the), **själva** (the very):
  hela tiden; halva dagen; själva poängen
- with **båda** (both), **förra** (last), **ena** (the one), **enda** (the only):
  båda flickorna; förra veckan; ena benet; enda barnet

And *often* in the following cases:

- in geographical locations:
  Gamla stan; Döda havet — the Old Town; the Dead Sea
- with nationality adjectives:
  franska revolutionen — the French Revolution
  brittiska öarna — the British Isles
- with colour adjectives:
  Röda armén — the Red Army

- with words for location:
  på högra sidan on the right hand side
  i mellersta lådan in the middle drawer

- with compass points:
  västra halvklotet the western hemisphere

- with ordinal numbers:
  första gången; andra våningen the first time; the first floor

Exercise 2

Complete the sentence using definite declension Type 3:

1 (Hel, kväll) gick de i skogen. 2 Värmland ligger i (väster, Sverige). 3 (Förr, år) såg Bill en älg för (först, gång). 4 Det är skönt att vandra i (frisk, luft). 5 De plockade bär (halv, eftermiddag).

Adjectives and adverbs

Some adverbs (but *not* the 'adverb' that has figured so far of the kind that modifies the meaning of the sentence as a whole) derive from adjectives by adding the ending **-t** to the stem of the adjective. They may, therefore, be confused with the **-t** forms of adjectives:

Ulla är *vacker*.	**Ulla sjunger *vackert*.**	**Rummet är *vackert*.**
Ulla is beautiful.	Ulla sings beautifully.	The room is beautiful.
ADJ	ADV	ADJ (**t**-form)

De plockar snabbt och effektivt. They pick quickly and effectively.
Alla kan vandra fritt. Everyone can walk freely.

Some adverbs are formed from adjectives by adding **-en** or **-tvis**:

Han kommer möjligen senare. He will probably come later.
Naturligtvis dricker Bill whisky. Naturally Bill drinks whisky.

Some other adverbs are not derivatives, e.g. **inte, ju, nog, väl, aldrig, här, där, hit, dit.**

Adverbs that end in **-t** are expressions of manner (MPT-expressions) and often come at the end of the clause. Adverbs that end in **-en**, **-tvis** are sentence adverbs like **inte** and go in the same position as **inte**.

Exercise 3

Which words are adverbs?

1 Huset är vackert. 2 Det är otroligt vackert. 3 Är det möjligt att han inte kommer? 4 Hon är inte särskilt vacker. 5 Han kan förmodligen jaga. 6 Han åkte långsamt. 7 Det är förbjudet att jaga. 8 Egentligen är han student.

Dialogue 13

Visst får du!

Of course you may!

Bill and Ulla discuss what you may and may not do

BILL: Får jag plocka vad som helst i skogen?
ULLA: Ja, det får du väl.
BILL: De här blommorna, kan jag plocka dem också?
ULLA: Det går bra.
BILL: Trevligt att man för en gångs skull kan göra vad man vill i det här stränga landet. Annars är det så mycket man inte får. Man får inte gå mot rött ljus, inte köpa vin på lördagar, inte . . .
ULLA: Du får visst gå mot rött ljus om det roar dig.
BILL: Och så ska du äta sex skivor bröd om dagen, gymnastisera, klä dig rätt, inte slå barnen . . .
ULLA: Lägg av! Inte vill du väl slå dina barn, och du får gärna äta en hel limpa om du vill eller inget bröd alls. Socialstyrelsen säger vad du *bör* göra.
BILL: Samma storebrorsfasoner. Och när man går ut med hunden måste man plocka bort hundskiten.
ULLA: Ja, vad är det för fel med det, om jag får fråga? England är underbart på många sätt, men i Sverige är det i alla fall rent.

Vocabulary

visst, of course
vad som helst, anything (at all)
för en gångs skull, for once
sträng -t -a, strict
annars, otherwise
gå mot rött ljus, cross the street against a red light
roa/ -r -de sig, amuse (oneself)
skiva -n -or, slice
gymnastisera/ -r -de, do exercises
klä/ -r -dde sig, dress
slå -r slog slagit, hit
lägg/a -er lade av, stop
limpa -n -or, loaf
Socialstyrelsen, Social Welfare Board
storebrorsfasoner, big brother attitude
hund -en -ar, dog
hundskit -en, dog dirt
ren -t -a, clean

Permission and prohibition

Find phrases in the text and dialogue meaning: 'That's all right, of course', 'You may . . . if you wish', 'One can do what one likes', 'It is (not) allowed', 'It is prohibited.'

Here are some other useful phrases:

Man får (inte) göra det.	You may (not) do that.
Förbud mot . . .	. . . is prohibited.
Var snäll och . . . inte!	Please do not . . . !
Man bör göra det.	One ought to/should do that.
Man har rätt att plocka svamp.	One is permitted to pick mushrooms.

Remember that måste is often a 'false friend':

Man måste göra det. — One must do that.

but:

Man måste inte göra det. — One does not need to do that.

and notice:

Man får/ska inte göra det. — One must/should not do that.

Reflexive pronouns and verbs

There is only one special reflexive pronoun form for the third person singular and plural. Ordinary object forms (see p.82) are used for first and second person:

Jag tvättar mig	I wash (myself)	**Vi tvättar oss**
Du tvättar dig	*etc.*	**Ni tvättar er**
Han tvättar sig		**De tvättar sig**
Hon tvättar sig		
Den tvättar sig		
Man tvättar sig		

The reflexive pronoun is used as the object of the verb or after a preposition but refers to the subject of the clause. The usage after a preposition is different from English:

Jag har skurit mig.	I have cut myself.
Han har skurit sig.	He has cut himself.
Stäng dörren efter dig.	Close the door behind you.
Han stängde dörren efter sig.	He closed the door behind him.
De hade inga pengar på sig.	They had no money on them.

Notice one difficult exception to the rule: in object + infinitive constructions (see p.171) the reflexive pronoun refers to the object and the object pronoun to the subject of the clause:

Han bad doktorn tvätta *sig*. He asked the doctor to wash himself.
OBJ <————

Han bad doktorn tvätta *honom*. He asked the doctor to wash him.
SUBJ <————————

A number of non-reflexive English verbs have reflexive equivalents in Swedish:

> **raka sig** (shave); **kamma sig** (comb one's hair); **klä sig** (get dressed); **gifta sig** (get married); **förkyla sig** (catch cold); **lära sig** (learn); **känna sig** (feel).

Many reflexive verbs indicate movement:

> **sätta sig** (sit down); **lägga sig** (lie down); **resa sig** (get up); **röra sig**, (move); **bege sig** (go); **vända sig** (turn round); **infinna sig** (present oneself); **förirra sig** (get lost); **skynda sig** (hurry); **närma sig** (approach).

Like other unstressed object pronouns, reflexive pronouns may come immediately after the verb (see p.208), rather than after the adverb which is the usual position for stressed objects.

Unstressed object pronouns (incl. reflexive pronouns):	*Stressed objects*:
Olle tvättar sig ˈaldrig.	**Olle tvättar aldrig ˈbilen.**
Olle köper den ˈinte.	**Olle köper inte ˈmattan.**

This happens only when there is a simple verb ($VERB_1$, i.e. present, past tense). If there is a complex verb or two-verb construction the unstressed object pronoun follows $VERB_2$:

Olle har inte tvättat sig idag.
Olle har inte tvättat den.
Olle tänker inte köpa den.

Exercise 4

What is the Swedish for:

1 He got up, moved to the chair and then sat down again. 2 We are getting married next Saturday. 3 I must wash and shave first. 4 The children got dressed and combed their hair. 5 He has not learned Swedish. 6 I didn't feel good. 7 We have caught a cold.

Present participles

Present participles end in **-nde:**

Verbs with stems ending in a consonant or **-a** add **-(a)nde**:

studera/	>	**studera/nde**	Conj. I
lev/a	>	**lev/ande**	Conj. II
skriv/a	>	**skriv/ande**	Conj. IV

Verbs with stems ending in a long vowel add **-ende**:

tro/	>	**tro/ende**	Conj. III
gå/	>	**gå/ende**	irregular verbs

Present participles are only rarely used as verbs in Swedish. For this reason the present participle is learned as a separate word, usually:

(a) an adjective:	**levande träd**	live (living) trees
	välsmakande svamp	pleasant tasting fungi
	stigande priser	rising prices

(b) a noun: **en studerande** a student
en sökande an applicant
ett förhållande a relationship

When N-gender the participle usually denotes a person, when T-gender a verbal abstract.

(c) an adverb: **fortfarande** still

Occasionally present participles are used after the verbs **komma**, **gå** and **bli** and verbs of motion in the same way as English '-ing' forms:

Älgen kom gående genom skogen.	The elk came walking through the forest.

But '-ing' forms are often translated by the Swedish infinitive, see p.171.

Factual text 13 📖

På våren

In the spring

Många traditioner är förknippade med våren i Sverige. I mars åker tusentals skidåkare de nästan nio milen från Sälen till Mora i Dalarna, samma väg som kung Gustav Vasa åkte år 1520 (fast han åkte åt andra hållet). Före reformationen fastade man i 40 dagar fram till påsk och flera traditioner har överlevt från den katolska tiden. Innan fastan började – på fettisdagen – brukade man äta upp den feta mat man inte fick äta under själva fastan. Ännu idag bakar svenskarna fettisdagsbullar eller semlor som innehåller vispgrädde och mandelmassa. Under fastan samlar man fortfarande björkris och pryder det med färgade hönsfjädrar och omkring påsk brister knopparna ut i fina ljusgröna blad. På skärtorsdagen klär småbarnen ut sig till påskkäringar – egentligen häxor – och tigger godis. På påskafton äter man målade ägg. Den sista april (eller 'Valborgsmässoafton') hälsar man äntligen våren välkommen med eldar och fyrverkeri. Valborg firas särskilt i studentstäderna med fester både ute och inne hela eftermiddagen och natten. Dagen därpå är det första maj, arbetarrörelsens högtidsdag, sedan 1938 en allmän helgdag i Sverige, med demonstrationer och politiska tal.

Vocabulary

förknippa/d -t -de, associated
åt andra hållet, in the other direction
överlev/a -er -de, survive
fastan, Lent
fettisdagsbullar, Shrove Tuesday buns
mandelmassa -n, almond paste
björkris -et, birch twigs
hönsfjädrar -na, hens' feathers
skärtorsdagen, Maundy Thursday
häxa -n -or, witch
tigg/a -er -de, beg
godis -et, sweets
Valborgsmässoafton, Walpurgis Eve
dagen därpå, the next day
arbetarrörelsen, the labour movement
allmän helgdag, public holiday
tal -et -, speech

Exercise 5

Här är några svar. Vad kan frågorna vara? Läs texten.

1 Från Sälen till Mora. 2 I Dalarna. 3 1520. 4 Fastan. 5 Man åt upp den mat man inte fick äta under fastan. 6 Semlor. 7 Färgade hönsfjädrar. 8 De tigger godis. 9 Man tänder eldar och har fyrverkerier. 10 I studentstäderna. 11 Sedan 1938.

Exercise 6

Revise the sections on adjectives on pp.62, 157, 169, 181. Then put the words in brackets in the correct form:

1 Man får inte plocka (någon, fridlyst) blommor. 2 (Ingen, bra) blåbär fick vi. 3 Vi måste hitta (en annan) ställe. 4 Den (vacker, engelsk) tjejen. 5 Den (kort, tystlåten) Erik. 6 Deras (liten, flicka) heter Lena. 7 Hon åkte dit för att lära sig (svensk, språk). 8 Han har samma (ful, jacka) på sig idag. 9 Bills (trevlig, bärutflykt). 10 Han hade med sig några (fin, gåva) till sina (god, vän). 11 Han ställer samma (dum, fråga) varje gång. 12 Ullas (egen, gammal) stuga.

14 Tidningar

Newspapers

In this lesson we will look at:

- comparison of adjectives
- how to express similarity and dissimilarity
- the definite forms of superlatives
- article use
- how to be understanding
- slang expressions
- political life in Sweden

Text 14

Tidningar

Newspapers

Kvällstidningen som Rebecca köper i tunnelbanekiosken verkar ha större och svartare rubriker än någonsin. Men den innehåller inga stora nyheter, bara några snyftreportage kring en olycka. Kvällspressen är likadan här som i England.

Rebecca prenumererar på en dagstidning, eftersom det är billigare än att köpa lösnummer, och hon får alltså varje morgon vid femtiden en tidning i brevlådan. Visserligen brukar hon titta på TV-nyheterna på kvällarna men att läsa tidningen är lite mer givande. Vid frukosten skummar hon första sidan och efter att ha kastat en snabb blick på ledaren och kultursidan bläddrar hon fram till utrikesnyheterna för att se om det hänt någonting i England. Det är ju lättast att läsa om sådant som man känner till.

Något som är annorlunda än i engelska tidningar är alla foton av glada brudpar på familjesidan. Eftersom Rebecca inte känner så värst många svenskar, hoppar hon över vigsel-, födelse- och dödsannonserna, fast ibland undrar hon om svenska brudpar är yngre eller äldre än engelska. De ser faktiskt rätt gamla ut på bilderna.

Någon gång läser hon filmrecensionerna. Platsannonserna och 'uthyres' är hon inte intresserad av. Hon söker varken plats eller lägenhet.

I ett avseende är svenska tidningar trevligare än engelska, tycker Rebecca. De sitter ihop. Erik tycker däremot bättre om det engelska lösbladssystemet. 'Det är väl bra att kunna dela med sig', säger han. 'Den ene, t ex jag, läser sporten. Den andre, t ex du, tar serierna.' Rebecca tycker bäst om serierna. Några är nämligen på engelska.

Vocabulary

kvällstidning -en -ar, evening paper
tunnelbanekiosk -en -er, kiosk at tube station
större, svartare, yngre, äldre, *etc.*, see 'Comparison of adjectives' below
rubrik -en -er, headline
någonsin, ever
nyheter-na, news
snyftreportage -t -, sob story
prenumerera/ -r -de, subscribe
dagstidning -en -ar, daily paper
lösnummer -numret -, single copy
brevlåda -n -or, letter box
visserligen, admittedly
givande, rewarding
skumma/ -r -de, skim through
sida -n -or, page
kasta/ -r -de, throw
kasta en blick, glance
ledare -n -, leader
kultursidan, the arts page
bläddra/ -r -de, leaf through
utrikesnyheter -na, foreign news
om det hänt = om det har hänt, see p.247
känn/a -er -de till, be familiar with
annorlunda än, different from, unlike
foto -t -n, photograph
brudpar -et -, bridal couple
familjesidan, the social page
inte så värst många, not that many
vigsel-, födelse- och dödsannonserna, notices of births, marriages and deaths
se/ -r såg . . . ut, look . . .
bild -en -er, picture
någon gång, occasionally
recension -en -er (*pron.* resansjon), review
platsannons -en -er, situations vacant advertisement
'uthyres', to let, vacant properties
avseende -t -n, respect
sitt/a -er satt ihop, be stuck together
lösblad -et -, loose page
dela/ -r -de med sig, share
tycker bäst om, prefers
sport -en -er, sport
serie -n -r, cartoon
nämligen, you see

Swedish newspapers

SVERIGES STÖRSTA MORGONTIDNING

DAGENS NYHETER.

SVENSKA DAGBLADET

Göteborgs-Posten

Comparison of adjectives

Swedish has four methods of comparing adjectives (i.e. forming the comparative and superlative forms) three of which are similar to English (cf. Eng. 'funny – funnier – funniest').

(a) Adds **-are, -ast**:

rolig (funny)	**roligare** (funnier)	**roligast** (funniest)

Most adjectives compare this way, including all in **-(l)ig**. *Note*: also **intelligent, intressant, modern, skicklig** (skilful) and **svår**, unlike their English equivalents.

(b) Vowel change and adds **-re**, **-st**:

stor (big)	**större** (bigger)	**störst** (biggest)

(c) Irregular comparison – changes stem:

liten (little)	**mindre** (smaller)	**minst** (smallest)

(d) Comparison with **mer**, **mest**:

komplicerad (complicated)	**mer komplicerad** (more complicated)	**mest komplicerad** (most complicated)
idyllisk (idyllic)	**mer idyllisk** (more idyllic)	**mest idyllisk** (most idyllic)

All past participles compare this way as well as all bisyllabic adjectives ending in **-isk** and an increasing number of others, especially long or polysyllabic adjectives. Notice that adjectives compared in this way have to agree with the noun in the indefinite or take a definite ending:

ett mer komplicera*t* problem, det mest komplicerad*e* problemet

As only a few adjectives compare according to methods (b) and (c) it is possible to list them and learn them individually:

Vowel change + **-re**, + **-st**

o > ö	**stor**	**större**	**störst**	big
	grov	**grövre**	**grövst**	coarse
å >ä	**låg**	**lägre**	**lägst**	low
	lång	**längre**	**längst**	long, tall (people)
	trång	**trängre**	**trängst**	narrow
	få	**färre**	—	few
	små	**smärre**	—	small
u > y	**ung**	**yngre**	**yngst**	young
	tung	**tyngre**	**tyngst**	heavy
ö	**hög**	**högre**	**högst**	high, tall (objects)

Irregular comparison

god/bra	**bättre**	**bäst**	good
god	**godare**	**godast**	good to eat
dålig	**sämre**	**sämst**	bad
dålig/ond	**värre**	**värst**	bad
gammal	**äldre**	**äldst**	old
liten	**mindre**	**minst**	little
många	**fler**	**flest**	many
mycket	**mer**	**mest**	a lot

Notice about the use of these last:

värre = more of an originally bad property
sämre = less of an originally good property

Compare:

den värsta lögn jag hört	the worst lie I had heard
byxor av sämre kvalitet än hans	trousers of worse quality than his

mer, mest are used only with non-count nouns
fler, flest are used only with count nouns

Compare:

Vill du ha mer kaffe?	Would you like more coffee?
Jag undervisar fler elever i år.	I teach more pupils this year.

Similarity and dissimilarity

Dissimilarity:

Whisky är stark*are än* öl.	Whisky is stronger than beer.
Whiskyn är *för* stark.	The whisky is too strong.
Hans dialekt är *annorlunda än* din.	His dialect is different from yours.
Hans dialekt är *olik* din.	His dialect is different from yours.
Hans bror är *olik* din.	His brother is different from yours.

Similarity:

Jag är *lik* min bror.	I am like my brother.
Jag *liknar* min bror.	I am like my brother.
Han är *lika* intelligent *som* jag.	He is as intelligent as me.

Han talar *samma* dialekt *som* jag.	He speaks the same dialect as me.
Din mössa är *likadan som* min.	Your cap is like mine.
Han talar *så* bra (*som*) han kan.	He speaks as well as he can.

Vigsel har ägt rum i Angelstads kyrka den 23 juni, 1995 mellan *Jan-Åke Nylén*, Halmstad, son till Arvid Nyhlén och hans maka Ulla-Lisa, f. Björk, och *Malin Brogren*, Angelstad, dotter till Mats Brogren och hans maka Kerstin f. Nyström. Vigselförrättare var Jörgen Westerberg.

Exercise 1

Give the adjectives and adverbs in the comparative form:

1 Är Henrik (gammal) än Rebecca? 2 Han ser faktiskt (ung) ut. 3 Är svenska tidningar (dyr) än engelska? 4 Ja, men de är mycket (bra). 5 Rebecca är (intresserad) av recensionerna. 6 Svenskarna läser (många) tidningar än andra nationaliteter. 7 Man läser en engelsk kvällstidning (snabb) än man läser en svensk. 8 De serverar (god) bakelser på Wahlströms konditori. 9 Han har alltid varit duktig men nu börjar han bli (dålig). 10 Svenskarna är kanske (idealistisk) än

engelsmännen. 11 Engelsmännen dricker kanske (mycket) öl än svenskarna, men (liten) sprit.

Definite forms of superlatives

The comparative does *not* inflect in the definite:

en vackrare flicka	**ett större hus**	**vackrare flickor/större hus**
den vackrare flickan	**det större huset**	**de vackrare flickorna/ de större husen**

But the superlative inflects:

1 Superlatives ending in **-ast** always add **-e**:

den vackrast*e* flickan

2 Superlatives ending in **-st** add **-a** (or **-e** with masculine singular):

den störst*a* flickan	**det störst*a* huset**	**de störst*a* flickorna/ husen**
den störst*e* pojken		

3 Superlatives using **mest** add **-a** (or **-e** for masc. sing.) to the adjective:

Hon är den mest intelligent*a* flickan i hela gruppen.
Han är den mest sympatisk*e* studenten i hela gruppen.

Några geografiska fakta om Sverige:

Den största sjön:	Vänern	5 585 km²
Den största ön:	Gotland	3 001 km²
Det största landskapet:	Lappland	109 729 km²
Det folkrikaste landskapet:	Västergötland	1 108 017 invånare
Det största länet:	Norrbottens län	98 906 km²
Den största staden:	Storstockholm	1 400 000 invånare
Det folkrikaste länet:	Stockholms län	1 524 266 invånare
Den längsta kanalen:	Dalslands kanal	225 km
Den längsta bron:	Ölandsbron	6 072 m

Några andra fakta:

Det största företaget:	ABB	200 000 anställda
Den största dagstidningen:	Expressen	418 300 exemplar
Den största veckotidningen:	Icakuriren	410 600 ex.
Den största månadstidningen:	Vår bostad	1 049 300 ex.
Den största serietidningen:	Kalle Anka & Co	139 300 ex.

Exercise 2

Study the table above and then insert the words in the correct form:

1 Den (lång, flod) i Sverige är Klarälven-Götaälv – 720 km. 2 Den (nordlig, punkt) i Sverige är Treriksröset. 3 Den (sydlig, punkt) är Smygehuk. 4 Den (djup, sjö) i Sverige är Hornavan – 221 m. 5 Det (hög, berg) i Sverige är Kebnekaise – 2111 m ö h. 6 Den (liten, fågel) i Sverige är kungsfågeln (*the goldcrest*). 7 Den (kall, månad) är februari. 8 Den (låg, temperatur) i Lappland kan ligga omkring 40–45 minusgrader.

Article use (2)

Use of indefinite and definite (end) articles in Swedish is often the same as in English, but notice the following difference:

No article in Swedish – definite article in English:

with instruments and machines:

Jag spelar piano.	I play the piano.
Vi tittar på TV.	We are watching (the) TV.
Hon lyssnar på radio.	She is listening to the radio.

with proper names:

Vi ska äta middag hos Olssons.	We are having dinner at the Olsson's.

with nouns after **nästa** (the next), **samma** (the same), **fel** (the wrong), **rätt** (the right), **följande** (the following), **föregående** (the previous):

Du ska fortsätta till nästa by.	You have to continue to the next village.
Han tog fel väg.	He took the wrong road.
Följande höst var torr.	The following autumn was dry.

Exercise 3

What is the Swedish for:

1 Aren't the headlines as big in the evening papers? They're bigger. 2 Is the newspaper as rewarding as the TV news? It's more rewarding. 3 Does she play as well as Erik? She plays better. 4 Are the boys like their father? They're taller. 5 Does Rebecca subscribe to the same paper

as you? Yes, but she pays less. 6 The sports pages are not the same as in English papers. They're fewer.7 The leader is more difficult to read. It is too difficult. 8 Sweden is very different from England. It's richer and more beautiful.

Dialogue 14

Jag begriper ingenting!

I don't understand anything!

After a lecture Rebecca is worried about her exam

REBECCA: Jag begrep inte ett ord av vad han sa.
ERIK: Det är väl inte så konstigt. Han talade fort och det var ett svårt ämne.
REBECCA: Men hur ska jag kunna klara mig om jag inte förstår vad han säger?
ERIK: Du vänjer dig. Oroa dig inte!
REBECCA: Fattar du inte? Det är bråttom. Jag tentar ju nästa vecka.
ERIK: Lugna dig! Det kommer att gå bra. Det har ju gått fint hittills. Du behöver inte vara orolig.
REBECCA: Vill du påstå att jag ska klara mig genom att gissa, eller ska jag fuska kanske?
ERIK: Jag har för mig att du sa att du var fena på att fuska i skolan.
REBECCA: Vad sa du? Nu begriper jag inte dig heller.

Vocabulary

begrip/a -er begrep, understand
konstig -t -a, strange
fort, quickly
ämne -t -n, subject
klara/ -r -de sig, cope
vänj/a -er vande sig, get used to
oroa/ -r -de sig, worry
fatta/ -r -de, understand, grasp
Det är bråttom. It's urgent.
tenta/ -r -de (= tentera), take an examination
lugna/ -r -de sig, calm down
hittills, so far, up to now
orolig -t -a, worried
påstå/ -r påstod, maintain
gissa/ -r -de, guess
fuska/ -r -de, cheat
har för mig, imagine
vara fena på (= fenomenal), be fantastic at something

Understanding and being understood

There are three ways of saying 'understand' in the dialogue. What are they? Here are one or two other expressions of the same kind:

Det antar jag.	I assume so.
Det förmodar jag.	I presume so.
Det undrar jag.	I wonder.
Det gissar jag.	That is my guess.

What are the three phrases Erik uses to tell Rebecca to calm down?

Slang (2)

See also p.164. Below are other frequent slang words and expressions (not already included in the dialogues) with their standard equivalents.

ball -t -a	**rolig**	fun
bergis (*indeclinable*)	**säker**	certain
bussig -t -a	**vänlig**	friendly, kind
deppig -t -a, deppad	**deprimerad**	depressed
dumburk -en -ar	**TV-apparat**	TV-set
extraknäck -en	**extra arbete**	moonlighting
fik -et -	**kafé**	café
funka/ -r -de	**fungera**	work, function
gaggig -t -a	**virrig, senil**	stupid, senile
grej -en -or (-er)	**sak, föremål**	thing
grunka -n -or	**sak, föremål**	thing
hoj -en -ar	**cykel**	bike
höjdare -n -	**högt uppsatt person**	'boss'
kass -t -a	**dålig, tråkig**	rotten, bad
klantig -t -a	**dum, fumlig**	stupid, clumsy
kul (*indeclinable*)	**rolig**	fun
käft -en -ar	**mun**	mouth
käk -et	**mat**	food
käka/ -r -de	**äta**	eat
kärra -n -or	**bil**	car
kåk -en -ar	**hus**	house
lira/ -r -de	**spela**	play (e.g. football)
läskig -t -a	**äcklig, obehaglig**	horrible
läbbig -t -a	**äcklig, obehaglig**	horrible

mack -en -ar	**bensinstation**	petrol station
macka -n -or	**smörgås**	sandwich
mugg -en	**toalett**	toilet
mygla/ -r -de	**fiffla, småstjäla**	fiddle, wangle
packad	**full**	drunk
pryl -en -ar	**sak**	thing, object
ragga/ -r -de upp	**skaffa (t ex flickor/ pojkar)**	get hold of, 'chat up'
sabba/-r-de	**sabotera**	sabotage
snask -et	**godsaker**	sweets
snut -en -ar	**polis -en -er**	cop, policeman
spänn	**kronor**	currency
stålar	**pengar**	money
toa -n	**toalett -en**	toilet
töntig -t -a	**dum, fånig**	stupid

Factual text 14

Det politiska livet

Political life

Svenskarna röstar i riksdagsval den tredje söndagen i september vart fjärde år, dvs. 1998, 2002 etc. och alla svenska medborgare som är över 18 år har rösträtt och får ställa upp som kandidater i valet. Valdeltagandet är högt – omkring 90% av väljarna brukar rösta. Det parti som får flest mandat (riksdagsledamöter) bildar regering antingen ensamt eller i koalition. Det finns 349 ledamöter i riksdagen uppdelade i block:

Det socialistiska blocket består av Arbetarepartiet–Socialdemokraterna (s) och Vänsterpartiet (Vp). Socialdemokraterna är mycket större än Vp. Det borgerliga blocket består av Folkpartiet liberalerna (fp), Centern (c) och det konservativa Moderata Samlingspartiet (m). De två blocken har ungefär lika många mandat.

Andra partier som får mindre än 4% av rösterna får inte vara med i riksdagen. Det finns också flera vänsterpartier som inte är så stora som Vp. Partier som är representerade i riksdagen får sedan 1966 statliga bidrag beroende på antalet mandat. Kring 4%-strecket ligger KdS (Kristdemokratiska samhällspartiet), ett borgerligt parti, och Miljöpartiet de gröna, som står utanför blocken.

Sverige har varit neutralt i krig och är inte medlem i NATO men gick med i EU 1995 och har samtidigt ett starkt samarbete med de övriga nordiska länderna. Två kända svenska statsmän från senare år är Dag Hammarskjöld, FNs generalsekreterare som omkom i Rhodesia under Kongokriget 1961 och Olof Palme, svensk statsminister som sköts ihjäl i Stockholm 1986.

Vocabulary

riksdagsval -et -, parliamentary election
medborgare -n -, citizen
rösträtt -en, right to vote
rösta/ -r -de, vote
valdeltagande -t, turnout
mandat -et -, seat
riksdagsledamot -en -ledamöter, member of parliament
regering -en -ar, government
bidrag-et, support, grant
beroende på, depending on
vare sig . . . eller, neither . . . nor
EU = Europeiska Unionen, the European Union
samarbete -t, co-operation
omkomm/a -er -kom, die (an unnatural death)
statsminister -n -rar, prime minister
ihjäl, dead

Exercise 4

Sätt ett kryss i rutan: (Place a cross in the box)	**rätt** (*right*)	**fel** (*wrong*)
Alla som är över 18 år brukar rösta.	☐	☐
Man får bli kandidat om man är över 18 år.	☐	☐
90% av alla över 18 år röstar.	☐	☐
Endast det parti som får 349 mandat får bilda regering.	☐	☐
Det socialistiska blocket har ungefär lika många mandat som Moderata samlingspartiet.	☐	☐
Socialdemokraterna är mycket större än kommunisterna.	☐	☐

Vp är det största vänsterpartiet efter socialdemokraterna. ☐ ☐

Alla politiska partier får statliga bidrag. ☐ ☐

Sverige är inte medlem i EU. ☐ ☐

Compounding

There are several compound nouns in the above text, i.e. nouns made up of two (or more) nouns joined together, of two main types:

NOUN + NOUN	**röst|rätt vänster|parti val|deltagande**
NOUN + **s** + NOUN	**kväll|s|press**

There are few firm rules for whether the link +-**s** is used, but it is found in the following cases:

- compounds in which the first part is itself a compound:

  fot|boll + lag = fotboll|s|lag

- nouns whose first part ends in **-(n)ing, -ling, -an, -nad, -(i)tet, -(a)tion**:

  koalition|s|regering
  regering|s|chef (head of government)

Further methods for compounding are:

- NOUN minus **-a/-e** + NOUN

  pojke + namn > pojk|namn
  flicka+ namn > flick|namn
  väljare + kår > väljar|kår

- NOUN + link vowel + NOUN

  familj + sida > familj|e|sida
  tunnelbana + kiosk > tunnel|ban|e|kiosk

- NOUN + old case ending + NOUN

  vecka + slut > vecko|slut
  vara + hus > varu|hus

This last method is now seldom used to form new compounds.

Exercise 5

What two nouns do the following compounds derive from?
Example:

ett läkarintyg	< en läkare	+ ett intyg	*doctor's certificate*
1 ett lärarrum	< . . .	+ . . .	*staff room*
2 en veckotidning	< . . .	+ . . .	*weekly newspaper*
3 ett hjärtbyte	< . . .	+ . . .	*heart transplant*
4 ett grannbarn	< . . .	+ . . .	*neighbour's child*
5 en soffkudde	< . . .	+ . . .	*sofa cushion*
6 en ficklampa	< . . .	+ . . .	*pocket torch*
7 en gatubild	< . . .	+ . . .	*street scene*
8 (en) kvinnokamp	< . . .	+ . . .	*feminist struggle*
9 en skoltermin	< . . .	+ . . .	*school term*
10 ett invånarantal	< . . .	+ . . .	*number of inhabitants*

15 Rebecca sätter igång och packar

Rebecca starts packing

In this lesson we will look at:

- reflexive possessive pronouns (**hans**, etc./**sin**, etc.)
- article use
- transitive and intransitive verbs
- the position of unstressed object pronouns
- how to express beginning, continuing and ending
- subjunctives
- emigration and immigration

Text 15

Rebecca satter igång och packar

Rebecca starts packing

Väckarklockan ringde ovanligt tidigt hos Rebecca den där morgonen, och först hörde hon den inte. Men hon vaknade, gnuggade sig i ögonen och satte sig på sängkanten. Hon sträckte sig efter telefonluren och slog numret till sin kompis, Pernilla, som hon lovat ringa och väcka. Pernilla svarade att hon redan var uppe. Hon hade vaknat i god tid, och eftersom hon avskydde att ligga och dra sig, hade hon redan packat sin ryggsäck och stod nu resklar med ytterkläderna på. Rebecca trevade med fötterna efter tofflorna, satte på sig morgonrocken och började lägga kläder i travar på sängen: några trosor, en bh, två långärmade T-shirts och en tjock olle, några blusar, en kjol, strumpbyxor. Högarna växte och hon tänkte i sitt stilla sinne att hon borde ha gjort detta föregående kväll.

De skulle resa norrut. Pernilla hade föreslagit att de skulle ta hennes bil och åka bort ett par dagar kring veckoslutet. De kunde behöva lite avkoppling från sina studier. Det var inte skidsäsong ännu, men det kunde vara så strålande vackert på senhösten och Pernilla ville visa Rebecca några av sina älsklingsställen. Rebecca hade förstås tackat ja till erbjudandet, men nu tittade hon förtvivlat på alla sina olika klädesplagg. Vad behövde man när det enligt väderleksrapporten skulle bli växlande molnighet och enstaka regnskurar i södra Norrlands inland och fjälltrakter?

Henrik hade lånat henne sitt regnställ, och hans råd hade varit att bara packa det nödvändigaste. Ju mindre, desto bättre. Rebecca beslöt att ta honom på orden, hoppade i jeansen, drog en tröja över huvudet, stoppade tandborsten i fickan, tog regnstället under armen och gick ner till den väntande bilen.

Vocabulary

sätt/a -er satte igång, start
packa/ -r -de, pack
hör/a hör -de, hear
vakna/ -r -de, wake up (*intrans.*)
gnugga/ -r -de, rub
sängkant -en -er, edge of the bed
sträck/a -er -te sig, reach, stretch
telefonlur -en -ar, telephone receiver
slå/ -r slog, hit; *here*: dial
väck/a -er -te, rouse, awaken (*trans.*)
svara/ -r -de, answer
ligga och dra sig, lie in bed (in the morning)
ryggsäck -en -ar, rucksack
resklar -t -a, ready to leave
ytterkläder -na, outdoor clothes
treva/ -r -de efter, grope for
toffla -n -or, slipper
morgonrock -en -ar, dressing gown
trave -n -ar, pile
trosor -na, knickers
bh -n -ar, bra
långärmad -t- de, long-sleeved
olle -n -ar, warm sweater
blus -en -ar, blouse
kjol -en -ar, skirt
strumpbyxor -na, tights
hög -en -ar, heap
väx/a -er -te, grow *(intrans.)*
i sitt stilla sinne, deep down
föreslå/ -r -slog, suggest
veckoslut -et -, weekend
avkoppling -en, break, relaxation
studie -n -r, study
skidsäsong -en -er, skiing season
strålande vackert, gorgeous
senhöst -en, late autumn
älsklingsställe -t -n, favourite place
tacka/ -r -de ja, accept
erbjudande -t -n, offer
förtvivlat, in desperation
klädesplagg -et -, article of clothing

väderleksrapport -en -er, weather report
växlande molnighet, cloudy with bright intervals
enstaka regnskurar, scattered showers
fjälltrakt -en -er, mountain area
inland -et, interior
regnställ -et -, waterproof
råd -et -, advice
det nödvändigaste, what was absolutely necessary
ju . . . desto . . ., the . . . the . . .
ta honom på orden, take him at his word
tandborste -n -ar, toothbrush
ficka -n -or, pocket
arm -en -ar, arm
vänta/ -r -de, wait

Reflexive possessive pronouns (hans etc./sin etc.)

English 'his', 'her', 'its', 'their' have two possible renderings in Swedish: **hans, hennes, dess, deras** (all indeclinable as they end in **-s**); **sin (sitt, sina)** which agrees with the noun following.

Han har en bil. *Hans* bil är gammal.	He has a car. His car is old.
Han har sålt *sin* bil.	He has sold his car.

Sin (sitt, sina) is reflexive. It may only qualify the object of the clause and always refers to possession by the subject of the clause.

Han har sålt *sin bil.*
SUBJ <—> OBJ (**sin** etc. qualifies the object of the clause.)
<————>
(**sin** etc. refers to the subject of the clause)

Sin (sitt, sina) *never* qualifies the subject of the clause:

***Hans bil* är gammal.**
SUBJ

One way of being sure of reference to the subject is to draw an arrow from the possessive to the possessor. If the possessor is subject of the clause *and* the noun that the possessive qualifies is object, then use **sin** *etc.*

He has sold *his* car. (i.e. A has sold A's car.)
<————>

Non-reflexive forms (**hans**, **hennes**, *etc.*) do not refer to the subject:

Olle är sur. Varför det? Åke gick ut med hans fru.
Olle is angry. Why? Åke went out with his (i.e. not Åke's own) wife.

Problems arise in the following cases:

- when there is more than one clause:

They think that their lessons are boring.
De tycker, att deras lektioner är tråkiga.

because 'their lessons' is the subject of the new sub clause.
(cf. They hate their lessons. = **De hatar sina lektioner.)**

- when there is a double subject:

He and his wife went away for the weekend.
Han och hans fru åkte bort för helgen.

because 'he and his wife' is all subject use **hans**.
(cf. **Han tog sin fru med sig.** = He took his wife with him.)

Exercise 1

Translate only the words in italics:

1 Pernilla rang *her friend* Rebecca. 2 It wasn't *her rucksack.* 3 She was packing *her case.* 4 *Her case* was heavy. 5 She put *her clothes* on the bed. 6 But are *her clothes* suitable for the country? 7 Pernilla was going to take *her own car.* 8 *Her car* never starts in the mornings. 9 Pernilla had to lend her *her warm sweater.* 10 She thinks that *her warm sweater* suits Rebecca. 11 *Pernilla and her friend* have a marvellous time in the country.

Exercise 2

Insert either **hans/hennes/dess/deras or sin/sitt/sina**:

Rebecca ville inte packa . . . blusar och strumpbyxor. . . . klädesplagg låg överallt på rummet. Pernilla kan inte få igång . . . bil. . . . bil startar aldrig på morgonen . . . motor krånglar. Rebecca kan inte få igen . . . väska. Hon tycker att . . . väska är besvärlig. Hon bad . . . kompis Henrik om råd och han sa att han tyckte att hon inte behövde ta med alla . . . kläder den gången. Hon följde till slut . . . råd. . . . regnställ hade hon fått i julklapp av Henrik.

Article use (3)

End article in Swedish – possessive pronoun in English

Notice that when the ownership is obvious, for example with parts of the body and clothing, Swedish does *not* use a possessive (see p.205).

Hon satte på sig morgonrocken.	She put on her dressing gown.
Hon drog en tröja över huvudet och stoppade tandborsten i fickan.	She pulled a sweater over her head and put her toothbrush in her pocket.
Hon tog av sig skorna.	She took off her shoes.
Hon ska tvätta håret.	She is going to wash her hair.
Han har ont i ryggen/magen/huvudet.	He has a pain in his back/a stomach ache/a headache.

Transitive and intransitive verbs

Transitive verbs take a direct object, intransitive verbs do not.

Hon	***hörde***	**väckarklockan.**	**Hon**	***sov***	**länge.**
	trans.	DO		intrans.	MPT (time)

Ditransitive verbs have both a direct and an indirect object: the indirect object is often a person and the direct object a thing:

Henrik	***lånade***	**henne**	**ett regnställ.**
	ditrans.	IO	DO

Whereas in English many verbs may be either intransitive or transitive, in Swedish there is often a sharp distinction in that separate verbs are used:

Transitive	*Intransitive*
He grows potatoes.	The potatoes are growing well.
Han *odlar* potatis.	**Potatisen *växer* bra.**

Churchill smoked cigars.	The chimney was smoking.
Churchill *rökte* cigarrer.	**Det *rykte* i skorstenen.**

There are a number of pairs of transitive/intransitive verbs in Swedish that are distinguished by different verb inflection (e.g. weak vs. strong):

Transitive		*Intransitive*	
sätt/a -er satte satt	put	**sitt/a -er satt suttit**	sit, be
lägg/a -er lade lagt	lay	**ligg/a -er låg legat**	lie, be
fäll/a -er -de -t	fell	**fall/a -er föll fallit**	fall
bränn/a -er -de -t	burn	**brinn/a -er brann brunnit**	burn
kyl/a -er -de -t	chill	**kallna/ -r -de -t**	cool
trött/a -r -de -t	tire	**tröttna/ -r -de -t**	get tired

Exercise 3

Choose one of the verbs and insert it in the correct form in the sentence:

sätta/sitta
Rebecca . . . på sängen och funderade. Hon kunde inte somna och hon tänkte . . . på radion. När hon hade . . . pa den, slutade hon fundera.

lägga/ligga
Jokkmokk är en liten stad som . . . i Lappland. Vi . . . brevet i brevlådan i går. Var har jag . . . mina byxor?

bränna/brinna
Har du . . . upp alla gamla tidningar? När han studerade . . . Lampan sent på natten. Jag har . . . mig på spisen.

Unstressed object pronouns

When object pronouns are unstressed they often move in front of the adverb, as in the text:

Först hörde hon den ˈinte.	(Cf. **Först hörde hon inte ˈden.**)
OBJ ADV	ADV OBJ

Cf. Noun (always stressed):	Pronoun (unstressed):
Hon gillar inte alls ˈpopkonst.	**Hon gillar den inte ˈalls.**
ADV OBJ	OBJ ADV

Cf. Stressed pronoun (for contrast):	Unstressed pronoun:
Jag känner inte ˈhonom (men	**Jag känner honom ˈinte.**
ADV OBJ	OBJ ADV
jag känner ˈhenne).	
(I don't know *him* (but I do know *her*.))	(I don't *know* him.)

Exercise 4

Replace the noun with a pronoun and re-arrange the word order as in the example:

Example: **Hon hörde inte väckarklockan. > Hon hörde den inte.**

1 Hon tog inte blusarna med sig. 2 Känner du inte Henrik? 3 Nej jag träffade aldrig Henrik. 4 Han gav mig inte regnstället. 5 Du glömmer väl inte ollen? 6 Du väcker väl inte Rebecca?

Dialogue 15

Det är bäst vi startar tidigt

We had better start early

Pernilla, an early riser, is keen to get going

REBECCA: God morgon, god morgon, det är dags att stiga upp.
PERNILLA: God morgon. Jag har varit vaken länge. Jag skulle just gå när du ringde.
REBECCA: Gå! Är du inte klok? Jag har precis vaknat, och nu ska jag sätta igång och packa. Jag vet inte var jag ska börja. Fy, vad det är jobbigt!
PERNILLA: Om jag vore du skulle jag bara ta lite underkläder, varma tröjor och någonting om vi går ut på kvällen. Det finns faktiskt ett disco däruppe. De håller igång hela natten.
REBECCA: Jag klarar inte det här. Varken min rutiga blus eller mina randiga skjortor passar till de rutiga långbyxorna. Något nytt enfärgat har jag inte råd med.
PERNILLA: Det problemet tar vi itu med när vi kommer fram. Mönster på mönster kan vara jättesnyggt. Sno dig nu! Resan tar

ganska lång tid, så det är bäst att vi startar tidigt. Jag kör nu . . . om jag får igång bilen.

REBECCA: Din bil startar aldrig på morgnarna så jag har en dryg halvtimme på mig att få igen väskan.

PERNILLA: Vi får se. Hej så länge.

REBECCA: Hej. Vi ses . . . om jag kommer upp ur sängen. Morgonpigga människor upphör aldrig att förvåna mig.

Vocabulary

starta/ -r -de, start
dags att, time to
stig/a -er steg upp, get up
vak/en -et -na, awake
inte klok, crazy
jobbig -t -a, hard work
vore, were (see 'Subjunctives' below)
underkläder -na, underclothes
håller igång, be in full swing
varken . . . eller . . ., neither . . . nor . . .
skjorta -n -or, shirt
passa/ -r -de (till), be suitable, go (with)
långbyxor -na, slacks
enfärgad -t -de, plain (*lit.* of a single colour)
ha råd med, afford
problem -et -, problem
ta/ -r tog itu med, deal with
mönster mönstret -, pattern
jättesnygg -t -a, stunning, very attractive
sno/ -r -dde sig, hurry up
få/ -r fick igång bilen, get the car started
en dryg halvtimme, a good half hour, at least half an hour
få igen väskan , get the case closed
morgonpigg, upphör, förvåna, dryg, see 'Beginning, continuing . . .' below

Beginning, continuing and ending

Find words in the text and dialogue which mean 'at first', 'already', 'for a couple of days', 'it is time to . . .', 'for a long time', 'I have just . . .', 'I have a good half hour to . . .'. There are also a number of expressions for beginning, continuing and ending:

Rebecca *började* lägga kläder i travar.	Rebecca began to lay out clothes in piles.
Nu ska jag *sätta igång och* packa.	Now I am going to start packing.

Starta is a 'false friend', meaning 'set out', 'start up' (engines), or 'take off' (aeroplanes).

Vi *startar* tidigt.	We will set out early.
Jag kan inte *få igång* motorn.	I can't start the engine.
Morgonpigga människor *upphör* aldrig att förvåna mig.	People who are lively in the morning never cease to amaze me.

Notice also: **hålla på och/hålla på med att** (be (engaged in) doing something):

Han håller på och lagar bilen. **Han håller på med att laga bilen.**	He is mending the car (i.e. right now).

Another word for 'continue' is **pågå**:

Matchen pågår ännu.	The match is still going on.

Another word for 'end, stop' is **sluta**:

Matchen har slutat.	The match has finished.
Det har slutat regna.	It has stopped raining.

Subjunctives

The subjunctive is rarely used in modern Swedish, and a special subjunctive form of the verb, ending in **-e**, is found only for a few verbs such as **vore** (from **vara**):

Det *vore* kul om du kunde komma ikväll.	It would be nice if you could come tonight.
(cf. **Det skulle vara kul . . .**)	

Usually the subjunctive is found in fixed expressions:

***Leve* brudparet!**	Long live the bridal couple!
Tack *vare* din hjälp . . .	Thanks to your help . . .

The past subjunctive of strong and irregular verbs is used now only as an alternative to the ordinary past tense in order to express unreal situations:

Om jag *vore* mycket rik skulle jag köpa ett slott i Frankrike.	If I were very rich I would buy a chateau in France.
(cf. **Om jag var . . .**)	

Factual text 15

Utvandring – invandring

Emigration – immigration

Mellan 1850 och 1920 utvandrade över 1 miljon svenskar till Nordamerika. De flesta kom från landsbygden, men arbetare från staden åkte också med. På 1800-talet förändrades Sverige mycket – befolkningen ökade hastigt och på landet betydde detta fler jordlösa och arbetslösa.

Under 1860-talet blev det missväxtår och många dog av hunger. Samtidigt erbjöd USA gratis jord och välbetalda arbeten i de växande städerna. I början sökte vissa svenskar också religionsfrihet i den nya världen. Senare reste socialister som Joe Hill (avrättad i Utah 1915) och unga män som inte ville göra den förlängda militärtjänsten (1901). Om tidig utvandring från Småland har författaren Vilhelm Moberg (1898–1973) skrivit i 'Romanen om utvandrarna' i fyra delar. Sedan andra världskriget har det kommit många arbetare och flyktingar till Sverige. Den största gruppen är finnar – omkring 250 000. På 60-talet och 70-talet kom många jugoslaver och greker. Grekerna flydde undan militärjuntan i Grekland 1967–74, och många chilenare flydde till Sverige efter kuppen mot president Salvador Allende år 1973. Det har kommit andra flyktingar från Iran och Somalia och på senare år från det forna Jugoslavien.

Trots att myndigheterna gör mycket för att hjälpa, trivs många invandrare inte i Sverige. De saknar sina hemländer och accepteras inte alltid av svenskarna.

Vocabulary

utvandra/ -r -de, emigrate
landsbygd -en, countryside
förändra/ -r -de, change
hastigt, rapidly
betyd/a -er -de, mean
missväxtår -et -, years when the harvest failed
frihet -en -er, freedom
avrätta/ -r -de, executed
militärtjänst -en, military service
författare -n -, writer
roman -en -er, novel
kupp -en -er, coup
myndigheterna, the authorities
det forna, former, ex-

Exercise 5

Hitta ett eller flera ord i texten som passar här:

1 Han kommer inte från staden utan från . . . 2 Den stora folkökningen på 1800-talet betydde att många hade varken . . . eller . . . 3 I USA kunde man få . . . 4 Religionsfrihet kunde man få i . . . 5 År 1901 förlängdes . . . 6 Joe Hill, den berömda . . . blev . . . i Utah. 7 Vilhelm Moberg är . . . till en . . . roman om utvandringen från . . . 8 Från södra Europa kom det många . . . till Sverige. 9 Militärled-ningen i Grekland kallades . . . 10 President Allende dog under . . . år 1973. 11 Från fjärran östern har det också kommit . . . , från . . .

16 Hos läkaren

At the doctor's

In this lesson we will look at:

- past participles
- particle verbs and their participles
- compound verbs
- the position of particles
- affixation
- words for parts of the body
- warnings
- words for people from certain towns and regions
- Linné, the flower king

Text 16

Hos läkaren

At the doctor's

Bill hade känt sig lite vissen en längre tid. Han hade en besvärande hosta, ihållande huvudvärk, ont i magen, plötsliga smärtor i korsryggen och dessutom skavsår på hälarna. Det sistnämnda tyckte han emellertid var för oheroiskt, så det ville han helst inte låtsas om.

Han kom ihåg att en vän hade sagt att man, om man blev sjuk, kunde gå till sjukhusakuten eller till en vårdcentral utan att först beställa tid. Bill blev omhändertagen trots att han saknade både personnummer och patientbricka. Han blev klämd på magen och knackad i ryggen, fick gapa och säga 'aah', blev stucken i långfingret för blodprov och fick kasta vatten för urinprov. Slutligen talade doktorn om för honom att hostan berodde på rökning, huvudvärken på alkohol, magplågorna på stress och ryggsmärtorna på den föga sittvänliga bilen. Han undrade om Bill kunde lägga av med cigaretterna, skära ner sin ölkonsumtion och koppla av på jobbet. Bill kunde hålla med om att det var en god idé, men när doktorn föreslog att han kunde ta långa stärkande promenader i stället för att sitta instängd i en obekväm, utsliten bil, tänkte Bill på sina skavsår och log sammanbitet.

Vocabulary

läkare -n -, doctor
viss/en -et -na, off colour
besvärande, troublesome
hosta -n, cough
ihållande, constant
huvudvärk -en, headache
ont i magen (see p.207), stomach ache
smärta -n -or, pain
korsrygg -en, small of the back
skavsår -et -, blister
häl -en -ar, heel
det sistnämnda, this last
emellertid, however
oheroisk -t -a, unheroic
inte låtsa/s -des om, ignore
sjukhusakuten, casualty department
vårdcentral -en -er, clinic, health centre
beställ/a -er -de tid, make an appointment
blev omhändertagen, was treated
sakna/ -r -de, lack, be without, have no
personnummer -numret -, personal identity number
patientbricka -n -or, patient card (a plastic medical card)
klämm/a -er klämde, squeeze, press
knacka/ -r -de, knock, tap
rygg -en -ar, back
gapa/ -r -de, open one's mouth
stick/a -er stack, prick, sting (of insects)
blodprov -et -, blood test
kasta/ -r -de vatten, urinate (hospital language)
urinprov -et -, urine test
slutligen, finally
bero/ -r -dde på, be due to
magplåga -n -or, stomach pain
ryggsmärta -n -or, back pain
föga sittvänlig, with poor seats
cigarett -en -er, cigarette
skär/a - skar ner, cut down
ölkonsumption -en, beer consumption
koppla/ -r -de av, relax
håll/a -er höll med om, agree with
stärkande, invigorating
promenad -en -er, walk
obekväm -t -a, uncomfortable
stäng/a -er -de in, shut in
slit/a -er slet ut, wear out
le/ -r log, smile
log sammanbitet, gave a dogged (polite) smile

Past participles

How to form past participles:

(a) Weak verbs that have a stem in **-a** or a voiced consonant (i.e. Conjugations I, II) add +-**d**:

packa/	(pack)	**packa/*d***	(packed)
stäng/a	(close)	**stäng/*d***	(closed)

(b) Weak verbs that have a stem in a voiceless consonant (**-k, -p, -s, -t, -x**, i.e. Conjugation IIb verbs) add **-t**:

köp/a	(buy)	**köp/*t***	(bought)

(c) Weak verbs that have a stem in a long stressed vowel (Conjugation III verbs) add **-dd**:

klä	(dress)	**klä/*dd***	(dressed)

(d) To form the past participle of a strong verb: delete the supine ending in **-it** and then add **-en:**

Infinitive	*Supine*	*Past participle*
skriv/a (write)	**skriv/it** (written)	**skriv/*en*** (written)

Using past participles:

The supine is an indeclinable form used together with **har, hade** to form the perfect and pluperfect tenses respectively (see p.116). The past participle of Swedish verbs is, however, a completely separate form which is used as an adjective in the indefinite and definite declensions (Roman numerals refer to verb conjugations):

Indefinite Predicative	*Indefinite Attributive*	*Definite Attributive*
I		
Stolen är nymåla/*d*	**en nymåla/*d* stol**	**den nymåla/*de* stolen**
The chair is newly painted.	a newly painted chair	the newly painted chair
Huset är nymåla/*t*	**ett nymåla/*t* hus**	**det nymåla/*de* huset**
The house is newly painted.	a newly painted house	the newly painted house

IIa		
Dörren är stäng/*d*	**en stäng/*d* dörr**	**den stäng/*da* dörren**
The door is closed.	a closed door	the closed door
Fönstret är stäng/*t*	**ett stäng/*t* fönster**	**det stäng/*da* fönstret**
The window is closed.	a closed window	the closed window
IIb		
Boken är oläs/*t*	**en oläs/*t* bok**	**den oläs/*ta* boken**
The book is unread.	an unread book	the unread book
Brevet är oläs/*t*	**ett oläs/*t* brev**	**det oläs/*ta* brevet**
The letter is unread.	an unread letter	the unread letter
III		
Enigheten är uppnå/*dd*	**en uppnå/*dd* enighet**	**den uppnå/*dda* enigheten**
Unity is achieved.	an achieved unity	the achieved unity
Resultatet är uppnå/*tt*	**ett uppnå/*tt* resultat**	**det uppnå/*dda* resultatet**
The result is reached.	the final result	the final result
IV		
Dikten är omskriv/*en*	**en omskriv/*en* dikt**	**den omskriv/*na* dikten**
The poem is rewritten.	a rewritten poem	the rewritten poem
Dramat är omskriv/*et*	**ett omskriv/*et* drama**	**det omskriv/*na* dramat**
The drama is rewritten.	a rewritten drama	the rewritten drama

Note: Both the N-form and T-form of Conjugation IIb past participles end in **-t**. The definite and plural form of past participles ending in **-ad** is **-e** irrespective of gender (cf. p.134). The definite and plural form of other past participles is **-a**. The past participles of strong verbs have the same root vowel as the supine:

dricka–dricker–drack–dr*u*ckit–dr*u*cken
slå–slår–slog–sl*a*git–sl*a*gen

Past participles are also used with forms of **bli** and **vara** to construct one type of passive (see p.229).

Exercise 1

Revise strong verbs (see p.146). Then insert the indefinite past participle form of the verbs provided:

1 (*skriva* IV) Är brevet . . .? 2 (*tvätta* I) Är kläderna . . .? 3 (*stressa* I) Bill har blivit . . . 4 (*steka* IIb/*grilla* I) Jag vill ha ett . . . ägg och en . . . korv, tack. 5 (*stänga* IIa) Är affärerna redan . . .? 6 (*bygga* IIa) Villorna blev . . . till slut. 7 (*gifta* IIb) De är . . . nu. 8 (*bjuda* IV) Är

vi båda . . . ? 9 (*sticka* IV) Olle blev . . . av ett bi. 10 (*tända* IIa) Är ljuset . . . ?

Exercise 2

Insert the definite past participle form:

1 (*duka* I) Det . . . bordet. 2 (*röka* IIb) Den . . . korven. 3 (*låsa* IIb) De . . . dörrarna. 4 (*känna* IIa) Den . . . filmstjärnan. 5 (*parkera* I) Den . . . bilen. 6 (*laga* I) Den . . . maten. 7 (*gifta* IIb) Det ny- . . . paret. 8 (*bebo* III) Den . . . stugan. 9 (*läsa* IIb) Den om- . . . boken. 10 (*beställa* IIa) De . . . biljetterna.

Particle verbs

Particles are stressed adverbs or prepositions which together with a verb form a particle verb, i.e. the two words together form one unit of meaning:

Jag *tycker om* dig.	I like you.
Du behöver *koppla av*.	You need to relax.
***Lägg av* med att röka!**	Stop smoking!

Prepositions may be used as particles. One difference between a preposition and a particle is that a preposition is unstressed and usually precedes a noun. There is often a difference in meaning:

Unstressed preposition **på**:	*Stressed particle* **på**:
Han sätter sig på ˈregnrocken.	**Han sätter ˈpå sig regnrocken.**
He sits on the raincoat.	He puts on the raincoat.

The following prepositions are, when stressed, often used as particles:

på	**Sätt på radion!**	Put the radio on!
av	**Stäng av stereon!**	Turn off the stereo!
med	**Olle håller inte med mig.**	Olle doesn't agree with me.
efter	**Jag skall se efter.**	I'll go and look.
om	**Gör inte om detta!**	Don't do that again!
	Hon klär om sig.	She is getting changed.
till	**Jag vill inte lägga till något.**	I don't wish to add anything.
över	**Blev det mycket vin över?**	Was there much wine left?
	Vi måste arbeta över idag.	We have to work late today.

The following adverbs are, when stressed, often used as particles:

omkring	**De gick omkring i Rom.**	They walked round in Rome.
runt	**Hon reste runt i Sverige.**	She travelled round in Sweden.
förbi	**Jag körde förbi skolan.**	I drove past the school.
tillbaka	**Hon lämnade tillbaka pennan.**	She gave back the pen.
kvar	**Vi stannar kvar och diskar.**	We'll stay and wash up.
igång	**När skall vi sätta igång?**	When are we going to start?
iväg	**Har du skickat iväg kortet?**	Have you sent off the card?
undan	**Tjuven kom undan polisen.**	The thief evaded the police.
omkull	**Jag slog omkull stolen.**	I knocked over the chair.
sönder	**Vem har slagit sönder vasen?**	Who has smashed the vase?
fast	**Spänn fast bältet!**	Fasten your belt!
loss	**Jag kan inte få loss muttern.**	I cannot loosen the nut.
ihop	**Har Åke och Eva flyttat ihop?**	Have Åke and Eva moved in together?
isär	**Nu har de flyttat isär.**	Now they have moved apart.
itu	**Pennan gick itu.**	The pen broke in two.
ikapp	**Du måste hinna ikapp.**	You must catch up.
ihjäl	**Fienden slog ihjäl honom.**	The enemy killed him.

Participles of particle verbs

In the present and past participle forms of particle verbs the particle becomes a prefix attached to the verb:

Vi *tycker om* vår lärare. We like our teacher.	**Hon är en mycket *omtyckt* lärare.** She is a very popular teacher.
Han *kastar bort* sin ölburk. He throws away his beer can.	**En *bortkastad* ölburk.** A discarded beer can.

Some examples from the text are: **instängd** (< **stänga in** 'shut in'); **utsliten** (< **slita ut** 'worn out'); **omhändertagen** (< **ta hand om** 'taken care of').

Exercise 3

Insert past participles in the correct form:

1 (*stänga av* II) Stereon är . . . 2 (*klä om* III) Hon var . . . 3 (*slå sönder* IV) Vasen är . . . 4 (*resa bort* IIb) Är de . . .? 5 (*köra om* IIa, =

'overtake') Han blev . . . av Porschen. 6 (*skriva upp* IV) Är alla priserna . . .? 7 (*kasta ut* I) Pojkarna blev . . . 8 (*spela in* I, = 'record') Alla sångerna är nyligen . . .

Compound verbs

There are two kinds of compound verb:

- with inseparable prefixes: **betala** (pay), **förklara** (explain), **oroa** (worry), **undkomma** (avoid)
- with separable prefixes: **känna igen/igenkänna** (recognise), **bjuda in/inbjuda** (invite)

The separable kind is similar to the particle verb, but has two alternate forms for every tense. The participle forms are always joined up. Generally speaking the separated forms of the separable compound verb have a lower style and/or have a concrete meaning, while the joined up forms have a higher style and/or an abstract meaning:

De *gick förbi* mig på vägen.
They walked past me on the road.

De *förbigick* mig i prisutdelningen.
They passed over me in the prize-giving.

Eleven *stryker under* ordet.
The pupil underlines the word.

Jag *underströk* sakens betydelse.
I underlined (i.e. stressed) the importance of the matter.

The position of particles

Front	*Verb*$_1$	*Subject*	*Adverb*	*Verb*$_2$	*Particle*	*Obj/Comp*	*MPT*
Nu	**tycker**	**jag**	**inte**	**—**	**om**	**dig**	**längre.**
Nu	**är**	**du**	**inte**	**omtyckt**	**—**	**—**	**längre.**
Då	**måste**	**vi**	**faktiskt**	**ringa**	**upp**	**honom.**	
Han	**har**	**—**	**—**	**blivit uppringd.**			
De	**kastade**	**—**	**—**	**—**	**ut**	**häcklaren.**	

Notice that in English the object comes before the particle, in Swedish after the particle: cf. 'ring him up', 'threw the heckler (**häcklaren**) out'.

Exercise 4

Using the verbs provided, translate into Swedish:

1 (*ringa upp*) Don't ring us before 7! 2 (*skriva ner*) Did you write the number down? 3 (*tycka om*) Didn't he like them? 4 (*kasta bort*) They never throw away old clothes. 5 (*slå sönder*) I didn't smash the window! 6 (*klä om sig*) Isn't she getting changed? 7 (*resa bort*) Don't they go away over the summer? 8 (*skicka iväg*) Hasn't he sent the letter?

Affixation

New words can be formed by adding a prefix before a stem or a suffix after a stem. Prefixes do not alter the word class or inflexion of the stem, but suffixes are often used for this very purpose:

o NEGATIVE PREFIX	+ **tacksam** + ADJ	> **o|tacksam** ADJ	= ungrateful
tacksam ADJ	+ **het** + NOUN SUFFIX	> **tacksam|het** NOUN	= gratitude

Below is a list of some common prefixes and suffixes with an indication of their meaning and function (< indicates derivation):

Prefixes

Negative:

o-	'not, opposite of'	**o|kokt**	uncooked
in-	'bad, wrongly'	**in|tolerant**	intolerant
miss-	'bad, wrongly'	**miss|förstå**	misunderstand
van-	'bad, wrongly'	**van|trivas**	be unsettled

Attitude:

sam-	'together with'	**sam|arbeta**	collaborate
med-	'together with'	**med|arbetare**	co-worker
mot-	'against'	**mot|stånd**	resistance

Time and place:

efter-	'after'	**efter|skrift**	postscript
gen-	'return'	**gen|ljud**	echo
ur-	'original, oldest'	**ur|skog**	primeval forest

Conversion – verb:

be- + -a	makes transitive	**be|bo**	(**< bo**)	inhabit, settle
för- + -a	'make into' + adj	**för|nya**	(**< ny**)	renew
be- + -a	'make into'	**be|fria**	(**< fri**)	set free, liberate

Suffixes

Nouns denoting people:

-are	**arbetare**	**< arbeta**	worker
-ande	**studerande**	**< studera**	student
-ende	**gående**	**< gå**	pedestrian
-ant, -ent	**emigrant**	**< emigrera**	emigrant
	konsument	**< konsumera**	consumer
-ing, -ist	**skåning**	**< Skåne**	inhabitant of Skåne
	cyklist	**< cykel**	cyclist

Feminines:

-inna	**värdinna**	**< värd**	hostess
-(er)ska	**städerska**	**< städare**	cleaner
-essa	**prinsessa**	**< prins**	princess

Conversion: verb > adjective:

-bar	**höjbar**	**< höja**	raisable
-lig	**begriplig**	**< begripa**	understandable
-ig	**bråkig**	**< bråka**	noisy
-abel	**diskutabel**	**< diskutera**	debatable

Conversion: noun > adjective:

-enlig	**avtalsenlig**	**< avtal**	according to the agreement
-mässig	**känslomässig**	**< känsla**	as regards feelings
-aktig	**pojkaktig**	**< pojke**	boyish, puerile
-(i)sk	**brittisk,**	**< britt,**	British
	germansk	**< german**	Germanic

Conversion: noun, adjective > verb:

-a	**tvätta**		wash
-era	**demonstrera**		demonstrate
-na	'become + adj'	**gulna**	go yellow
-ja	'become + adj'	**vänja (< van)**	grow accustomed to

Dialogue 16

Låt bli!

Stop it!

Bill goes to the doctor's

DOKTORN: Var så god och stig in.
BILL: Tack.
DOKTORN: Det går bra att sitta på den här britsen. Nu ska vi se . . . Det var hosta och buksmärtor.
BILL: Ja, och så gör det ont här över höfterna när jag böjer mig, och jag har jämt en otäck huvudvärk vid tinningarna.
DOKTORN: Var snäll och lägg upp benen här så får jag känna lite på magen. Sådär ja. Känns det något om jag trycker här?
BILL: Ja, det känns lite obehagligt. Det sticker till liksom.
DOKTORN: Hmmm. Nu kan ni sitta upp igen. Andas djupt! . . .
BILL: Är det något farligt?
DOKTORN: Det ska vi väl inte tro. Såvitt jag förstår är det ingenting som ni inte själv kan ändra på. Låt bli cigaretterna och var försiktig med spriten. Glöm inte att du kan få magsår av stress och låt bli att alltid köra bil till arbetet! Och så tänk på att en rask promenad är bra inte bara för ryggen utan för alla de andra krämporna också!
BILL: Man skulle inte kunna få ett par nya skor i stället för medicin?

Vocabulary

låt/a -er lät bli, stop
stig/a -er steg in, step inside
brits -en -ar, couch
buksmärta -n -or, abdominal pain
gör/a - gjorde ont, be painful
höft -en -er, hip
böj/a -er -de, bend
otäck -t -a, terrible
tinning -en -ar, temple
ben -et -, leg
känn/a -er kände, feel
tryck/a -er -te, press
obehaglig -t -a, unpleasant
anda/s - andades, breathe
farlig -t -a, *here*: serious
såvitt, as far as
ändra/ -r -de på, change
stress -en, stress
försiktig -t -a, careful
magsår -et -, stomach ulcer

rask -t -a, brisk
krämpa -n -or, ailment
i stället för, instead of
medicin -en -er, medicine

Parts of the body

A number of parts of the body are mentioned in the text and dialogue. Some other useful ones are:

hand -en händer (hand); **fot -en fötter** (foot); **tand -en tänder** (tooth); **arm -en -ar** (arm); **vrist -en -er** (ankle); **handled -en -er** (wrist); **tå -n -r** (toe); **nacke -n -ar** (back of neck); **hals -en -ar** (throat); **axel -n axlar** (shoulder); **bröst -et -** (breast, chest); **stjärt-en -ar** (bottom); **lår -et -** (thigh); **öga -t ögon** (eye); **öra -t öron** (ear); **hjärta -t -n** (heart); **hjärna -n -or** (brain); **lever -n** (liver); **njure -n -ar** (kidney); **lunga -n -or** (lung)

Warnings

Find in the text and dialogue phrases meaning 'Remember that . . .', 'Don't forget that . . .', 'Leave off the cigarettes', 'The doctor suggested that . . .', 'Be careful with . . .', 'Bear in mind that . . .', 'Is it dangerous?'

Warnings on signs are not always immediately obvious:
Varning! (Warning!); **Obs(ervera)!** (Look out!); **Livsfarlig ledning!** (Danger. High voltage!); **Vådligt. Farligt att förtära** (Danger. Not to be taken); **Gift** (Poison); **Frätande** (Corrosive); **Explosionsfara** (Danger of explosion).

Exercise 5

If you are unlucky enough to have to visit the **sjukhus** or **lasarett** and the problem is urgent you go to **akutmottagning** (or **akuten**). If it is routine you may be sent from the **mottagning** to the **väntrum**. If you have fallen over you may be sent to the **röntgen**, and if you cannot be patched up immediately you will be sent to a **vårdavdelning** where you will be looked after by a **sjuksköterska** and we can come and visit you during **besökstid**. If you need more serious attention you may go to **kirurgi** and be attended to by the **kirurg**, but let's hope all that is needed is a **recept** from the **läkare** for some medicine from the **apotek**.

Can you guess what these are in English?

Factual text 16

Blomsterkungen

The Flower King

1700-talet är en vetenskapens guldålder i Sverige, och Carl von Linné var ett av landets största naturvetenskapliga snillen. Han föddes i södra Småland 1707, son till en fattig kyrkoherde som lärde honom uppskatta naturen. I Lund läste Linné medicin men hans egentliga kärlek var till botaniken. I Uppsala lärde han sig ingenting av föreläsningarna, men år 1732 fick han stipendium till en forskningsresa i det då nästan okända Lappland. På våren red Linné norrut från Uppsala och i fem månader vandrade han över 500 mil genom Nordkalottens vildmarker. Varje dag förde han dagbok med noggranna observationer av flora, fauna och folkliv. Han var den förste forskaren som i detalj redogjorde för samernas liv (i boken *Lapplandsresan*). Som forskare gjorde han sin främsta insats inom botaniken och zoologin med *Systema naturae* (1735), en klassifikation av naturens tre riken (dvs. växter, djur, mineraler) med. för växtlivets del, sexualsystemet. I *Species plantarum* beskriver han de då kända växtarterna. Han hittade på latinska namn åt inte mindre än 8000 växtarter och 4400 djurarter, ett bestående arbete.

Senare kom *Flora suecica* och *Fauna suecica* i vilka han skildrar Sveriges växt- respektive djurvärld. Linné var professor i medicin och naturhistoria i Uppsala 1741–77 och blev Kungliga vetenskapsakademiens förste president 1739.

Men för eftervärlden är Linné mest känd för de friska och omedelbara reseskildringar där han ingående beskriver olika provinser: *Öländska och gotländska resan* (1745), *Västgötaresan* (1747) och *Skånska resan* (1751) som än i dag ger de bästa beskrivningarna av hur 1700-talets Sverige såg ut.

Vocabulary

vetenskap -en -er, science
snille -t -n, genius
föd/as -s -des, be born
kyrkoherde -n -ar, rector
uppskatta/ -r -de, appreciate
kärlek -en, love
forskningsresa -n - or, investigative journey
Nordkalotten, the arctic area of Scandinavia, *lit.* 'the northern cap'
redogör/a -gör -gjorde för, give an account of
insats -en -er, contribution
växt -en -er, plant
växtart -en -er, species of plant
hitta/ -r -de på, think up
bestående, lasting
reseskildring -en -ar, travelogue
ingående, detailed

Exercise 6

Find synonyms in the text for the following words: **beskriver**; **beskrivning**; **flora**; **fauna**; **geni**; **präst**; **ödemarken**; **landskap**; **lapparna**.

Skåningar and Stockholmare

Someone from Stockholm or Göteborg is **en stockholmare** or **en göteborgare**. Someone from Lund is, however, **en lundensare**.

To form an adjective merely add **-sk**: **göteborgsk, stockholmsk**.

The dialects spoken in these towns are: **göteborgska, stockholmska**.

Someone from the province of Skåne is **en skåning**. This method is used for several provinces:

Värmland	**en värmlänning** (pl. **-ar**)
Småland	**en smålänning**
Närke	**en närking**

Notice, however:

Östergötland	**- en östgöte**
Västergötland	**- en västgöte**

The adjective from Skåne is **skånsk,** cf. **värmländsk, lappländsk.** Dialects spoken are: **skånska, värmländska, småländska, västgötska, östgötska.**

People who live in towns usually add **-bo** (pl. **-r**) to the name of the place: **en Gävlebo, en Londonbo.**

Some provinces are difficult:

Dalarna -	**en dalmas** (pl. **-er**)	male inhabitant
	en dalkulla (pl.**-or**)	female inhabitant
	dalmål	dialect

Exercise 7

What is someone called who comes from: Norrland, Dalsland, Halland; the towns of Jönköping, Kristianstad, Märsta? What dialect is spoken in: Gotland, Sö(de)rm(an)land?

17 Två skadade vid seriekrock

Two injured in multiple collision

In this lesson we will look at:

- passives
- the position of passive agents
- independent clauses
- words for males and females
- abbreviation
- some frequent abbreviations
- Swedish industry

Text 17

Två skadade vid seriekrock

Two injured in multiple collision

Två personer skadades lindrigt, då tre personbilar på fredagseftermiddagen kolliderade på en skogsväg i närheten av riksväg 81 utanför Sveg. Olyckan inträffade när en Saab, som färdades söderut, av okänd anledning kommit över på fel sida av vägen och föraren, en engelsk affärsman, sökte väja för en mötande Volvo. Båda bilarna bromsade kraftigt för att avvärja en frontalkrock, och vid inbromsningen påkördes Volvon bakifrån av en Toyota, som ej sett Saaben närma sig.

I bilarna färdades inalles sex personer. Engelsmannen och en ung engelsk studentska fördes till sjukhus för att plåstras om men kunde snart återvända till olycksplatsen, där bilarna lämnats kvar. Volvon framfördes av en medelålders ingenjör från Stockholm och Toyotan av en 20-årig kvinna. Samtliga inblandade befinner sig väl.

Vocabulary

skada/ -r -de, injure, hurt
seriekrock -en -ar, multiple collision
lindrigt, slightly
personbil -en -ar, (private) car
kollidera/ -r -de, collide
i närheten av, in the vicinity of
riksväg -en -ar, an 'A' road, major route
utanför, outside
inträffa/ -r -de, occur
färda/s färdas -des, travel
okänd -t -da, unknown
anledning -en- ar, reason
förare -n -, driver
affärsman -mannen -män, businessman
sök/a -er -te, attempt
väja/ -er -de, swerve to avoid
mötande, oncoming
bromsa/ -r -de, brake
kraftigt, hard
avvärj/a -er -de, prevent
frontalkrock -en -ar, head-on collision
inbromsning -en, braking
kör/a kör -de på, drive into
bakifrån, from behind
närma/ -r -de sig, approach
inalles, in all
person -en -er, person
studentska -n -or, (female) student
för/a för -de, carry, take
plåstra/ -r -de om, patch up
olycksplats -en -er, scene of the accident
lämnats kvar, had been left
samtliga, all
inblanda/d -t -de, involved
befinn/a -er befann sig väl, be doing well

Passives

Before trying to construct the passive it is advisable to revise s-forms of verbs (see p.160) and forms of past participles (see p.216). The reason is that passives are formed in one of three different ways:

1 **s**-passives, which use the s-form of the verb (the most common type)
2 **bli**-passives which use forms of **bli** + a past participle
3 **vara**-passives which use forms of **vara** + a past participle

First compare the sentences below:

Active: ***En svensk*** **uppfann** ***skiftnyckeln.***
SUBJ OBJ
(+ agent)
(A Swede invented the adjustable spanner.)

Passive: ***Skiftnyckeln* uppfanns *av en svensk.***
SUBJ AGENT
(The adjustable spanner was invented by a Swede.)

Only transitive verbs (see p.207) can be used in the passive form. The passive is most often used when the person carrying out the action is unknown or unimportant in the context. The agent is then omitted:

Bernadotte föddes i Frankrike år 1763.	Bernadotte was born in France in 1763. (who bore him is unimportant here)
Middag serveras kl 8.	Dinner is served at 8 o'clock. (who serves it is unimportant here)

S-passives are often used to express a repeated action and often have no agent:

Dörrarna öppnas kl 7.	The doors are opened at 7 o'clock.

S-passives are often found in objective newspaper style, as in the text above:

Två personer skadades.	. . . were injured	(no agent)
En studentska fördes till sjukhuset.	. . . was taken	(no agent)
Volvon kördes av en ingenjör.	. . . was driven	(agent)
Volvon påkördes av en Toyota.	. . . was driven into	(agent)

Bli-passives are often used to express a single action and frequently have an agent. The agent is then usually significant:

England blev slaget 2–3 av Sverige i finalen.	England was beaten 2–3 by Sweden in the final.
Han har blivit påkörd av en motorcykel.	He has been run over by a motorcycle.
Han intervjuades av Olle Olsson.	He was interviewed by Olle Olsson.

Vara-passives are often used to express the result of an action and are descriptive:

Himlen är täckt av moln.	The sky is covered in clouds.
Huset är sålt.	The house is (i.e. has been) sold.

Exercise 1

Re-write using the s-passive (see also p.207) as in the example:

Example: **Man klämde honom på magen. > Han klämdes på magen.**

1 Man knackade honom i ryggen. 2 Man stack honom i fingret. 3 Man försäkrade bilen. 4 Man lämnar tillbaka pennan. 5 Man skickar iväg kortet. 6 Man behöver en sittvänlig bil. 7 Man stänger av stereon. 8 Man har sålt huset. 9 Man har öppnat dörrarna. 10 Man ska servera middag. 11 Man ska plåstra om henne.

Exercise 2

Translate into Swedish using the s-passive:

1 Driver is sought by the police. 2 Their names are written down by the policeman. 3 The Saab was not seen by the other driver. 4 A head-on collision was avoided. 5 The car should be left behind. 6 An appointment was made yesterday with the doctor. 7 Bill's beer consumption must be cut down. 8 Long walks have been suggested by the doctor. 9 The case had been packed that morning. 10 All the newspapers will be burned. 11 Potatoes are grown there.

The position of passive agents

Front	*Verb$_1$*	*Subj*	*Adv*	*Verb$_2$*	*Obj/ Comp*	*Agent*	*MPT*
Bilen	**kördes**	—	**ofta**	—	— —	**av en ung flicka**	**på den tiden.**
Älgen	**sköts**	—	—	—	—	**av jägaren**	**vid sjön.**
Älgen	**blev**	—	—	**skjuten**	— —	**av jägaren**	**vid sjön.**
Himlen	**var**	—	**ju**	**täckt**	—	**av moln**	**igår.**

The passive agent goes after VERB$_2$ and before the MPT-expression. There is no object in the passive clause.

Exercise 3

Change the passive sentences in the fictitious headlines below (to texts 11 to 17 in this book) into active sentences, if necessary introducing as subject the word man.

Knattefotboll uppmuntras av aktiva pappor.

Valborg firas i Lund med fester hela natten.

Dagstidning läses av 95% i Sverige.

Fjällvärlden invaderas av turister på senhösten.

Alkoholkonsumtionen måste skäras ner.

Läkarbesök förorsakas allt oftare av stress.

Engelsmän förs till sjukhus efter bilolycka.

Dialogue 17

Att jag kunde vara så dum!

How could I be so stupid!

After the car crash

BILL: Vilket elände! Att det ska vara så svårt med höger och vänster! Jag tar naturligtvis på mig skulden. Det var mitt fel.

JAN: Ja, det råder det väl knappast något tvivel om, men du ska nog ändå inte dra några förhastade slutsatser. Vi kan väl i och för sig göra upp i godo, men eftersom den här unga damen också är inblandad, kanske vi ändå ska tillkalla polis. Om det bara fanns telefon i närheten!

PERNILLA: Det låg några stugor bakom kurvan. Jag går dit och frågar.

BILL: Behövs inte. Jag har en yuppienalle. Ska jag ringa med detsamma, eller . . .?

JAN: Vi kan ju skriva upp varandras namn och försäkringsbolag så länge. Min bil står i mitt namn.
BILL: Jag har ju lånat den här bilen av en bekant. Han visade mig att alla handlingar låg här i handskfacket. Jag borde kanske meddela honom med detsamma. Själv är jag försäkrad i England.
EVA: Ta och vänta lite med allt det där! Du, Bill, verkar lite omtumlad. Sätt dig här i gräset och hälsa på Rebecca som också kommer från England, så tar jag fram förbandslådan och kaffetermosen. Det är bäst att inte stressa
BILL: Jag ser inte några större bucklor på bilarna.
REBECCA: Minsta rispa är en katastrof för en svensk.

Vocabulary

vilket elände!, what rotten luck!
ta/r tog på sig skulden, take the blame on oneself
råd/a -er -de inget tvivel om, be no doubt about
dra förhastade slutsatser, jump to conclusions
göra upp i godo, arrive at an amicable settlement
dam -en -er, lady
tillkalla/ -r -de, send for
kurva -n -or, bend
yuppienalle -n, mobile phone (**nalle** = teddy bear)
försäkringsbolag -et -, insurance company
stå/r stod stått, stand; *here*: is registered
bakom kurvan, beyond the bend
en bekant bekanta, acquaintance
handling -en -ar, document
handskfack -et -, glove box
meddela/ -r -de, inform
med detsamma, immediately
försäkra/ -r -de, insure
omtumla/d -t -de, shaken up
gräs -et, grass
förbandslåda -n -or, first aid box
kaffetermos -en -ar, coffee thermos
inte stressa, keep calm
buckla -n -or, dent
rispa -n -or, scratch
katastrof -en -er, catastrophe

Independent clauses

An independent clause is a sub clause that stands alone as a sentence and does not form part of a main clause sentence (see also pp.148–9).

Kanske vi ändå ska tillkalla polis?	Perhaps we should call the police anyway?
Att jag kunde vara så dum!	That I could be so stupid!
Om jag ändå var rik!	If only I were rich!

The word order is that of the sub clause, i.e. S(ubject) – **I(nte)** –V(erb). Many independent clauses are either exclamations or the result of ellipsis:

(Jag trodde inte) att jag kunde vara så dum!

Answers to questions are often of this kind:

(Varför har du plåster på fingret?)
(Jag har plåster på fingret . . .) För att jag just har skurit mig.

Exercise 4

Re-order the words in the different answers to the question:

Varför säger du det?	För att	aldrig/jag/tyckt/har/henne/om
	För att	jag/dig/med/håller/faktiskt inte
	För att	du/fel/har/egentligen
	För att	göra/något/vi/måste/verkligen
	För att	möjligen/dutborde/om/dig/klä

Male and female

The distinction between male and female is indicated in a number of different ways:

(a) By adding a suffix (see p.222):

Male	*Female*	
vän	**väninna**	(friend)
kassör	**kassörska**	(cashier)
skådespelare	**skådespelerska**	(actor)
massör	**massös**	(masseur)
aktör	**aktris**	(actor)

Sexist job titles are declining, so that a female teacher is no longer called **en lärarinna** but **en lärare**, a female cleaner is not **en städerska** but **en städare.**

(b) By adding the endings **-e** (male)/**-a** (female) to an adjective (see p.159):

den gamle	the old man	**den gamla**	the old woman

cf. **en make/maka** (spouse); **en hane/hona** (male/female); **Helge/ Helga**; **Tore/Tora**. (Exceptions: **Ola** is male, **Signe** is female.)

(c) By different words: **tupp/höna** (cockerel/hen); **hingst/sto** (stallion/ mare); **kung/drottning** (king/queen).

Some nouns not denoting females have feminine gender:

Hur mycket är klockan? Hon (Den) är fem.
Människan – hon.
Solen – hon (den).

Some nouns denoting persons are T-words: **ett barn**, **ett statsråd** (cabinet minister), **ett vittne** (witness), **ett biträde** (assistant), **ett geni**, **ett snille** (genius)

Exercise 5

Are the following males or females?:

1 en servitris 2 en frisör 3 Åke 4 Åsa 5 en ägarinna 6 den sjuke 7 en sjuksköterska 8 en dansös 9 en författarinna 10 den mörka?

Abbreviation

Different parts of a word may be lost in abbreviations:

the beginning:	**(bi)cykel, (automo)bil**
the middle:	**mo(torveloci)ped, flex(ibel arbets)tid**
the end:	**el(ektricitet), rea(lisation)** (= 'sale')

Reduction may go so far that only the initial letters are left:

LO (Landsorganisationen) (= Swedish TUC)
SAAB (Svenska aeroplans aktiebolag)

Acronyms (words consisting of initials) are of two kinds:

1 Alphabetisms (pronounced as the individual letters): **bh (bysthållare)**, **UD (Utrikesdepartementet)**.
Sometimes these are re-spelled: **behå, teve.**

2 Acronyms pronounced as words: **NATO, SAAB, SAS.**
Sometimes hybrid forms emerge: **T-bana (tunnelbana), u-båt (undervattensbåt), p-plats (parkeringsplats).**

Some frequent abbreviations

See also p.71.

AB	**aktiebolag**	plc, Co. Ltd
ATP	**Allmän tjänstepension**	state retirement pension
e Kr	**efter Kristus**	AD
em	**eftermiddag**	p.m.
f Kr	**före Kristus**	BC
fm	**förmiddag**	a.m.
forts	**fortsättning**	continued
fr o m	**från och med**	from
följ	**följande**	following
ggr	**gånger**	times
häft	**häftad**	paperback
i-land	**industriland**	industrialised country
inb	**inbunden**	bound
inv	**invånare**	inhabitant
jvstn	**järnvägsstation**	railway station
m fl	**med flera**	etc.
NB	**Nedre botten**	lower ground (floor)
omkr	**omkring**	about
PM	**promemoria**	memo
s	**sida**	page
	substantiv	noun
	subjekt	subject
sa	**summa**	total
s k	**så kallad**	so-called
st	**styck(en)**	number
tr.	**trappa (trappor)**	floor
UD	**Utrikesdepartementet**	Foreign Ministry
u-land	**utvecklingsland**	developing country
ung.	**ungefär**	approx.
vard.	**vardagar**	weekdays
v g v	**var god vänd**	PTO

Exercise 6

Try your hand at abbreviating the following:

1 Statens järnvagar
2 Dagens Nyheter (*newspaper*)
3 världsmästarskapet (*world championship*)
4 Sveriges meteorologiska och hydrologiska institut
5 meromsättningsskatt (*VAT*)
6 Arbetsmarknadsstyrelsen (*Labour Market Board*)
7 biograf (*cinema*)
8 kylskåp (*refrigerator*)
9 konsumentföreningen (*Coop*)
10 legitimation (*ID*)
11 flexibel arbetstid
12 verkställande direktör (*managing director*)
13 varudeklaration (*declaration of contents*)

Factual text 17

Svensk industri

Swedish industry

En stor del av den svenska befolkningen arbetar – 91% av männen mellan 20–64 år och 75% av kvinnorna. Traditionella skillnader mellan manligt och kvinnligt arbete håller på att suddas ut. 90% av landets industri är i privat ägo medan 55% av arbetskraften arbetar inom den privata sektorn. På 90% av de mer än 43 000 bolagen arbetar mindre än 5 personer. Bara 800 bolag har mer än 500 anställda. Många svenska företag har dotterbolag utomlands och många utländska firmor har dotterbolag inom Sverige.

Sverige exporterar maskiner och utrustning, skogsprodukter, fordon och malm, och importerar olja och petroleumprodukter, maskiner och verkstadsprodukter, råvaror, kemiska produkter och matvaror. Mer än hälften av export- och importhandeln sker med EU och en fjärdedel med det övriga Europa.

Sverige har höga löner och ett mycket högt antal (80–90%) fackligt anslutna.

Svenska produkter är kända världen runt – personbilar, lastbilar och bussar från Volvo och Saab-Scania, elektriska varor från Electrolux, telefonsystem från Ericsson.

Enbart Electrolux har 130 000 anställda, mer än ¾ av dem i sina 360 bolag i mer än 40 länder. Skånska Cementgjuteriet som bygger mycket utomlands har tagit bort den lilla ringen över a-et och har blivit 'Skanska' som är lättare för utlänningar att uttala.

Välkända i utlandet är också sådana varor som köksmaskiner (Husqvarna), svenskt glas (Orrefors, Kosta, Boda) och svenska möbler (IKEA).

Vocabulary

sudda/ -r -de ut, erase; *here*: blur
bolag -et -, company
anställ/a -er -de, employ
utrustning -en, equipment
fordon -et -, vehicle
malm -en -er, ore
råvara -n -or, raw material
ske/ -r -dde, happen, occur; *here*: be carried on
arbetslöshet -en, unemployment
fackligt ansluten -et -na, member of a trade union
lastbil -en -ar, truck
vara -n -or, goods, product
cementgjuteri -et, cement works

Exercise 7

Hitta ord i facktexten (Factual text) som betyder detsamma som:

1 invånarna i Sverige 2 olikheter 3 företag 4 människor 5 i utlandet 6 främmande 7 bilar 8 halva 9 25% 10 många

Exercise 8

Vad kan du säga om:

1 hur stora de flesta bolag är i Sverige? 2 hur många kvinnor som arbetar? 3 hur många som arbetar inom den statliga sektorn? 4 vilka länder Sverige säljer till och köper ifrån? 5 vilka svenska varor som är kända i utlandet? 6 varför det numera heter 'Skanska'?

18 Två brev och ett vykort

Two letters and a picture postcard

In this lesson we will look at:

- how to write letters
- sub clauses with main clause word order and conditional clauses
- determinative pronouns
- differences between written and spoken constructions
- punctuation
- schools and colleges

Text 18

Två brev och ett vykort

Two letters and a picture postcard

Bradford den 5 september 1996

Kära Erik!

Hur har du det? Själv har jag det bra. Resan gick fint, vädret var vackert för att vara i England och här kan jag frossa i indisk mat igen, men gud, vad jag saknar Stockholm – och dig. Du sitter väl i en skärgårdsbåt nu eller flanerar i Kungsan . . .

Min lärare trodde inte det skulle vara omöjligt för mig att få ett stipendium, och i så fall kan jag börja mina doktorandstudier i Sverige när jag är klar med min examen här. Då får du en engelsk sambo. Men innan dess ses vi till jul och till påsk. Jag kommer att längta efter snön och mörka vinterkvällar och våren och galna soldyrkare och ljusa nätter, och så universitetet förstås – men mest av allt efter *dig*.

Stor kram

Rebecca

****

Pryl och Grej AB
Marknadsavdelningen

1996 05 11

Push and Pull plc

Beställningsorder – plasthandtag

Vår firma hade nyligen besök av Er representant, Bill Morris, som gav oss utförliga upplysningar om Era nyligen lanserade plasthandtag. Vid en jämförelse med produkter saluförda av en firma i Japan har vi övertygats om att Era priser och leveransvillkor är de för oss mest fördelaktiga och vi beställer härmed

5 000 (5 tusen) plasthandtag, artikelnummer 353 27, enligt försäljningsvillkor i brev av den 5 april.

Vi önskar också tillägga att vi är synnerligen nöjda med den klara och vederhäftiga presentation av varan som Er representant lät oss ta del av på oklanderlig svenska.

Med vänlig hälsning

Dag Fristedt
marknadschef

Postadress	Besöksadress	Telefon	Postgiro
Box 345	Mölndalsvägen 83	031/31 87 54	641929–5
412 63 Göteborg		Telefax	
		031/31 87 75	

****

Tjena!

Du skulle hängt med på konserten alltså. Soundet var suveränt bra och du skulle ha sett gitarristens amp. Den var på 500 kalla w. Sångaren hade tryckt till med en häftig make alltså. Det var precis att jag hann med burken efteråt. Du har banne mig gått miste om något, José. Hehe.

Hälsningar

Jocke

Tjena!
Du skulle hängt med på konserten alltså. Soundet var suveränt bra och du skulle ha sett gitarristens amp. Den var på 500 kalla W. Sångaren hade tryckt till med en häftig make alltså. Det var precis att jag hann med burken efteråt. Du har banne mig gått miste om något José. HeHe.

Hälsningar
Jocke

Vocabulary

frossa/ -r -de, gorge oneself
indisk -t -a, Indian
sakna/ -r -de, *here*: miss
skärgårdsbåt -en -ar, boat to the archipelago
flanera/ -r -de, wander
Kungsan = Kungsträdgården, park in central Stockholm
omöjlig -t -a, impossible
stipendi/um -et -er, grant, scholarship
doktorandstudier, studies for a doctorate
vara klar med, complete
examen (ett), (university) degree
sambo -n -r, live-in girl- (or boy-) friend
innan dess, before that
längta/ -r -de efter, long for
soldyrkare -n -, sun worshipper
kram -en -ar, hug
marknadsavdelning -en -ar, marketing department
nyligen, recently
ha besök av, receive a visit from
representant -en -er, representative
utförlig -t -a, detailed, full
upplysningar -na, information
lansera/ -r -de, bring onto market, introduce
jämförelse -n -r, comparison
saluför/a -för -de, offer (for sale)
övertyga/ -r -de, convinced
leveransvillkor -et -, terms of delivery
fördelaktig -t -a, advantageous
beställ/a -er -de, order
härmed, hereby
plasthandtag -et -, plastic handle
försäljningsvillkor -et -, terms of sale
artikelnum/mer -ret -, part number

enligt, according to
önska/ -r -de, wish
tillägg/a -er tillade, add
synnerligen, most, extremely
nöjd -a, pleased
vederhäftig -t -a, reliable
presentation -en -er, introduction, presentation
vara -n -or, product
ta del av, inform oneself
oklanderlig -t -a, impeccable
marknadschef -en -er, marketing director
tjena! = tjänare, hi!
häng/a -er -de med, come, go
konsert -en -er, concert
soundet = ljudet, sound
gitarrist- en -er, guitarist
amp = förstärkare-n, amplifier
kalla 500 w., a cool 500 watts
suverän, häftig , terrific
sångare -n - , singer, vocalist
tryckt till med = lagt sig till med, put on
make = sminkning, make up
burken = bussen, the bus
banne mig = verkligen, really
gå/ -r gick gått miste om, miss out on

Writing letters

For most letters it is not necessary to use an especially formal kind of Swedish. In private letters your detailed address is written on the back of the envelope, and only the town and date at top right of the letter itself. Business stationery often has the address printed at the bottom and you add the address of the person you are writing to at top left.

There are two common forms for the date: **960724** or **den 24 juli 1996.**

There is no equivalent in Swedish to 'Dear Sir'. Either insert a heading outlining the purpose of the letter or start straight in. For friendly letters use: **Kära John!** or **Hej!**

To end a formal letter use: **Med vänlig hälsning**. To end a friendly letter use: **Hjärtliga hälsningar** or just: **Hälsningar**. The word **Kram** (Love) is becoming frequent.

For layout study the letters above.

Exercise 1

Write a letter:

(a) from Pryl & Grej AB to Sayonara Enterprises thanking them politely for their offer but rejecting it.

(b) from Erik to Rebecca in answer to her letter, saying what he and their friends have been doing, and planning a visit to Bradford at Christmas.

Sub clauses with main clause word order and conditional clauses

There are two kinds of sub clause which form part of the main clause and yet do *not* have the usual (S-I-V) sub clause order. Instead they have main clause word order. They are:

(a) **Att** clauses beginning with a non-subject (rather than beginning with the subject – see p.149). If a non-subject comes immediately after **att**, then the clause has main clause order (and the verb and subject are inverted):

Janne säger att imorgon *tänker* han *inte* åka hem.
NON-SUBJ VERB SUBJ INTE

Cf.

Janne säger att han *inte tänker* åka hem imorgon.
S I V

This is now common in both spoken and written Swedish.

(b) **Att**-clauses *in the spoken language only*:

Han sa att han *kunde inte* komma.

This is *not* acceptable in written Swedish but is heard in spoken Swedish.

(c) Some conditional clauses with yes/no question word order.

Most conditional clauses are introduced by **om/ifall**:

Om du inte bjuder henne blir hon ledsen.

But conditional clauses are also found that have no **om/ifall** and rely on inverted order to express the condition. These clauses have the same order as in the yes/no question, but they are *not* questions:

Bjuder du inte henne, (så) blir hon ledsen.
(Cf. the yes/no question: **Bjuder du inte henne?**)

Clauses somewhat similar to this occur in English:

Had I known you were coming, I would have waited.

Exercise 2

Alter the following sentences so that the conditional clauses have main clause order:

1 Om Rebecca får ett stipendium, kan hon börja sina doktorandstudier.
2 Om Rebecca blir doktor, blir hon kanske så småningom professor.
3 Om Bill blir VD, kan han betala reparationskostnaderna.
4 Om José hade hängt med, skulle han hört en suveränt bra konsert.
5 Om Erik åker till Bradford, får han frossa i indisk mat.

Determinative pronouns

Compare the following forms:

Demonstrative pronoun:	***Den*** **mann*en* var full.**
Determinative pronoun:	***Den*** **man som var full ramlade i golvet.**

The determinative pronoun is a kind of demonstrative (see p.95) used with a following **som**-clause where this clause is *necessary* to complete the meaning. The noun after the determinative has no end article.

De **turister*na* har fått mycket sol.** (Demonstrative)
Those tourists . . .

De **turister som åkte till Island har fått mycket sol, medan de turister som åkte till Italien har fått regn varje dag.**
(Determinative)
Those tourists who . . .

Notice that a contrast is usually implied. Demonstratives are increasingly used instead of determinatives in informal written and spoken Swedish.

Exercise 3

Re-write the sentences below, using where necessary either a determinative or demonstrative pronoun:

1 Engelska firmor som har svensktalande representanter får fler order från svenska företag.

2 Engelska studenter som studerar flitigt i Sverige får höga betyg i sina examen.
3 En svensk kille som jag känner sambor med en engelsk flicka.
4 En utförlig presentation som Bill förmedlade i Göteborg ledde omedelbart till en beställning.
5 En av Bill Morris framlagd (*made*) presentation, som jag råkade vara med på, förmedlades helt på oklanderlig svenska.

Dialogue 18

Då säger vi det!

That's all right then!

Bill Morris gives everyone a pleasant surprise

BILL: Kan jag få anknytning 343?
VÄXELN: Ett ögonblick.
JAN: Jan Forsberg.
BILL: Hej, det är Bill, Bill Morris som körde sönder din bil.
JAN: Nämen hej! Är du i Sverige igen?
BILL: Nej då, inte ännu, men det kommer nog inte att dröja länge. Nej, jag ringer för att erbjuda mig att betala alla kostnader i samband med krocken.
JAN: Det var det värsta. Man tackar. Hur kommer det sig?
BILL: En annan har liksom kommit på grön kvist. Mina affärsframgångar och mina svenskkunskaper har gjort mig till VD i mitt företag. Vad säger du om det?
JAN: Jag är stum. Jag får verkligen gratulera. Så roligt!
BILL: Ja, det kan man säga. Men skicka mig alla uppgifter och kontakta Pernilla också, så ordnar sig allt.
JAN: Det ska jag göra.
BILL: Då säger vi det.
JAN: Det gör vi.
BILL: Hej då. Hälsa familjen!
JAN: Hej, hej . . . Jösses, nästa gång är det väl Rebecca som blivit professor i litteraturvetenskap.

Vocabulary

kör/a kör -de sönder, smashed up
inte dröja länge, not be long
erbjud/a -er erbjöd, offer
kostnad -en -er, cost
i samband med, in connection with
Det var det värsta. Well I never!
komm/a -er kom sig, come about, happen
en annan = jag, 'yours truly'
liksom, sort of
komma på grön kvist, end up 'in clover'
affärsframgång -en -ar, business success
svenskkunskaper -na, knowledge of Swedish
VD = verkställande direktör, managing director
stum -t -ma, dumb; *here*: speechless
gratulera -r -de, offer congratulations
uppgift -en -er, detail
kontakta/ -r -de, get in touch with
ordnar sig allt, everything will be sorted out
hälsa/ -r -de, give one's regards
Jösses! Blimey!
professor -n -er, professor
litteraturvetenskap -en, Theory of Literature

Written and spoken constructions

Features of spoken and less formal written Swedish are:

(a) Omission of **att** after verbs of saying and thinking:

Hon sade hon hade fått brevet.
Cf. **Hon sade att . . .**

(b) Omission of **som** as object:

Mannen jag pratade med heter Johansson.
Cf. **Mannen som jag pratade med . . .**

(c) Use of duplicates (this is very colloquial, see p.176):

Erik, han är hemskt intelligent, han.

(d) Use of main clause word order after **att** (see 'Sub clauses with main clause word order' above):

Hon var arg på honom därför att han kom aldrig i tid.
Cf. **. . . därför att han aldrig kom . . .**

Features of more formal written Swedish:

(e) Omission of **har/hade** in the sub clause:

Han påstod att han blivit bestulen.
Cf. **Han påstod att han hade blivit bestulen.**

(f) Leftward movement of MPT-expressions (to the adverb position):

Han har stannat hemma *under de senaste dagarna.* →
Han har *under de senaste dagarna* stannat hemma.

(g) Fronting of heavy elements such as sub clauses and infinitive phrases:

***Att tillverka ett gott bröd enligt det gamla traditionella receptet med användande av modern teknik och kontroll* är en princip för företaget.**

(h) Use of nouns rather than verbs:

Krocken hade *skadat* bilens lackering (= 'paintwork'). →
Krocken hade *anställt skadegörelse* på bilens lackering.

(i) Use of the s-passive:

Man förde dem* till sjukhus för att *man skulle plåstra om dem. →
De fördes* till sjukhus för att *omplåstras.

Punctuation

There are only a few significant differences from English:

(a) There is no comma:

before an **att**-clause:
Han sade att han tänkte komma.

after introductory or closing phrases in letters:

Bäste herr Olsson!

Med vänlig hälsning
Erik

(b) There is no apostrophe before or after genitive **-s**:

pojkens far; pojkarnas far

(c) The exclamation mark is used more frequently in Swedish:

Vad vackert det är här! **Lycka till!** **Obs!**

(d) The hyphen is used in some cases where there is a common element:

på låg- och mellanstadiet = på lågstadiet och mellanstadiet.

Swedish school timetable

Schema klass 7 B

	Måndag	Tisdag	Onsdag	Torsdag	Fredag
8.15 – 9.15	Tyska 201	Engelska 211	Tyska 211	Engelska 201	Svenska 201
9.25 – 10.25	Svenska 201	Naturorient. Biologi 318	Naturorient. Fysik 306	Matematik 211	Engelska 201
10.35 – 11.35	Lunch	Lunch	Lunch	Lunch	Idrott
11.40 – 12.40	Naturorient. Biologi 301	Samhälls-orient. 214	Engelska 201	Samhälls-orientering 214	Lunch
12.50 – 13.50	Samhälls-orientering 214	Idrott	Musik	Svenska 201	Bild
14.05 – 15.05	-"-	Matematik 205	Elevens val. Historia 117	Slöjd	Matematik 211
15.15 – 16.15			-"-		

Factual text 18 📖

Skolor och hogskolor

Schools and Colleges

I Sverige ansvarar kommunerna för de flesta skolor. Det finns mycket få privatskolor. Den obligatoriska utbildningen – grundskolan – är nioårig och omfattar alla barn mellan 7 och 16 år. Det finns ingen uppdelning på linjer efter begåvning eller kunskaper, och skolan är examensfri. Betyg sätts endast i klasserna 8 och 9. På låg- och mellanstadiet, d v s under de första sex åren sköts undervisningen av klasslärare som undervisar i de flesta ämnena. På högstadiet meddelas undervisningen av ämneslärare. Engelska är ett obligatoriskt ämne, som barnen börjar läsa tidigt – ibland redan i första klass. Senare lär de sig ofta tyska och franska eller något annat språk. Över 90% av alla 16-åringar fortsätter i gymnasieskolan, där de väljer mellan 16 olika nationella program. Fjorton av dessa är yrkesinriktade, t ex estetiska programmet, handels- och administrationsprogrammet och omvårdnadsprogrammet och två är studieförberedande, nämligen naturvetenskapsprogrammet och samhällsvetenskapsprogrammet. Alla programmen är treåriga och f o m årskurs 2 väljer eleverna gren. I samhällsvetenskapliga programmet finns då möjlighet att välja ekonomisk, humanistisk, samhällsvetenskaplig eller EU-inriktning. Även en elev som läst ett yrkesinriktat program kan fortsätta med högskolestudier, eftersom alla programmen ger allmän behörighet för studier på högskola.

Det finns numera sju universitet (de två äldsta är Uppsala och Lund) och över 20 statliga högskolor. Högskoleutbildningen är avgiftsfri och de flesta studenter får ett statligt studiebidrag samt ett lån som utgör större delen av studiemedlen. Då kurser ofta också ges på kvällstid och i långsam takt kan man studera vid sidan om förvärvsarbetet. Något över hälften av antalet högskolestuderande är kvinnor, och det finns många äldre studerande.

Vocabulary

ansvara/ -r -de, be responsible for
utbildning -en, education
grundskola -n, compulsory school for 7–16 year olds
begåvning -en, intelligence,
kunskap -en -er, knowledge
betyg -et -, grade, mark
undervisa/ -r -de, teach
ämne -t -n, subject
samtidigt, at the same time
fortsätt/a -er fortsatte, continue
gymnasieskola -n, sixth form college
yrkesinriktat, skill-oriented
studieförberedande, preparatory to higher education
naturvetenskap, (natural) science
samhällsvetenskap, social science
behörighet, matriculation
avgiftsfri -tt -a, free of charge
studiebidrag -et -, grant
takt -en -er, pace
förvärvsarbete -t -, paid work
studerande -n -, student

Exercise 4

Svara på frågorna:

1 Hur många år måste man gå i skolan i Sverige? 2 Hur ofta får man betyg? 3 Vad undervisar klasslärare? och ämneslärare? 4 Vilka språk undervisas? 5 Hur många fortsätter sin utbildning efter 16 år? 6 Hur många väljer teoretiska linjer på gymnasieskolan? 7 Hur finansieras studierna på högskola eller universitet? 8 Vilka sorters studenter studerar i långsam takt eller på kvällstid?

Key to exercises

Lesson 1

Exercise 1

1 Är det ett päron? 2 Vad är det? 3 Det är en persika. 4 Har hon ett äpple? 5 Är det en högskola? 6 Nej, det är en fabrik. 7 Det är ett äpple. 8 Är det Rebecca? 9 Nej, det är Sven. 10 Är han hungrig?

Exercise 2

1 Studerar de? 2 Kommer hon? 3 Har ni ett päron? 4 Är det Sven? 5 Är det en stor högskola?

Exercise 3

1 De läser. 2 Vi studerar. 3 Hon bor i Stockholm. 4 Studerar du? 5 Kommer de?

Exercise 4

1 Ja, det är du. 2 Nej, det är de inte. 3 Ja, det har jag. 4 Nej, det har hon inte. 5 Ja, det är det. 6 Nej, det har vi inte. 7 Ja, det är han. 8 Nej, det är jag inte.

Exercise 5

hot dog stand; hot dogs; *lit.* 'street kitchen'; café or coffee shop; restaurant; self service; menu; tray; plate; glass; cutlery; today's special; with bread and butter, milk or light beer or coffee; till; no smoking; return trays.

Exercise 6

Kan jag få en skinksmörgås och ett glas öl, tack. Kan jag få en kopp te och en bulle, tack. Kan jag få en kopp kaffe och en kaka, tack. Kan jag få en ostsmörgås och ett glas öl, tack. Varsågod! Tack så mycket!

Exercise 7

1 Ja, det är det. 2 Det är också ett land. 3 De talar engelska. 4 De talar svenska. 5 Ja, det har det. 6 Den heter Stockholm. 7 Ja, det är det. 8 Nej, det har det inte. 9 Ja, det har det. 10 Nej, det har sällan mycket snö på vintern. 11 Nej, det har man inte.

Lesson 2

Exercise 1

ha; läsa; hata; göra; kommer; heter; åker; skriver.

Exercise 2

1 Han läser. 2 Han är student. 3 De åker. 4 Vi bor i Stockholm. 5 Jag bor i England. 6 Jag åker till London. 7 Vi har en lägenhet. 8 Jag läser (studerar) svenska. 9 De kommer från London. 10 Väckarklockan ringer klockan åtta. 11 Hon börjar klockan sex på morgonen. 12 De hatar väckarklockan.

Exercise 3

uppsatsen; lägenheten; landet; dagen; äpplet; flickan; kakan; kilot; koppen; en fabrik; en bulle; ett år; en skinka; en pojke; en industri; en tunnelbana; en klocka; ett vin.

Exercise 4

1 Hon kommer från England. 2 Ofta åker hon till Stockholm. 3 Hon åker tunnelbana. 4 På morgonen läser (studerar) hon svenska. 5 Just nu är hon på universitetet. 6 Hon börjar just nu. 7 Ibland sitter hon på biblioteket. 8 Klockan åtta tar hon tunnelbanan. 9 Klockan sex ringer väckarklockan.

Exercise 5

1 Läser de? 2 Bor de i Stockholm? 3 Förstår du? 4 Vad heter de? 5 Var bor du? 6 Vad läser du? 7 Vad gör de? 8 Var kommer han ifrån? 9 Vem är hon? 10 När kommer de? 11 Talar du med Rebecca? 12 Läser hon? 13 Förstår han svenska?

Exercise 6

Hej! Jag heter . . . Jag studerar svenska. Jag är . . . år. Jag kommer från England. Jag bor i . . .

Exercise 7

fel; fel; rätt; rätt; fel; fel; rätt; rätt; rätt; fel.

Lesson 3

Exercise 1

1 Det är inte ett företag. 2 Hon bor inte i Stockholm. 3 Hon heter inte Maria. 4 De studerar inte svenska. 5 Jag tar inte kaffe. 6 Jag vill inte ha en kopp te. 7 Vi träffar inte representanter. 8 Han åker inte buss. 9 Han bor inte där.

Exercise 2

1 Han reser aldrig utomlands. 2 Han tar ofta tunnelbanan. 3 Han tar alltid taxi. 4 Det tar alltid en timme. 5 De köper aldrig plasthandtag av Bill. 6 Han flyger inte till Sverige. 7 De tillverkar inte plasthandtag. 8 Han tar inte tunnelbanan till Arlanda. 9 Det tar nästan två timmar till Köpenhamn med flyg. 10 Han tar alltid in på ett hotell.

Exercise 3

1 Har man inte tunnelbana i Bradford? 2 Kommer ni inte från England? 3 Är du inte svensk? 4 Börjar vi inte klockan Åtta? 5 Läser hon inte svenska? 6 Förstår de inte engelska? 7 Bor du inte i staden? 8 Åker vi inte buss? 9 Ligger stationen inte i centrum?

Exercise 4

1 firmans produkter; 2 Londons flygplats; 3 en timmes resa; 4 firmans representanter; 5 studentens lägenhet; 6 Stockholms universitet; 7 flickans uppsats.

Exercise 5

railway station; departures; platform; train to Oslo; 'where in the train the carriage is'; luggage; left luggage office; all tickets; those who just got on at Hallsberg.

Exercise 6

1 klockan elva; 2 halv fyra; 3 kvart i sju; 4 fem minuter i halv nio (tjugofem minuter över åtta); 5 klockan (Hon; Den) är fem; 6 kvart över två; 7 fem minuter i tolv; 8 tjugotre och tjugofem (tjugofem minuter över elva, fem minuter i halv tolv); 9 hur dags flyger Bill till London?

Exercise 7

1 Jag ska åka till London imorgon. 2 Bill tänker fortsätta till Oslo. 3 Måste det vara icke-rökare? 4 Kan jag få en enkel till Märsta, tack? 5 Vi ska köpa kaffe imorgon. 6 Du måste studera idag. 7 Vill du komma till Sverige?

Exercise 8

1 The roads are good. 2 Because Swedes are careful drivers. 3 Because of the cheap rail tickets. 4 Bigger and more comfortable but slower. 5 Because it is difficult to drive in the centre of towns and because of the cheap monthly rail pass. 6 Inexpensive local trains running in Western Skåne. 7 Gothenburg and Norrköping. 8 There are no railways left.

Lesson 4

Exercise 1

1 Du måste alltid göra som jag säger! 2 Jan brukar aldrig köra bil på semestern. 3 Här tänker de inte övernatta. 4 Eva vill ofta titta på gamla kyrkor. 5 Man serverar alltid god mat i Skåne.

Exercise 2

1 timmar; 2 invånare; 3 björnar; 4 byar; 5 miljoner; 6 sjöar; 7 år; 8 portioner; 9 finnar; 10 länder.

Exercise 3

1 en trevlig dialekt; 2 ett vackert slott; 3 underbara kyrkor; 4 ett högt fjäll; 5 en vänlig svensk; 6 en varm dag; 7 kallt öl; 8 ett rikt folk; 9 fattiga studenter; 10 tråkiga popskivor.

Exercise 4

1 Firman är stor. 2 Företaget är stort. 3 Deras produkter är dyra. 4 Kaffet är varmt. 5 Domkyrkan var underbar. 6 Slottet var gammalt. 7 Resan var mycket lang. 8 Studenter är ofta roliga. 9 Klimatet är kallt. 10 Är Skåneslätten tråkig?

Exercise 5

boarding house or cheap hotel; youth hostel; dining room; gents (toilet); ladies (toilet); lift; wardrobe; tub; shower.

Exercise 6

1 I år besöker Forsbergs staden Lund som ligger i södra Sverige. 2 De brukar servera smörgåsbord på gästgiveriet på kvällen. 3 Joakim äter en enorm hamburgare på hotellet. 4 För bara tre hundra år sedan var landskapet en del av Danmark. 5 Efter lunch vill de titta på domkyrkan. 6 Den ligger precis om hörnet. 7 Jag måste beställa två enkelrum för i natt. 8 Skulle du kunna hjälpa mig? 9 Vi har två stora rum på fjärde våningen med dusch och toalett. 10 Kan du vara så snäll och skicka ett vykort till Olle? 11 Ikväll tänker vi övernatta på ett traditionellt skånskt gästgiveri. 12 Deras son är inte alls intresserad av god mat.

Exercise 7

1 Knut den store. 2 Ett astronomiskt ur från 1300-talet. 3 Konstmuseet, Botaniska trädgården, Kulturhistoriska museet. 4 Ett friluftsmuseum med en samling av gamla byggnader från olika delar av södra Sverige. 5 År 1658. 6 20 000 studenter. 7 Mer än 3 miljoner böcker.

Exercise 8

1 1600-talet; 2 900-talet; 3 1400-talet; 4 70-talet; 5 50-talet; 6 80-talet; 7 1990-talet; 8 1820-talet.

Lesson 5

Exercise 1

Just nu bor Rebecca i Stockholm. I år läser hon svenska vid Stockholms universitet. Varje dag åker hon tunnelbana till universitetet. Ofta börjar hon klockan åtta på morgonen. På biblioteket sitter hon och antecknar. Ibland skriver hon en uppsats. Sju gånger i veckan går Rebecca på föreläsningar. Efteråt dricker hon kaffe. Kaffe tycker hon om. Sedan åker hon tunnelbana hem.

Exercise 2

1 elektrikern; 2 exemplet; 3 systern; 4 fingret; 5 professorn.

Exercise 3

affärer, biljetter, fjäll, fabriker, hamburgare, glas, hotell, katoliker, invånare, kronor, maskiner, bullar, firmor, miljoner, människor, namn, olyckor, portioner, päron, drottningar, skolor, skottar, stugor, timmar, byten, toaletter, kyrkor, turister, veckor, ägg, ökningar.

Exercise 4

ett förkläde, en fiskpinne, en kaka, ett glas öl, en gång, en dag, en bondstuga, ett museum, ett hus, ett vykort, en olycka, en lärare, en timme, en människa, ett hotell, en väckarklocka.

Exercise 5

1 Kalla mig för Janne, är du snäll! 2 Köp en ny bil till billigt pris! 3 Servera alltid vitt vin till fisk! 4 Tala bara svenska i Sverige! 5 Använd inte socker om du inte vill bli tjock! 6 Läs artikeln högt så vi kan höra! 7 Skriv ett vykort till Eva när ni kommer fram! 8 Res till Grekland i sommar! 9 Ställ flaskan på bordet, är du snäll! 10 Håll tyst!

Exercise 6

1 Ställ mjölken i kylskåpet, är du snäll! 2 Hon mumsar alltid på en kex. 3 Vi behöver några burkar öl. 4 Tala om skräpmat! 5 De äter tre gånger om dagen. 6 Svenskarna dricker alltid kallt brännvin. 7 Jag använder inte socker i te. 8 Har du alltid grädde i kaffe? 9 Du måste smaka riktigt engelskt öl. 10 De äter fiskpinnar framför teven.

Exercise 7

Kan du . . . äta det? . . . hjälpa oss? . . . tala med henne? . . . sälja dem? . . . hämta honom? . . . köpa det? . . . följa mig? . . . träffa honom? . . . träffa oss. Kan vi . . . tro på henne? . . . beställa dem? . . . titta på det? . . . följa dig? . . . skicka honom? . . . hjälpa er? . . . läsa det? . . . träffa dig?. . . bjuda dem? . . . prata med er? . . . se det?

Exercise 8

1 Maten är dålig. 2 Grädden är tjock. 3 Ölet är kallt. 4 Deras bakelser är underbara. 5 Några gula lökar och några tunna skivor potatis (potatisskivor). 6 En annan kokbok med ett annat recept. 7 Inget namn och ingen adress. 8 Vi har inga kex och inga kakor. 9 Det är underbart, det är roligt . . . det är dyrt! 10 Vilken tråkig bok! 11 Vilket stort glas! 12 Vilka stora kakor! 13 Vilka enorma portioner! 14 Att laga mat är roligt. 15 Att äta pommes frites hela tiden är tråkigt. 16 Vi äter ingenting varmt till lunch. 17 Ingenting är tråkigt.

Exercise 9

1 Nordens Venedig. 2 Birger Jarl, år 1252. 3 Tre små öar mellan sjön Mälaren och Östersjön. 4 På Norrmalm. På Östermalm. 5 En miljon. 6 I Gamla stan. 7 I Gamla stan. 8 En samling klassisk konst. 9 På Skansen. 10 Nordiska djur, t ex varg, lo och älg. 11 Ett krigsskepp som sjönk i hamnen 1628 och som man bärgade för trettio år sedan. 12 På ett av utekaféerna.

Lesson 6

Exercise 1

1 Deras lägenhet är stor och gammal. 2 Affischerna är vackra. 3 De har inte råd att köpa en djup bekväm fåtölj. 4 Han ligger och läser på

soffan. 5 Eva vill ha en stor bordslampa till vardagsrummet. 6 Han ramlar i golvet hela tiden därför att hans säng är så smal. 7 Vi vill skaffa en tavla till ett hyggligt pris. 8 Eva tycker inte alls om skrivbordet. 9 De behöver några breda runda stolar till arbetsrummet.

Exercise 2

1 nakna flickor; 2 enkla möbler; 3 rött; 4 ett runt bord; 5 ett brett rum; 6 ett nytt skrivbord; 7 gammalt; 8 slitna; 9 hårt; 10 milt; 11 vackert; 12 vackra; 13 små, litet; 14 gott; 15 gamla; 16 nyktra; 17 ledsna.

Exercise 3

(a) tand; bokstäver; bönder; bok. (b) kor; stadsbor; hustru; bastu; aktie. (c) vintrar; aftnar; muskel; finger.

Exercise 4

sale; reduced prices; bargain; department store; shop; boutique or shop; ground floor; first floor; basement; lift; escalator; stand on the right; walk on the left; exit.

Exercise 5

(a) gamla; långsamma; tunna; dumma. (b) ett program; en man; ett hem; ett nummer; (ett) timmer. (c) en vän; en sommar; en mun; en trädstam.

Exercise 6

(a) Götaland; Svealand; mer än hälften; 1,2 miljoner; finska; samerna; renskötare; åtta veckor; midnattssolen; vandra; järnväg; bil; Norge. (b) Man ser inte solen på åtta veckor i norra Norrland. Midnattssolen är en stor turistattraktion på sommaren. Viktiga naturtillgångar finns också här. Man byggde en järnväg för att kunna utnyttja järnmalmsfyndigheterna. En ny bilväg blev färdig för ett par år sedan.

Lesson 7

Exercise 1

1 och; 2 för; 3 eller; 4 men; 5 för.

Exercise 2

år åren; vintrar vintrarna; rum rummen; veckor veckorna; timmar timmarna; skivor skivorna; skor skorna; passagerare passagerarna; landskap landskapen; länder länderna; hotell hotellen; hamburgare hamburgarna; förkläden forkladena; besökare besökarna; biljetter biljetterna.

Exercise 3

1 Deras hus är mycket ovanligt. 2 Vårt hotell är mycket litet och enkelt. 3 Mitt kontor ligger i London. 4 Var är dina skor? 5 Jag måste växla mina resecheckar. 6 Hennes man är tjock men han är mycket trevlig. 7 Hans fru är vacker men hon är hemskt tråkig. 8 Bill går längs Kungsportsavenyn med dess dyra affärer.

Exercise 4

1 på, i; 2 på, på; 3 på, i; 4 i, på; 5 från, till, med; 6 hos, på; 7 i, (genom) längs; 8 vid; 9 in i; 10 ut ur, till.

Exercise 5

1 Vart ska du (gå)? 2 Jag ska ut snart. 3 Var är du nu? 4 Jag är härhemma. 5 Kan du komma in hit genast för jag ska ut snart? 6 Finns det en bank där? 7 Var ligger banken? 8 Det ligger därborta vid kanalen. 9 Jag vet en bank där du kan växla dina resecheckar.

Exercise 6

1 Affärerna ligger i centrum – gå rakt fram och de ligger till höger. 2 Hans kontor ligger på den här sidan parken, förbi konstmuseet. 3 Gå över kanalen och ta sedan till vänster. 4 Ta sedan spårvagn nummer sju. 5 Gå längs floden och det ligger nära kyrkan innan man (du) kommer till stationen. 6 Det är inte särskilt långt härifrån – högst tre minuter.

Exercise 7

1 den 23 mars 1980. 2 12. 3 inga kärnkraftverk. 4 den bevisar att kärnkraften är farlig. 5 för att deras renar förblir radioaktiva i många

år. 6 kol, sol, vind, torv och markvärme. 7 nej. 8 ja. 9 de är rädda för att nya vattenkraftverk på norrlandsälvarna kommer att förstöra miljön.

Lesson 8

Exercise 1

1 anmälde sig; 2 köpte; 3 lärde känna; 4 började titta; 5 var; 6 ställde sig.

Exercise 2

1 har pratat; 2 har antecknat; 3 har vågat ställa; 4 har behövt slå upp; 5 har ställt; 6 har frågat; 7 har tyckt; 8 har skrivit.

Exercise 3

kraftverken; miljövännerna; kollegieblocken; ordböckerna; orden; somrarna; språken; kurserna; stockholmarna; frågorna; föreläsningarna.

Exercise 4

1 Det ligger ett konditori vid kanalen. 2 Det går ett tåg till Göteborg kl. 8. 3 Det kommer en lärare hit till Rebecca. 4 Det står många studenter i kön. 5 Det finns en miljon böcker på universitetsbiblioteket .

Exercise 5

1 När Rebecca kommer in i salen sitter ett trettiotal studenter där. 2 Ifall du behöver slå upp några ord måste du ha en ordbok. 3 Eftersom hon ställer en fråga kommer några fram och pratar med henne. 4 Om vi jobbar hårt kommer vi att kunna förstå stockholmarna. 5 Fastän jag har läst boken tidigare har jag svårt att följa med.

Exercise 6

1 ett gratis vykort; 2 goda bakelser; 3 ett bra konditori; 4 ett samtida drama; 5 ett stort kollegieblock; 6 äkta intresse; 7 ett främmande ord; 8 ett fint konstmuseum.

Exercise 7

1 Hela sommaren har de andra solat sig, men Rebecca har arbetat hårt. 2 Till föreläsningen hade hon tagit med ett kollegieblock som hon köpte i bokhandeln. 3 Efteråt frågar ett par studenter varifrån hon kommer och hur länge hon har studerat svenska. 4 Svenska lärare är hemskt svåra att förstå, eller hur Rebecca? 5 Ja, det stämmer. 6 Men om man har läst lite innan man kommer till Sverige kan man förstå svenskarna. 7 Är det lika dåligt som det verkar i Stockholm. 8 Nej, inte alls. 9 Jag håller med dig (om) att det är anonymt och jag föredrar egentligen Bradford. 10 Att bli kär i en svensk kille är det bästa sättet att lära sig förstå landet.

Exercise 8

fel; rätt; rätt; rätt; fel; rätt; fel; fel; rätt; rätt.

Lesson 9

Exercise 1

1 ordnar; 2 åker; 3 behöver; 4 vill ha; 5 ska de köpa; 6 tänder; 7 kostar; 8 blir; 9 anländer; 10 mår; 11 lever; 12 använder.

Exercise 2

1 stannade; 2 skulle köpa; 3 valde; 4 handlade; 5 glömde; 6 köpte; 7 tyckte; 8 rökte; 9 stämde; 10 avskydde; 11 hörde; 12 lärde; 13 gjorde; 14 satte; 15 sa; 16 ställde sig.

Exercise 3

1 den trevliga festen; 2 den saftiga persikan; 3 det stora bordet; 4 den goda maten; 5 det danska brännvinet; 6 den fina äppelkakan; 7 det svenska ölet; 8 det hårda brödet; 9 den unge pojken, 10 det gröna äpplet

Exercise 4

1 Det är Pernilla som är kär i Henrik. 2 Det var han som lurade henne att läsa svenska. 3 Det är hon som kommer från England. 4 Är det du som pratar så bra svenska? 5 Är det i kaffekön som han har ställt sig? 6 Är det här som man får röka? 7 Det är Bradford som jag föredrar.

8 Det är hennes kunskaper som läraren blir imponerad av.

Exercise 5

1 Imorgon ska (tänker) jag läsa Strindberg. 2 Igår köpte vi mat till festen. 3 Nästa vår åker de till England. 4 På kvällen brukar vi titta på TV. 5 På tisdag ska jag börja en ny kurs. 6 Nästa juni kan du se midnattssolen. 7 I julas var jag hemma.

Exercise 6

1 Jag tycker om sådana vindruvor. 2 Har ni några äpplen? 3 Ja, men vi har inga persikor. 4 Hon försökte köpa någon ost men de har ingen. 5 Ska vi köpa något öl? 6 Vi har inget hemma. 7 Någon har glömt servetterna. 8 Men du dricker ingenting! 9 Det var en sådan trevlig fest.

Exercise 7

bread; fruit; vegetables; meat; drinks; canned goods; dairy produce; butter; milk; sour milk; deep frozen; fish fingers; rapid till (max. 5 items).

Exercise 8

1 union; 2 unionstiden; 3 befrielsekrig; 4 skatt; 5 regeringstid; 6 reformationen; 7 uppror; 8 västeuropeiskt.

Lesson 10

Exercise 1

1 dotterson; 2 brorson; 3 systerson; 4 kusin; 5 morfar; 6 farbror; 7 morbror; 8 moster. 9 Jan är född år 1955. 10 Vilhelm dog år 1991. 11 Kent är född år 1956. 12 Ingrid dog 1981.

Exercise 2

1 led; 2 sprang; 3 skröt; 4 sjöng; 5 satt; 6 stack; 7 hann; 8 kom.

Exercise 3

1 dör; 2 ger ut; 3 sover; 4 äter; 5 får; 6 ser; 7 tiger; 8 sitter.

Exercise 4

1 Han sa, att Jans pappa inte var stockholmare. 2 Han sa, att han aldrig drack sprit. 3 Hon undrade, om han alltid varit förälskad i henne. 4 När han äntligen fick dagisplats, kunde Eva börja utbilda sig. 5 Han undrar, om hon ofta träffar sina kusiner.

Exercise 5

1 Sven säger att han inte är sjuk. 2 Jan förklarar att han genast blev förälskad i henne. 3 Vi undrar om Jan fortfarande har släktingar i Norrland. 4 Jan frågar om hans gamla mor ännu lever. 5 Eva förklarar att Joakim alltså har flera kusiner.

Exercise 6

1 De har inte ätit några persikor. 2 De har inte fått några fler barn. 3 De har inte druckit något kaffe. 4 Det har inte blivit någon fest. 5 Vi har inte gjort någonting. 6 Hon har inte skrivit några brev. 7 De har inte bjudit några flickor. 8 Han har inte sett några älgar.

Exercise 7

1 Jag förklarade att det inte finns några älgar i Stockholm. 2 Olle undrar om han inte drack någon sprit igår. 3 Joakim säger att han inte har några syskon. 4 Biträdet sa att de inte hade några bananer. 5 Olle undrar om det inte finns något kaffe hemma.

Exercise 8

1 Less than 100 years. 2 Gustavus Adolphus and Charles XII. 3 He founded a number of towns, created high schools and revitalised the army and the national economy. 4 Kristina had intellectual interests, especially philosophy. 5 She was an intellectual and a woman in a male chauvinist society. 6 He marched his army over the sea ice to Denmark. 7 He gained the provinces of Skåne, Halland and Blekinge. 8 Tsar Peter. 9 He was shot while fighting in Norway. 10 Her Baltic provinces.

Lesson 11

Exercise 1

1 den dåliga filmen; 2 det vanliga barnet; 3 den trevliga boken; 4 den goda maten; 5 de intressanta människorna; 6 den snälle pojken; 7 den vackra systern; 8 de små sportskorna; 9 det lilla ljuset; 10 den danska osten; 11 det växande intresset.

Exercise 2

1 den där unge killen; 2 det där stora bordet; 3 de där nya glasen; 4 den där gamla täckjackan; 5 det där milda vädret; 6 de där gröna äpplena; 7 de där andra studenterna; 8 det där nya kollegieblocket; 9 den där medelålders damen; 10 det där bra fotbollslaget; 11 de där saftiga persikorna.

Exercise 3

(a) den korta; den livliga; den blonda; den mörka; den vackra; den intelligenta. (b) den länge; den tystlåtne; den lille; den tråkige; den snygge; den fule.

Exercise 4

1 tycks; 2 talades vi vid; 3 ses; 4 följdes de åt; 5 funnits; 6 trängdes; 7 lyckats; 8 umgicks.

Exercise 5

Jag undrar . . . vem den korte är; . . . vad Jocke gör; . . . vem som går neråt stan; . . . vad de köper; . . . vem som har min röda tröja; . . . vad som har hänt med den; . . . vem som spelar fotboll; . . . vem hon träffar ikväll; . . . vad José tycker om; . . . vem han talar med?

Exercise 6

1 De där unga pojkarna trivs mycket bra ihop. 2 José och hans kompisar brukar samlas (träffas) på lördagarna. 3 Måste du ha den nya? 4 Det enda som han gillar (tycker om) är att spela fotboll. 5 Kristoffer är den länge mörke i sportskor. 6 Jocke är helt olik den allvarlige Mårten. 7 Han ser inte alls ut som Jocke. 8 Liknar

ungdomarna (de unga pojkarna) varandra? 9 Skyll dig själv om du inte kan hålla reda på dina kläder.

Exercise 7

idrott; vandra i skogen; utförsåkning; simbassäng; stjärna; fjällen; lägga ned pengar; årligen; familjesport; tycker om; sportintresserade; klubbanslutna spelare; upplyst motionsspår; jogga.

Lesson 12

Exercise 1

1 Bills gamle vän Gunnar; 2 Bills svenska bil; 3 nästa lilla avtagsväg; 4 samma vackra stuga; 5 Jockes röda tröja; 6 pappas egen röda träningsoverall; 7 Värmlands stora skogar; 8 männens långa affärssamtal; 9 deras lilla by; 10 denna krångliga resa.

Exercise 2

1 Rebecca borde läsa den här boken. 2 Hon skulle läsa boken om hon kunde hitta den. 3 Men kommer hon att läsa den? 4 Och vill hon läsa den? 5 Sven får inte dricka så mycket öl. 6 Han måste inte dricka så mycket. 7 Vill du ha en kopp kaffe? 8 Jag måste dricka kaffe på morgnarna.

Exercise 3

1 Han tänker ha fest. 2 De lyckades hitta hit. 3 Vi slutade röka. 4 Man (Du) kan höra dem spela. 5 Att jogga är bra för hälsan. 6 Vi slipper köra på de stora vägarna.

Exercise 4

filling station; petrol pump; turn off your engine; car-wash; spare parts; workshop; service; air; water.

Exercise 5

1 salt; 2 stekt salt, potatis; 3 torka, syra (grava); 4 bränna brännvin; 5 surströmming; 6 kräftor; 7 stora, runda; 8 på stanger (under taket); 9 svamp, bär; 10 kaffe.

Lesson 13

Exercise 1

1 staden, måndagarna; 2 älg; 3 svenskarna, naturen; 4 eld; 5 svamp; 6 hösten, bär, skogen.

Exercise 2

1 hela kvällen; 2 västra Sverige; 3 förra året, första gången; 4 friska luften; 5 halva eftermiddagen.

Exercise 3

otroligt; inte; inte särskilt; förmodligen; långsamt; egentligen.

Exercise 4

1 Han reste sig, rörde sig till stolen och sedan satte han sig igen. 2 Vi gifter oss nästa lördag. 3 Jag mÂste tvätta mig och raka mig först. 4 Barnen klädde (på) sig och kammade sig. 5 Han har inte lärt sig svenska. 6 Jag kände mig inte bra. 7 Vi har förkylt oss.

Exercise 5

1 Vilken väg åkte kung Gustav Vasa år 1520? 2 Var ligger Mora? 3 När åkte Gustav Vasa till Mora? 4 Vad heter de 40 dagarna fram till påsk? 5 Vad brukade man göra på fettisdagen? 6 Vad heter fettisdagsbullarna? 7 Vad pryder man björkriset med? 8 Vad gör påskkäringar? 9 Hur firar man Valborg? 10 Var firas Valborg särskilt? 11 Hur länge har första maj varit högtidsdag?

Exercise 6

1 några fridlysta; 2 inga bra; 3 ett annat; 4 vackra engelska; 5 korte tystlåtne; 6 lilla flicka; 7 svenska språket; 8 fula jacka; 9 trevliga bärutflykt; 10 fina gåvor; 11 goda vänner; 12 dumma fråga; 13 egen gamla.

Lesson 14

Exercise 1

1 äldre; 2 yngre; 3 dyrare; 4 bättre; 5 mer intresserad; 6 fler; 7 snabbare; 8 godare; 9 sämre; 10 mera idealistiska; 11 mer; 12 mindre.

Exercise 2

1 längsta floden; 2 nordligaste punkten; 3 sydligaste punkten; 4 djupaste sjön; 5 högsta berget; 6 minsta fågeln; 7 kallaste månaden; 8 lägsta temperaturen.

Exercise 3

1 Är inte rubrikerna lika stora i kvällstidningarna? De är större. 2 Är tidningen lika givande som TV nyheterna? Den är mer givande. 3 Spelar hon lika bra som Erik? Hon spelar bättre. 4 Liknar pojkarna fadern? De är längre. 5 Prenumererar Rebecca på samma tidning som du? Ja, men hon betalar mindre. 6 Sportsidorna är inte samma som i engelska tidningar. De är färre. 7 Ledaren är svårare att läsa. Det är för svårt. 8 Sverige är mycket olikt England. Det är rikare och vackrare.

Exercise 4

ätt; rätt; rätt; fel; fel; rätt; rätt; fel; rätt.

Exercise 5

1 en lärare/ett rum; 2 en vecka/en tidning; 3 ett hjärta/ett byte; 4 en granne/ett barn; 5 en soffa/en kudde; 6 en ficka/en lampa; 7 en gata/en bild; 8 en kvinna/en kamp; 9 en skola/en termin; 10 en invånare/ett antal.

Lesson 15

Exercise 1

1 sin vän; 2 hennes ryggsäck; 3 sin väska; 4 hennes väska; 5 sina kläder; 6 hennes kläder; 7 sin egen bil; 8 hennes bil; 9 sin olle; 10 hennes olle; 11 Pernilla och hennes vän.

Exercise 2

sina; hennes; sin; hennes; dess; sin; hennes; sin; sina; hans; sitt.

Exercise 3

satt, sätta, satt; ligger, lade, lagt; bränt, brann, bränt.

Exercise 4

1 Hon tog dem inte med sig. 2 Känner du honom inte? 3 Nej jag träffade honom aldrig. 4 Han gav mig det inte. 5 Du glömmer det väl inte? 6 Du väcker henne väl inte?

Exercise 5

1 landsbygden; 2 jord, arbete; 3 gratis jord och välbetalda arbeten; 4 den nya världen; 5 militärtjänsten; 6 socialisten, avrättad; 7 författare, Småland; 8 jugoslaver och greker; 9 juntan; 10 kuppen; 11 flyktingar, Vietnam.

Lesson 16

Exercise 1

1 skrivet; 2 tvättade; 3 stressad; 4 stekt, grillad; 5 stängda; 6 byggda; 7 gifta; 8 bjudna; 9 stucket; 10 tänt.

Exercise 2

1 dukade; 2 rökta; 3 låsta; 4 kända; 5 parkerade; 6 lagade; 7 nygifta; 8 bebodda; 9 omlasta; 10 beställda.

Exercise 3

1 avstängd; 2 omklädd; 3 sönderslagen; 4 bortresta; 5 omkörd; 6 uppskrivna; 7 utkastade; 8 inspelade.

Exercise 4

1 Ring inte upp oss före sju! 2 Skrev du ner numret? 3 Tyckte han inte om dem? 4 De kastar aldrig bort gamla kläder. 5 Jag slog inte sönder

fönstret. 6 Klär hon inte om sig? 7 Åker de inte bort över sommaren? 8 Har han inte skickat iväg brevet?

Exercise 5

hospital; hospital; casualty; reception; waiting room; X-ray; ward; nurse; visiting hours; surgery; surgeon; prescription; doctor; chemist's.

Exercise 6

skildrar, skildring, växter, djur, snille, kyrkoherde, vildmarken, provins, samerna.

Exercise 7

norrlänning, dalslänning, hallänning, Jönköpingsbo, Kristianstadsbo, Märstabo, gotländska, sörmländska.

Lesson 17

Exercise 1

1 Han knackades i ryggen. 2 Han stacks i fingret. 3 Bilen försäkrades. 4 Pennan lämnas tillbaka. 5 Kortet skickas iväg. 6 En sittvänlig bil behövs. 7 Stereon stängs av. 8 Huset har sålts. 9 Dörrarna har öppnats. 10 Middag ska serveras. 11 Hon ska plåstras om.

Exercise 2

1 Förare söks av polisen. 2 Deras namn skrivs ner av polisen. 3 Saaben sågs inte av den andra föraren. 4 En frontalkrock undveks. 5 Bilen borde lämnas kvar. 6 En beställning gjordes hos läkaren igår. 7 Bills ölkonsumtion måste skäras ner. 8 Långa promenader har föreslagits av läkaren. 9 Väskan hade packats den morgonen. 10 Alla tidningarna ska brännas. 11 Potatis odlas där.

Exercise 3

1 Aktiva pappor uppmuntrar knattefotboll. 2 Man firar Valborg i Lund med fester hela natten. 3 95% i Sverige läser dagstidning. 4 Turister invaderar fjällvärden på senhösten. 5 Man måste skära ner

alkoholkonsumptionen. 6 Stress förorsakar allt oftare läkarbesök. 7 Man för engelsmän till sjukhus efter bilolycka.

Exercise 4

För att jag aldrig har tyckt om henne. För att jag faktiskt inte håller med dig. För att du egentligen har fel. För att vi verkligen måste göra något. För att du möjligen borde klä om dig.

Exercise 5

1 a waitress; 2 a hairdresser *M*; 3 boy's name; 4 girl's name; 5 an owner *F*; 6 the sick person *M*; 7 a nurse *F*; 8 a dancer *F*; 9 an author *F*; 10 the dark one *F*.

Exercise 6

1 SJ; 2 DN; 3 VM; 4 SMHI; 5 moms; 6 AMS; 7 bio; 8 kyl; 9 konsum; 10 leg; 11 flextid; 12 VD; 13 VDN.

Exercise 7

1 befolkningen; 2 skillnader; 3 bolag; 4 personer; 5 utomlands; 6 utländsk; 7 fordon; 8 hälften; 9 en fjärdedel; 10 ett mycket högt antal.

Exercise 8

1 de flesta bolag är mycket små; 2 75%; 3 45%; 4 Sverige säljer mest till och köper mest från EU och det övriga Europa; 5 bilar, elektriska varor, telefonsystem, köksmaskiner, glas och möbler; 6 företaget hette Skånska förr men har tagit bort den lilla ringen över a-et.

Lesson 18

Exercise 2

1 Får Rebecca ett stipendium, kan hon . . . 2 Blir Rebecca doktor, blir hon . . . 3 Blir Bill VD, kan han . . . 4 Hade José hängt med, skulle han . . . 5 Åker Erik till Bradford, får han . . .

Exercise 3

1 De engelska firmor som har . . . 2 De engelska studenter som studerar . . . 3 Den svenske killen som jag känner . . . 4 Den utförliga presentation som Bill förmedlade . . . 5 Den av Bill Morris framlagda presentationen, som . . .

Exercise 4

1 9 år. 2 I klasserna 8 och 9. 3 Klasslärare undervisar i alla ämnen. Ämneslärare undervisar ett eller två ämnen. 4 Engelska plus tyska, franska eller något annat språk. 5 Mer än 90%. 6 Över hälften. 7 Högskolestuderande får ett statligt studiebidrag plus ett lån. 8 De som förvärvsarbetar vid sidan om.

Swedish–English glossary

The order of the alphabet in this list is as in Swedish: **A . . . ZÅÄÖ**. Thus **bränn/a** follows **bryt/a**, **då** follows **dyr**, etc.

abdikation-en-er abdication
absolut definitely, really
acceptera/s - -des be accepted
adelsman -nen -män nobleman
adjö goodbye
administrativ -t -a administrative
adress -en -er address
affisch -en -er poster
affär -en -er shop; (pl.) business
affärscentrum (ett) business district
affärsman -nen -män businessman
affärssamtal -et - business discussion
affärsvän -nen -ner business contact
afton -en aftnar evening
Akademibokhandel -n university bookshop
akta/ -r -de sig för watch out for
aktie -n -r share in a company
Aktuellt TV news programme
aldrig never
alkohol -en alcohol
all -t -a all
allemansrätten the right of common access
allmän helgdag public holiday
alltför too
alltid always
alltså therefore
allvarlig -t -a serious
alternativ -t -a alternative
amatör -en -er amateur
amerikansk -t -a American
anda/s - -des breathe
andra second
anknytning -en -ar (telephone) extension
anledning -en -ar reason
anländ/a -er -e arrive
anmäl/a -er de sig (till) enrol (for)
annan annat andra other
annars otherwise
annorlunda (än) different (from)
anonym -t -a anonymous
ansjovis -en- ar anchovy
anställ/a -er -de employ
anställd -a employee
ansvara/ -r -de be responsible for
antal -et number

anteckna/ -r -de	take notes
antingen . . . eller	either . . . or
använd/a -er -e använt	use
april	April
arbeta/ -r -de	work
arbetare -n -	worker
arbetarkvarter -et -	working class area
arbetarrörelse -n	labour movement
arbete -t -n	work
arbetskraft -en	labour
arbetslös -t -a	unemployed
arbetslöshet -en	unemployment
arbetsrum -met -	study
arbetstillstånd -et -	work permit
areal -en -er	area
arg -t -a	angry
arktisk -t -a	arctic
arm -en -ar	arm
armé -n -er	army
art -en -er	species, type
artikelnummer -numret -	part number
arton	eighteen
astronomisk -t -a	astronomical
att	that
augusti	August
av	of, by
avfall -et -	waste
avgiftsfri -tt -a	free of charge
avkoppling -en	relaxation
avrätta/ -r -de	execute
avseende -t -n	respect, regard
avsky/ -r -dde	hate, detest
avsluta/ -r -de	complete
avstånd -et -	distance
avsäg/a -er avsade avsagt sig	renounce
avtagsväg -en -ar	side road
avundsjuk -t -a	envious
avundsvärd -t -a	enviable
avveckla/s - -des	be phased out
avvärj/a -er -de	prevent
axelvadd -en -ar	shoulder pad(ding)
bada/ -r -de	swim, bathe
badrum -met -	bathroom
bagagelucka -n -or	boot (of car)
baka/ -r -de	bake
bakelse -n -r	pastry, cake
bakifrån	from behind
bakom	behind
Balticum	the Baltic area
bana -n -or	track, rink
banan -en -er	banana
bank -en -er	bank
banktjänsteman -mannen -män	bank clerk
bara	only, just
barn -et -	child
barnslig -t -a	childish
barnvakt -en -er	babysitter
bastu -n -r	sauna bath
be/ -r bad bett	ask (someone to do something)
be/ -r bad om lov	ask someone's permisson
befinn/a -er befann sig väl	be doing well
befolkning -en -ar	population
befria /-r -de	liberate
befrielsekrig -et -	war of liberation
begrip/a -er begrep	understand
begåvning -en -ar	intelligence, ability
behöv/a -er -de	need
bekant (en) bekanta	acquaintance
bekväm -t -a	comfortable
ben -et -	leg
bensinmätare -n -	fuel gauge
bensinpris -et -er	petrol price
bensinstation -en -er	filling station
berg -et -	mountain
bero/ -r -dde på	be due to

beroende på	depending on
beröva/ -r -de	deprive
beskriv/a -er beskrev	describe
beskrivning -en -ar	description
beslut/a -er beslöt sig för	decide to
bestå -r bestod (av)	consist (of)
beställ/a -er -de	order, book
beställ/a -er -de tid	make an appointment
beställning -en -ar	order
bestämm/a -er bestämde	decide
bestå/ -r bestod bestått	consist
bestående	lasting
besvik/en -et -na	disappointed
besvär -et	trouble, bother
besvärande	troublesome
besök/a -er -te	visit
besökare -n -	visitor
betrakta/ -r -de	regard
betungande	burdensome
betyd/a -er -de betytt	mean
betydelse -n -r	importance, significance, meaning
betyg -et -	grade, mark
bevisa/ -r -de	prove
bh (behå) -n -ar	bra
bibel -n biblar	Bible
bibliotek -et -	library
bidrag -et -	support, grant
bil -en -ar	car
bild -en -er	picture
bilda/ -r -de	form
bilist -en -er	motorist
biljett -en -er	ticket
biljettlucka -n -or	ticket window
biljettpris -et -	cost of a ticket
billig -t -a	cheap, inexpensive
bind/a -er band	bind, tie
bio(graf) -en -er	cinema
biskopssäte -t -n	bishopric

bit/a -er bet	bite
bjud/a -er bjöd	invite, offer
björkris -et	birch twig
björn -en -ar	bear
blad -et -	leaf
bland	among
bland annat (bl a)	among other things
bli kär i	fall in love with
bli/ r blev	be, become
blick -en -ar	glance
block -et -	block; group; writing pad
blodprov -et -	blood test
blomma -n -or	flower
blomsterkrans -en -ar	flower garland
blomstra/ -r -de	flower
blus -en -ar	blouse
blå blått blå(a)	blue
blåbär -et	bilberry
bläddra/ -r -de	leaf through
bo/ -r -dde	live
bok -en böcker	book
bokhandel -n bokhandlar	bookshop
bokstav -en bokstäver	letter of alphabet
bolag -et -	company
bonde -n bönder	peasant, farmer
bondgård -en -ar	farm
bondstuga -n -or	peasant cottage
bord -et -	table
bordslampa -n -or	table lamp
borgerlig -t -a	middle-class, non-socialist
borra/ -r -de	bore
bort	away (direction)
borta	away (location)
bostadskvarter -et -	residential area
botanik -en	botany
botten	awful
Bottniska viken	the Gulf of Bothnia
bra	good, well, fine

bred brett breda	broad, wide
bred/a -er -de brett	spread
bredvid	beside
brev -et -	letter
brevlåda -n -or	letter box
brevväxla/ -r -de	correspond (by letter)
brinn/a -er brann	burn (*intrans.*)
brist/a -er brast	burst
brits -en -ar	couch
bro -n -ar	bridge
broms -en -ar	brake
bromsa/ -r -de	brake
bror brodern bröder	brother
brudgum -men -mar	bridegroom
brudpar -et -	bridal couple
bruka/r -de	usually (do something)
bry/ r -dde sig om	worry/care/ bother about
brygga -n -or	jetty
bryt/a -er bröt	break
bränn/a -er -de	burn (*trans.*); distil
brännvin -et	schnapps
bröd -et -	bread
bröst -et -	breast, chest
buckla -n -or	dent
buksmärta -n -or	abdominal pain
bulle -n -ar	bun
burk -en -ar	can, tin
buss -en -ar	bus
bussig -t -a	kind
busskö -n -er	bus queue
by -n -ar	village
bygg/a -er -de	build
bygga ut	expand, develop
byggnad -en -er	building
byggnadsarbetare -n -	building worker
byråkrati -n -er	bureaucracy
byte -t -n	change
byxor -na	trousers
båda	both
både . . . och . . .	both . . . and . . .
båt -en -ar	boat
bär -et -	berry
bär/a - bar	carry, wear
bärga/ -r -de	salvage
bärutflykt -en -er	berry-picking expedition
böj/a -er -de	bend
böra bör borde bort	ought to, should
börja/ -r -de	begin
början	(the) beginning
central -t -a	central
centrum (ett)	town centre
chilenare -n -	Chilean
cigarett -en -er	cigarette
cykel -n cyklar	bicycle
dag -en -ar	day
dagbok -en -böcker	diary
dagis -et - (daghem -met -)	nursery school
dags att	time to
dagstidning -en -ar	daily paper
dam -en -er	lady
Danmark	Denmark
dans -en -er	dance
dansk -t -a	Danish
de	they
december	December
del -en -ar	part
dela/ -r -de	divide
dela/ -r -de med sig	share
dem	them
demonstration -en -er	demonstration
den (det, de) övriga	the rest of
den (N-words)	it
den där	that (one)
den här	this
denna	this, that (N-words)
deras	their

dess	its
dessa	these, those
dessutom	besides
det (T-words)	it
detalj -en -er	detail
detta	this, that (T-words)
dialekt -en -er	dialect
dig	you (*object*)
dill -en	dill
din ditt dina	your
direkt	direct
dit	there (direction)
djup -t -a	deep
djur -et -	animal
djärv -t -a	daring
doktor -n- er	doctor
doktorandstudier -na	studies for a doctorate
dol/d -t -da	hidden
dom	they, them
dominans -en	domination
dominera/ -r -de	dominate
domkraft -en -er	jack
domkyrka -n -or	cathedral
dotter -n döttrar	daughter
dotterbolag -et -	subsidiary company
dra/ -r drog dragit igen	zip up
dra/ -r drog sig	lie in bed (in the morning)
dragig -t -a	draughty
dramatik -en	drama
drick/a -er drack	drink
drottning -en -ar	queen
druva -n -or	grape
dryg	about, a good
dröj/a -er -de	be long, delay
drömm/a -er drömde	dream
du	you (sing.)
dubbelrum -met -	double room
dug/a -er dög	be acceptable, good enough
duka/ -r -de	set the table
duka/ -r -de fram	unpack, set out (food)
dum -t dumma	stupid
dunka/ -r -de	pound
dusch -en -ar	shower
dygn -et	day, 24 hours
dyr -t -a	expensive, dear
då	then
då och då	now and then
då så	now then
dålig -t -a	bad
däck -et	tyre
där	there, where
därborta	over there
däremot	on the other hand
därför	therefore, this is why
därför att	because
därifrån	from there
dö/ -r dog dött	die
död -en	death
effektiv -t -a	efficient
effektförvaring -en -ar	left luggage office
efter	after
eftermiddag -en -ar	afternoon
efterrätt -en	sweet course
eftersom	as, because
eftervärlden	posterity
efteråt	afterwards
eg/en -et -na	own
egentlig -t -a	real
egentligen	really, actually
ej	not, no
ekonomi -n -er	economy
eld -en -ar	fire
eldfast -a	ovenproof
elektricitet -en (= el)	electricity
elektrisk -t -a	electric(al)

eller or
eller hur see text
elva eleven
elände -t bad luck
emellertid however
en (N-words) a, one
ena/ -r -de unite
endast only
energi -n energy
enfärga/d -t -de plain
engelsk -t -a English
engelska English (language)
engelsman -nen engelsmän English(man)
enkel -t enkla simple, single (e.g. ticket)
enkelrum -met - single room
enkrona -n -or 1 krona coin
enligt according to
enorm -t -a enormous
ense agreed
ensam -t -ma lonely, alone
enstaka odd
er you (*object*)
er ert era your
erbjud/a -er erbjöd offer
erbjudande -t -n offer
ett (T words) one
EU =Europeiska Unionen the European Union
Europa Europe
evighet -en -er eternity, ages
examen (ett) (university) degree
examensfri -tt -a without examinations
fabrik -en -er factory
fackligt anslutlen -et -na member of a trade union
faktiskt actually
faktum faktum/ faktumet faktum/ fakta fact
familj -en -er family
familjenöje -t -n place of entertainment for the whole family
familjesida -n -or social page
fantastiskt incredibly
farfar farfadern (paternal) grandfather
farlig -t -a dangerous, serious
fasta/ -r -de fast
fastan Lent
fast(än) although
fatta/ -r -de understand, grasp
fattig -t -a poor
februari February
fel - wrong
fem five
fempoängskurs -en -er 5-week course
femte fifth
femtio fifty
femtilapp -en -ar 50 kronor note
femton fifteen
fest -en -er party
fet -t -a fat(ty)
fettisdagen Shrove Tuesday
ficka -n -or pocket
figur -en -er figure
fika/ -r -de drink coffee
fil -en yoghurt
filosof -en -er philosopher
fin -t -a fine
finger fingret fingrar finger
finnas finns fanns be, exist
finnas kvar remain, still exist
finne -n -ar Finn
finsktalande Finnish-speaking
fira/ -r -de celebrate
firma -n -or firm

fiska/ -r -de	fish
fiske -t	fishing
fiskeby -n -ar	fishing village
fiskpinne -n -ar	fish finger
fixa/ -r -de	fix, mend
fjorton	fourteen
fjäll -et -	fell, mountain
fjälltrakt -en -er	mountain area
fjärde	fourth
flanera/ -r -de	wander
flaska -n -or	bottle
fler	more
flera	several
flicka -n -or	girl
flitigt	assiduously
flod -en -er	river
fly/ -r -dde	flee, escape from
flyg/a -er flög	fly
flygplats -en -er	airport
flykting -en -ar	refugee
fogde -n -ar	sheriff
folk -et -	people
folkliv -et -	way of life of the people
folkomröstning -en -ar	referendum
fordon -et -	vehicle
form -en -ar	baking dish
forskare -n -	researcher
forskningsresa -n -or	investigative journey
fort	quickly
fortfarande	still
fortsätt/a -er -satte -satt	continue
fot -en fötter	foot
fotboll -en	football
fotbollslag -et -	football team
fotbollsplan -et -	football pitch
foto -t -n	photo
fram	forward
framför	in front of
framgång -en -ar	success
framme	in front, there
framtid -en	future
fransk -t -a	French
franskbröd -et -	French bread
fredag -en -ar	Friday
freestyle -n -s	personal stereo
frestelse -n -r	temptation
fridlyst - -a	protected
frihet -en -er	freedom
friluftsmuseum museet -museer	open air museum
frisk -t -a	fresh
fritt	freely
frontalkrock -en -ar	head-on collision
frossa/-r -de	gorge oneself
frukost -en -ar	breakfast
frukt -en -er	fruit
frus/en -et -na	frozen
fråga -n -or	question
från	from
främmande -	foreign, alien
främst	foremost, leading
ful -t -a	ugly
fundera/ -r -de	think, ponder
fungera/ -r -de	work, function
furubord -et -	pine table
fuska/ -r -de	cheat
fyll/a -er -de	fill
fyndighet -en -er	find
fyra	four
fyrkant -en -er	rectangle
fyrkantig -t -a	rectangular
fyrtio	forty
fyrverkeri -et -er	firework
fysik -en	physics
få	few
få får fick fått	have, get; be able to; be permitted
få/ -r fick igen något	get something shut
få/ -r fick igång något	get something going
få/ -r fick reda på	learn

få/ -r fick tag på	get hold of
fågel -n fåglar	bird
fåtölj -en -er	armchair
fängelse -t -er	prison
färda/s - des	travel
färdig -t -a	ready, complete
färg -en -er	colour
färga/d -t -de	coloured
färgteve -n -ar	colour TV
Färöarna	the Faroes
födelse -n -r	birth
föd/as -s -des fötts	be born
följ/a -er -de (med)	follow, accompany
följande	the following
för	because, for
för all del	by all means
för att	because
för det mesta	mostly
för en gångs skull	for once
för . . . sedan	ago
för/a för -de	carry, take
för/a för -de dagbok	keep a diary
för/a för -de krig	wage war
för/a för -de samtal	carry on a conversation
förare -n -	driver
förbandslåda -n -or	first aid box
förbered/a -er -de	prepare
förbi	past
förbjud/en -et -na	prohibited
förbli/ -r förblev	remain
förbud mot	is prohibited
fördelaktig -t -a	advantageous
föredra/ -r -drog framför	prefer . . . to . . .
föregående	the previous
föreläsning -en -ar	lecture
föreläsningssal -en -ar	lecture room
föremål -et -	object
förena/d -t -de	united
föreslå/ -r föreslog	suggest
företag -et -	company
författare -n -	author, writer
förfärligt	terribly
förklara/ -r -de	explain
förkläde -t -n	apron
förknippa/d -t -de	associated
förlora/ -r -de	lose
förlåt	sorry, excuse me
förläng/a -er -de	extend
förmiddag -en -ar	morning
förnya/ -r -de	renew
förort -en -er	suburb
förr	before
förresten	by the way, incidentally
försiktig -t -a	careful
försiktigt	carefully
förskräckligt	terribly
först	first
första	first
förstå/ -r förstod förstått	understand
förstås	of course
förstör/a - -de	destroy
försvinn/a -er försvann	disappear
försäkra/ -r -de	insure
försäkringsbolag -et -	insurance company
försäljningsvillkor -et -	terms of sale
försök/a -er -te	try, attempt
förtvivlat	in desperation
förut	earlier
förvåna/ -r -de	surprise, astonish, amaze
förvärvsarbete -t	paid employment
förälder -n föräldrar	parent
förälska/d -t -de	in love
förändra/ -e -de	change
gal/en -et -na	crazy, mad
Gamla stan	the Old Town (in Stockholm)
gammal -t gamla	old
gammaldags -	old-fashioned

ganska	rather, fairly
gapa/ -r -de	open mouth
garage -t -	garage
garderob -en -er	cupboard, wardrobe
gardin -en -er	curtain
gatukorsning -en -ar	junction
ge/ -r gav ut	spend
genast	immediately
generös -t -a	generous
genom	through
genomför/a -för -de	carry out
gift -a	married
gift/a -er -e sig (med)	get married (to)
giftig -t -a	poisonous
gilla/ -r -de	like
gissa/ -r -de	guess
gitarrist -en -er	guitarist
givande - -	rewarding
glaciär -en -er	glacier
glad glatt glada	happy
glas -et	glass
glass -en	ice cream
glesbefolka/d -t -de	sparsely populated
glömm/a -er glömde glömt	forget
gnugga/ -r -de	rub
god gott goda	good
goddag	how do you do?
godis -et	sweeties
golv -et -	floor
granne -en -ar	neighbour
gratis -	free, gratis
gratulera/ -r -de	congratulate
grej -en -er	thing
grek -en -er	Greek
grilla/ -r -de	grill
gropig -t -a	potholed
grunda/ -r -de	found
grundläggare -n -	founder

grundskolelärare -n -	schoolteacher in basic school
grupp -en -er	group
grusväg -en -ar	dirt road
grym -t -ma	cruel
grå grått grå(a)	grey
grädda/ -r -de	bake
grädde -n	cream
gräll -t- a	loud, garish
gränd -en -er	alley
gräs -et	grass
grön -t -a	green
gul -t -a	yellow
guldålder -n	golden age
gymnasi/um -et -er	grammar school
gymnasieskola -n -or	sixth form college
gymnastisera/ -r -de	take exercise
gå miste om	miss out on
gå/-r gick gått	go, walk
gång -en er	time, occasion
gård -en -ar	farm
gäll/a -er -de	be valid, apply
gäng -et -	gang
gärna	willingly, by all means; really
gäst -en -er	guest
gästgiveri -et -er	inn
gör/a gjorde gjort	do, make
gör/a gör gjorde ont	be painful
ha besök av	receive a visit from
ha roligt	have fun, enjoy oneself
ha råd (med)	afford
ha rätt (i)	be right (about)
ha/ -r -de haft	have
hage -n -ar	meadow
haka/ -r -de upp sig	stick
hall -en -ar	hall
halmtak -et -	thatched roof
halv (en)	half

halvtimme -n -ar	half hour
hamburgare -n -	hamburger
hamn -en -ar	harbour
hamna/ -r -de	end up
han	he
hand -en händer	hand
handel -n	trade
handla/ -r -de	shop
handling -en -ar	document
handskfack -et -	glove box
handskrift -en -er	manuscript
hans	his
hastig -t -a	rapid
hastighetskontroll -en -er	(police) speed trap
hata/ -r -de	hate
hav -et -	ocean
hej	hello
hela	the whole, all
helg -en -er	holiday, weekend
heller	either
helst	preferably
hem -met -	home
hemland -et -länder	home country
hemma	at home
hemskt	awfully
hennes	her(s)
het/a -er hette hetat	be called
hink -en -ar	bucket
hinn/a -er hann (med)	catch, have time to
hiss -en -ar	lift
hit	(to) here
hitta/-r -de hit	find one's way here
hitta/ -r -de på	think up
hitta/ -r -de	find
hittills	so far, up to now
hjälp -en	help
hjälp/a -er -te	help
hon	she
honom	him
hoppas hoppas hoppades	hope
hosta -n	cough
hota/ -r -de	threaten
hotell -et -	hotel
hund -en -ar	dog
hundra	(a) hundred
hundralapp -en -ar	100 kronor note
hundskit -en -ar	dog dirt
hunger -n	starvation, hunger
hur	how
hur dags?	what time?
hur länge	how long
hur som helst	in any case
hus -et -	house
husmanskost -en	traditional food
hustru -n -r	wife
huvud -et -en	head
huvudsakligen	mainly
huvudstad -en -städer	capital city
huvudvärk -en	headache
hyfsa/d -t -de	nice, OK
hyfsat	not so bad
hygglig -t -a	reasonable; nice, friendly
hål -et -	hole
håll -et -	direction
hålla -er höll	hold, keep
håll/a -er höll med (om)	agree with (about)
håll/a -er höll reda på	look after
hård hårt hårda	hard
hårt bröd	crispbread
häl -en -ar	heel
hälft -en -er	half
häll/a -er -de	pour
hälsa -n	health
hälsa/ -r -de någon	give someone one's regards (love)
häls/a -r -de på	visit

hämta/ -r -de	fetch
händ/a -er hände	happen, occur
häng/a -er -de	hang
häng/a -er -de med	come, go (along with someone)
här	here
härifrån	from here
härlig -t -a	wonderful
härmed	hereby
häromkvällen	the other night
häruppe	up here
häxa -n -or	witch
höft -en -er	hip
hög -en -ar	heap
hög -t -a	high, tall (of things)
höger	right
höglju/dd -tt -dda	noisy
högskola -n -or	college, university
högst	at most
högstadi/um -iet	school classes for 16-year-olds
högtid -en -er	celebration, festival
hönsfjäder - n -fjädrar	hen's feather
hör/a hör -de	hear
höst -en -ar	autumn
i	in
i affärer	on business
i alla fall	anyway
i natt	tonight
i närheten av	in the vicinity of
i samband med	in connection with
i stället för	instead of
i telefon	on the telephone
ibland	sometimes
icke	not, non-
icke-rökare -n -	non-smoker
idag	today
idé -n -er	idea
idrott -en -er	sport
ifall	in case, whether
igår	yesterday
ihjäl	to death
ihjälskjut/en -et -na	shot to death
ihop	together
ihållande	constant
i kväll	this evening
illa	bad
imorgon	tomorrow
imorgon bitti	tomorrow morning
i morse	this morning (earlier)
imponera/d -t -de	impressed
imponerande	impressive
in	in (direction)
in i/in på	into
inalles	in all
inblanda/d -t -de	involved
inbromsning -en -ar	braking
indier -n -	Indian
indisk -t -a	Indian
industri -n -er	industry
industriland -et -länder	industrial country
ing/en -et -a	no, none, no-one
ingenjör -en -er	engineer
ingenstans	nowhere
ingenting	nothing
ingående	in detail
ingång -en	entrance
inköp -et -	purchases
inlagd sill	pickled herring
inland -et	interior
innan (dess)	before (that)
inne	in (location)
innehåll/a -er -höll	contain
inomhus	indoor(s)
inrikta/d -t -de på	concentrating on
insats -en -er	contribution

institution -en -er	university department
inte	not
inte alls	not (. . .) at all
inte ett dugg	not a bit
inte farligt	not bad
inte . . . heller	not . . . either
inte klok -t -a	crazy
inte mycket	not much
inte sant?	isn't it?
inte särskilt	not very
inte så noga	not matter
inte . . . utan	not . . . but
intellektuell -t -a	intellectual
intressant - -a	interesting
intressera/d -t -de (av)	interested (in)
introducera/ -r -de	introduce
inträffa/ -r -de	occur
invandring -en -ar	immigration
invånare -n -	inhabitant
irländare -n -	Irishman
is -en	ice
isbana -n -or	skating rink
isfri -tt -a	ice free
Island	Iceland
italiensk -t -a	Italian
ja	yes
ja visst	of course
jag	I
jaga/ -r -de	chase, hunt
jaha	I see
jaktlag -en -ar	hunting law
januari	January
jaså	oh, really
jobba/ -r -de	work
jobbig -t -a	hard work
jogga/ -r -de	jog
jordgubbe -n -ar	strawberry
jordlös -t -a	landless
jordnöt -en -nötter	peanut
ju	you know
ju . . . desto . . . (comparative)	the . . . (comparative) the . . .
jugoslav -en -er	Yugoslav
juli	July
juni	June
just	precisely
just nu	at present
jämförelse -n -r	comparison
jämt	all the time, always
järnmalm -en -er	iron ore
järnväg -en -ar	railway
järnvägststation -en -er	railway station
jättelik - -a	gigantic
jättesnygg -t -a	stunning, really attractive
kafeteria -n -or	cafeteria
kaffe -t	coffee
kaffetermos -en -ar	coffee thermos
kaka -n -or	cake
kal -t -a	bare, treeless
kall -t -a	cold
kalla/ -r -de	call
kallna/ -r -de	grow cold
kanal -en -er	channel, canal
kandidat -en -er	candidate
kanske	perhaps, maybe
kant -en- er	edge, corner
karta -n -or	map
kasta/ -r -de en blick	glance
kasta/ -r -de vatten	urinate
katastrof -en -er	catastrophe
katolik -en -er	Catholic
katolsk -t -a	Catholic
kemisk -t -a	chemical
kex -et -	biscuit
kille -n -ar	boy
kilo -t	kilogramme
kjol -en -ar	skirt
klara/ -r -de (sig)	manage, get out of, solve

klase -n -ar	bunch
klass -en -er	class (in school)
klassifikation -en -er	classification
klassisk -t -a	classical
klicka/ -r -de ut	put knobs of butter on top
klimat -et -	climate
klubbanslut/en -et -na	member of a club
klä/ -r -dde sig	dress
kläder -na	clothes
klädesplagg -et -	article of clothing
klämm/a -er klämde	squeeze
knacka/ -r -de	knock, tap
knopp -en -ar	bud
knappast	hardly
knäckebröd -et	crispbread
ko -n -r	cow
koalition -en -er	coalition
kokbok -en -böcker	cook book
kol -et	coal
kolla/ -r -de	check
kollegieblock -et	note pad
kollidera/ -r -de	collide
komm/a -er kom att + infinitive	will, is going to
komm/a -er kom fram till	go up to
komm/a -er kom fram	come out
komm/a -er kom ihåg	remember
komm/a -er kom kommit	come
komm/a -er kom sig	come about
kommun -en -er	local authority
kommunikation -en -er	communication
kompis -en -ar	friend, buddy
kompromiss -en -er	compromise
konditori -et -er	coffee shop
konduktör -en -er	ticket collector
konflikt -en -er	conflict
konsert -en -er	concert
konservera/ -r -de	preserve
konst -en -er	art
konstig -t -a	strange
konstmuseum -museet -museer	art gallery
konsumption -en	consumption
kontakta/ -r -de	get in touch with
kontor -et -	office
konung -en -ar	king
kopp -en -ar	cup
koppla/ -r -de av	relax
korg -en -ar	basket
korsrygg -en	small of the back
kort - -a	short
korv -en -ar	sausage
kosta/ -r -de	cost
kostnad -en -er	cost
kraft -en -er	power, strength
kraftigt	substantially; markedly, hard
kraftverk -et -	power station
kram -en -ar	hug
kreditkort -et -	credit card
krig -et -	war
krigarkung -en -ar	warrior king
krigsskepp -et -	warship
kring	around
krona -n -or	unit of currency
kryp/a -er kröp	creep
krånglig -t -a	difficult, troublesome
kräfta -n -or	crayfish
krämpa -n -or	ailment
kudde -n -ar	pillow
kul	fun
kultur -en -er	culture
kultursida -n -or	arts page
kung -en -ar	king
kungamakt -en	royal authority
Kungliga slottet	the Royal Palace
kunna kan kunde kunnat	can, be able

kunskap -en -er	knowledge
kupp -en -er	coup
kurs -en -er	course
kurva -n -or	bend
kusin -en -er	cousin
kust -en -er	coast
kvar	remaining, behind
kvinnlig -t -a	female
kvist -en -ar	branch
kväll -en -ar	evening
kvällstidning -en -ar	evening newspaper
kyl/a -er -de	chill (*trans.*)
kyla -n	cold
kylskåp -et -	refrigerator
kyrka -n -or	church
kyrkoherde -n -ar	rector
käk -et	food
källa -n -or	source, spring
källare -n -	basement
känn/a -er -de till	be familiar with, know
känn/a -er kände	feel, know
kän/d -t -da	famous
kärlek -en	love
kärnkraft -en	nuclear power
kärnkraftverk -et -	nuclear power station
kö -n -er	queue
kök -et -	kitchen
köksbord -et -	kitchen table
köksmaskin -en -er	kitchen equipment
köp/a -er -te	buy
Köpenhamn	Copenhagen
kör/a kör -de om	overtake
kör/a kör -de på	drive into
kör/a kör -de	drive
kött -et	meat
laboratorium laboratoriet -ier	laboratory
laga/ -r -de	mend; prepare (a meal)
lager lagret -	layer; store, stock
lagfärg -en -er	team colour
land -et länder	country
landsbygd -en	countryside
landsdel -en -ar	part of the country
landskap -et -	province
landsvägsbuss -en -ar	rural bus
lansera/ -r -de	market, launch
lastbil -en -ar	truck
latinsk -t -a	Latin
lax -en -ar	salmon
le/ -r log	smile
ledare -n -	leader article
ledsen ledset ledsna	sad, sorry
legitimation -en	identification
leta/ -r -de efter	look for
lev/a -er -de	live
levande	live
leveransvillkor -et -	terms of delivery
lid/a -er led	suffer
ligg/a -er låg legat	lie, be (located)
lika . . . som	as . . . as
likadan -t -a	alike, similar
like	equal
likna/ -r -de	be like, similar to
liksom	sort of
lila	mauve
limpa -n -or	loaf
lina -n -or	line
lindrigt	slightly
linje -n -r	line, band
lita/ -r -de på	trust
lite	a little
lite av varje	a bit of everything
lite grann	a little
liten litet små	little, small

liter -n	litre
litteratur -en -er	literature
litteraturvetenskap -en	theory of literature
livlig -t -a	lively
ljus -t -a	light
lo -n -ar (lodjur -et -)	lynx
locka/ -r -de	attract
loge -n -ar	barn
lokaltåg -et -	local train
lova/ -r -de	promise
luddig -t -a	fluffy, downy
luft -en	air
lugg -en -ar	fringe
lugna/ -r -de sig	calm down
lunch -en -er	lunch
lunginflammation -en	pneumonia
lura/ -r -de	deceive
lutfisk -en -ar	stockfish
lyckas lyckas lyckades	succeed
lyft/a -er -e	lift
lykta -n -or	headlamp
lys/a -er -te upp	brighten, illuminate
lyssna/ -r -de	listen
låg -t -a	low
lågpris	budget, economy
lån -et -	loan
låna/ -r -de	borrow; lend
lång -t -a	long, tall
långbyxor -na	slacks
långsam -t -ma	slow
långt	far
långtråkig -t -a	boring
långärma/d -t -de	long-sleeved
låt/a -er lät bli	stop
låtsa/s låtsas -des inte om	ignore
läge -t -n	situation, location
lägenhet -en -er	flat
lägg/a -er lade av	stop, lay off
lägg/a -er lade in	pickle
lägg/a -er lade ned	spend
lägg/a -er lade lagt	lay, put
lämna/ -r -de	leave
läkare -n -	doctor
längre	(any) longer
längre bak	further back
längre fram	further on
längs	along
längta/ -r -de efter	long for
lär/a lär -de	teach
lära känna	get to know
lärare -n -	teacher
läs/a -er -te	read
läsk -en	soft drink
lätt - -a	easy, light
lättöl -et	light beer
läxläsning -en	homework
lök -en -ar	onion
lön -en -er	wage
löpning -en	running
lördag	Saturday
lös/a -er -te	solve
lösblad -et -	loose page
lösnummer -numret	single copy
löv -et -	leaf
mage -n -ar	stomach
mager -t magra	thin (person)
magplåga -n -or	stomach pain
magsår -et -	stomach ulcer
maj	May
majstång -en -stänger	maypole
makt -en -er	power
mallig -t -a	stuck up
malm -en -er	ore
mamma -n -or	mummy
man	one
man -nen män	man, husband
mandat -et -	(parliamentary) seat
mandel -n mandlar	almond
mandelmassa -n	almond paste

manlig -t -a	male
manssamhälle -t -n	male-dominated society
mark -en	ground
marknadsavdelning -en -ar	marketing department
marknadschef -en -er	marketing director
markägare -n -	landowner
marmelad -en	jam, marmalade
mars	March
maskin -en -er	machine
mat -en	food
matematik -en	mathematics
matlagning -en	cookery
matsked -en -ar	dessertspoon
matte = matematik	maths
matvara -n -or	foodstuff
matvrå -n -r	dining alcove
med	with
medborgare -n -	citizen
meddela/ -r -de	inform; communicate; give (tuition)
medan	while
medeltida	medieval
medelålders -	middle-aged
medicin -en -er	medicine
medlem -men -mar	member
melittafilt/er -ret	coffee filter
mellan	between
mellersta	central
men	but
mer	more
mest	most, mostly
meter -n -	metre -
metod -en -er	method
middag -en -ar	dinner
midnatt	midnight
midnattssol -en	midnight sun
midsommar -en -somrar	Midsummer
midvinter -n	midwinter
mig	me
mil (en)	Swedish mile = 10 km or 6.2 English miles
mild milt milda	mild
militärtjänst -en	military service
miljon -en -er	million
miljö -n -er	environment
miljövän -nen -ner	environmentalist
miljövård -en	environmental protection
min mitt mina	my, mine
mineral -en -er	mineral
minnas minns mindes	remember
minne -t -n	memory, reminder
missnöj/d -t -da	displeased
misstänksamhet -en -er	suspicion
missväxtår -et -	year when harvest fails
mitt i	in the middle of
mjölk -en	milk
mor modern mödrar	mother
morbror -brodern -bröder	(maternal) uncle
morgon -en morgnar	morning
morgonrock -en -ar	dressing gown
mormor -modern -mödrar	grandmother
morsa -n	mum
mossmark -en -er	bog
mot	to(wards)
motionsgymnastik -en	keep fit
motionsspår -et	running/skiing track
motorhuv -en -ar	car bonnet
mumsa/ -r -de	nibble, chew
mun munnen munnar	mouth
museum museet museer	museum
musik -en	music
muskel -n muskler	muscle
muttra/ -r -de	mutter

mycket	very, much, a lot
myndigheter -na	authorities
mynt -et -	coin
myr -en -ar	marsh
mysig -t -a	cosy, charming
må/ -r -dde illa	feel sick
måla/-r-de	paint
månad -en -er	month
månadskort -et -	monthly rail pass
måndag	Monday
många	many
måste -	must, have to
människa -n -or	person
märk/a -er -te	notice
möbel -n möbler	(piece of) furniture
möjligen	possibly
mönster mönstret -	pattern
mörk -t -a	dark
mötande	oncoming
möte -t -n	meeting
namn -et -	name
Napoleonbakelse -n -r	type of cream cake
nationalstat -en -er	nation state
natt -en nätter	night
natur -en -er	nature, countryside
naturligtvis	naturally, of course
naturtillgång -en -ar	natural resource
naturvetenskap -en -er	physical science
ned	down
nederlag -et -	defeat
nej	no
ner	down (direction)
nere	down (location)
nervös -t -a	nervous
neutral -t -a	neutral
ni	you (pl.)
nio	nine
nittio	ninety
nitton	nineteen
njut/a -er njöt av	enjoy
noggran/ -nt -na	careful
nord-	northern
Norden	Scandinavia
Nordirland	Northern Ireland
nordisk -t -a	Nordic, Scandinavian
Nordkalotten	arctic Scandinavia
Norge	Norway
norr	north
norra	northern
norrländsk -t -a	from the province of Norrland
november	November
nu	now
numera	nowadays; at present
nummer numret	number
nuförtiden	nowadays
ny nytt nya	new
nyhet -en -er	piece of news, news
nykter -t nyktra	sober
nyligen	recently
någon något några	some, any
någonsin	ever
någonting	something, anything
nämligen	you see
när	when
nära	almost
närhet-en	vicinity
närma/ -r -de sig	approach
näröppet (ett)	corner shop
nästa	(the) next
nästan	almost
nödvändig -t -a	necessary
nöj/d -t -da	pleased
nöjespark -en -er	amusement park

obehaglig -t -a	unpleasant
obekväm -t -a	uncomfortable
obligatorisk -t -a	compulsory
observation -en -er	observation
och	and
också	also, too
ofta	often
ogärna	(be) reluctant (to)
oheroisk -t -a	unheroic
oklanderlig -t -a	impeccable
oktober	October
okän/d -t -da	unknown
olik -t -a	different (from)
olja -n -or	oil
olle -n -ar	warm sweater
olycka -n -or	accident
om	if, whether
omedelbar -t -a	immediate
omedelbart	immediately
omfatta/ -r -de	comprise, apply to
omgivning -en -ar	environs, surroundings
omkomm/a -er -kom	die (an unnatural death)
omkring	about
område -t -n	area, land
omtumla/d -t -de	shaken up
omöjlig -t -a	impossible
ond ont onda	evil
onsdag	Wednesday
ont i magen	stomach ache
ord -et -	word
ordbok -en -böcker	dictionary
ordentligt	properly
ordna/ -r -de	organise, fix, sort out
oroa/ -r -de sig	worry
orolig -t -a	worried
oss	us
ost -en -ar	cheese
ostsmörgås -en -ar	cheese sandwich
osäker -t osäkra	uncertain
otäck -t -a	terrible
ovanlig -t -a	unusual
packa/ -r -de	pack
packa/ -r -de ur	unpack
pappa -n -or	daddy
papper -et -	(piece of) paper
par -et -	couple, pair
park -en -er	park
parkera/ -r -de	park
parti -et -er	political party
pass -et -	passport
passa/ -r -de (till)	be suitable, go (with)
passa/ -r -de in i	fit into
patientbricka -n -or	patient card
pendeltåg -et -	commuter train
pendla/ -r -de	commute
pengar -na	money
pensionär -en -er	pensioner
period -en -er	period
persika -n -or	peach
person -en -er	person
personbil -en -ar	private car
personnummer -numret	personal identity -number
pittoresk -t -a	picturesque
plasthandtag -et -	plastic handle
plats -en -er	place, seat
platsannons -en -er	situations vacant ad
platta/ -r -de till	flatten
plocka/ -r -de	pick
plugg/a -r -de	study, swot
plåstra/ -r -de om	patch up
plötslig -t -a	sudden
pojke -n -ar	boy
polis -en -er	police(man)
politik -en	politics, policy
politiker -n -	politician
politisk -t -a	political

pommes frites chips
popgrupp -en -er pop group
populär -t -a popular
portion -en -er portion
postkontor -et - post office
potatis -en -/-ar potato
potatischips crisps
praktiskt taget practically
prata /-r -de talk
precis just, precisely, quite
prenumerera/ -r -de subscribe
present -en -er present
presentation -en -er introduction, presentation
pris -et - price
privat - -a private
privatbilism -en private motoring
privatskola -n -or private school
problem -et - problem
produkt -en -er product
professor -n -er professor
program -met - programme
promenad -en -er walk, stroll
prova/ -r -de try, test
provins -en -er province
pryd/a -er- de decorate
pump -en -ar pump
pumpa/ -r -de pump
punktering -en -ar puncture
på at, in
på grund av because of
påsk -en Easter
påskkäring -en -ar 'Easter witch'
påstå/ -r påstod påstått maintain
pärm -en -ar folder
päron -et - pear
rad -en -er line
radioaktiv -t -a radioactive
raffig -t -a stunning
rak -t -a straight
ramla/ -r -de fall
rand -en ränder stripe
randig -t -a striped
rask -t -a brisk
rast -en -er break
recension -en -er review
recept -et - recipe; prescription
redan already, as early as
redogör/a -gör -gjorde för give an account of
reformation -en Reformation
regel -n regler rule
regent -en -er monarch
regering -en -ar government
regeringstid -en -er reign
regn -et rain
regnskur -en -ar (rain) shower
regnställ -et - waterproof
rejäl -t -a solid
relativ -t -a relative
religion -en -er religion
ren -en -ar reindeer
ren -t -a clean
renat unflavoured schnapps
renovera/ -r -de renovate
renskötare -n - reindeer farmer
representant -en -er representative
representera/ -r -de represent
resa/ -n -or journey
res/a -er -te travel; raise
resecheck -en -ar traveller's cheque
reservhjul -et - spare wheel
reseskildring -en -ar travelogue
resklar -t -a ready to leave
respektive respectively
rest -en -er remainder, rest
restaurang -en -er restaurant
restaurangvagn -en -ar buffet car

resultera/ -r -de i	result in
riddare -n -	knight
rik -t -a	rich
rike -t -n	kingdom, realm; sphere
rikedom -en -ar	riches
Riksdagen	the Swedish Parliament
Riksdagshuset	the Parliament building
riksdagsledamot -n -ledamöter	member of parliament
riksdagsval -et -	general election
riksväg -en -ar	major road
riktig -t -a	real
riktigt	really
ring -en -ar	ring
ring/a -er -de	ring
rinnande	running (water)
risig -t -a	tatty, battered
rispa -n -or	scratch
roa/ -r -de sig	amuse oneself
roddbåt -en -ar	rowing boat
rolig -t -a	fun(ny); interesting
roman -en -er	novel
rubrik -en -er	headline
rufsig -t -a	unkempt
rum rummet -	room
rund runt runda	round
rundvandring -en -ar	tour
rutig -t -a	checked
rygg -en -ar	back
ryggsmärta -n -or	back pain
ryggsäck -en -ar	rucksack
rymlig -t -a	roomy, spacious
rå/ -r -dde om någon	have someone to oneself
råd -et	advice
råd/a -er -dde inget tvivel om	be no doubt about
råka/ -r -de	happen, chance
råvara -n -or	raw material
rädd -a	afraid
rätt	right, really
rätt -en	right
rätt -en -er	dish, course
rätta -n	justification, justice
röd rött röda	red
röd avgång	cheap rate (train ticket)
rök/a -er -te	smoke
rökare -n -	smoker
rökning -en	smoking
röst -en -er	vote
rösta/ -r -de	vote
rösträtt -en	right to vote
saftig -t -a	juicy
sakna/ -r -de	lack; miss, have no
salt - -a	salty
salt -et	salt
saluför/a - -de	offer (for sale)
samarbete -t -n	co-operation
sambo -n -r	live-in girl/boyfriend
same -n -r	Sami, Lapp
samhällsvetenskap -en	social science
samiska -n	Sami, Lappish (language)
samla/ -r de	collect
samlas samlas samlades	gather, meet
samling -en -ar	collection
samma	(the) same
samt	and
samtida	contemporary
samtidigt	at the same time
samtliga	all
sann sant sanna	true
schema -t -n	timetable

se/ -r såg . . . ut look
se/ -r såg sett see
sedan then, when, since
sedel -n sedlar (bank)note
sedelautomat -en -er automatic petrol pump
segelbåt -en -ar sailing boat
segling -en sailing
sekel seklet sekler century
semester -n semestrar holiday
senare later
senast -e latest, recent
senhöst -en late autumn
september September
serie -n -r cartoon
seriekrock -en -ar multiple collision
servera/ -r -de serve
servett -en -er napkin
ses ses sågs setts meet
sex six
sextio sixty
sexton sixteen
sida -n -or side, page
siffra -n -or figure
sill -en herring
simbassäng -en -er swimming pool
sitt/a -er ihop be stuck together
sitt/a -er satt sit
sittplatsbiljett -en -er seat reservation
sju seven
sjukhus -et - hospital
sjukhusakuten casualty department
sjung/a -er sjöng sing
sjunk/a -er sjönk sink
sjuttio seventy
sjutton seventeen
själv -t -a self
självsäker self-confident
sjätte sixth
sjö -n -ar lake
skada/ -r -de injure, hurt
skaffa/ -r -de (sig) get, acquire; have (children)
skala/ -r -de peel
Skandinavien Scandinavia
skapa/ -r -de create
skapligt not so bad
skatt -en -er tax
skavsår -et - blister
ske/ -r -dde happen, occur
skick/a -r -de send
skida -n -or ski
skidsäsong -en -er skiing season
skidåkare -n - skier
skidåkning -en skiing
skildra/ -r -de depict
skillnad -en -er difference
skinka -n -or ham
skinksmörgås -en -ar ham sandwich
skit/a -er sket i do not care about
skitig -t -a dirty
skiva -n -or slice; gramophone record; party
skivaffär -en -er record shop
skjorta -n -or shirt
skjut/a -er sköt shoot
sko -n -r shoe
skog -en -ar forest
skogsland -et -länder forested country
skojig -t -a fun
skola -n -or school
skola skall skulle skolat will, shall
skoltrött - -a tired of school
skorpsmulor -na breadcrumbs
skotte -n -ar Scot
Skottland Scotland
skramla/ -r -de rattle
skridsko -n -r skate
skridskobana -n -or skating rink
skrik/a -er skrek yell
skriv/a -er skrev write

skrivbord -et -	desk
skryt/a -er skröt	boast
skräpmat -en	junk food
skuld -en -er	blame; guilt; debt
skumma/ -r -de	skim (read) through
skyll/a -er -de sig själv	have oneself to blame
Skåne	schnapps flavoured with aniseed
skånsk -t -a	of Skåne
skåp -et -	cupboard
skär/a ner -	cut down
skära skär skar	cut
skärgårdsbåt -en -ar	boat to the archipelago
skärtorsdagen	Maundy Thursday
skön -t -a	beautiful
sköt/a -er -te om sig	look after oneself
sköt/as -s -tes	be looked after
slag -et -	battle
slags (ett)	kind of
slalomåkare -n -	slalom skier
slit/a -er slet ut	wear out
slit/en -et -na	worn
slott -et -	castle
slut -et -	end
slut -	finished
sluta/ -r -de (med)	finish, stop
slutligen	finally
slå/ -r slog sig ner	sit down
slå/ -r slog slagit	hit; strike; dial; chime
slå/ -r slog upp	look up
släkting -en -ar	relative
släpp/a -er -te	let drop
slätt -en -er	plain
smaka/ -r -de	taste
smal -t -a	narrow
smit/a -er smet	avoid, get out of
småpengar -na	small change
smärta -n -or	pain
smör -et	butter
smörgås -en -ar	sandwich
smörgåsbord -et -	smörgåsbord, cold table
smörj/a -er smorde	grease
snabb -t -a	quick
snagg -en	crew cut
snaps -en -ar	akvavit, spirits
snille -t -n	genius
snö/ -r -dde sig	hurry up
snorkig -t -a	superior (*negative*)
snyftreportage -t -	sob story
snygg -t -a	attractive
sno -n	snow
socialdemokrat -en -er	Social Democrat
socialist -en -er	socialist
socialistisk -t -a	socialist
Socialstyrelsen	Social Welfare Board
socker sockret	sugar
soffa -n -or	sofa
sol -en -ar	sun
sola/ -r -de sig	sunbathe
soldyrkare -n -	sun worshipper
som	which, that
sommar -en somrar	summer
sommarlov -et -	summer holidays
son -en söner	son
sort -en -er	sort, kind
sovrum -met -	bedroom
spad -et	juice; stock
spara/ -r -de	save
spela/ -r -de	play
spela/ -r -de in	record
spelare -n -	player
sport -en -er	sport
sporta/ -r -de	pursue a sport
sporthall -en -ar	sports hall

sportskor -na	trainers
spring/a -er sprang	run
sprit -en	spirits
språk -et -	language
spy/ -r -dde	vomit
spår -et -	platform
spårvagn -en -ar	tram
späd/a -er -de	dilute
stad -en städer	town
stadsbo -n -r	town dweller
stadsdel -en -ar	quarter, area of town
stanna/ -r -de	stop
starta/ -r -de	start
statlig -t -a	state-run, national, government
statsman -nen -män	statesman
statsminister -n -ministrar	prime minister
stearinljus -et -	candle
stek/a -er -te	fry
stick/a -er stack	go off, disappear; prick, sting
stig/a -er steg	step, come, rise
stig/a -er steg in	come inside; step inside
stig/a -er steg upp	get up
stink/a -er stank	smell
stipendi/um -et -er	grant, scholarship
stjärna -n -or	star
stockholmare -n -	Stockholmer
stol -en -ar	chair
stoppa/ -r -de	stop, prevent; stuff
stor -t -a	big
Storbritannien	Great Britain
storebrorsfasoner	big brother attitude
Storkyrkan	the Cathedral (in Stockholm)
stormakt -en -er	great power
strand -en stränder	beach, shore
treck -et -	line
stress -en	stress
stress/a -r -de	get agitated
strumpbyxor -na	tights
strunta/ -r -de i	not care
sträck/a -er -te	reach
sträng -t -a	strict
strö/ -r -dde	sprinkle
student -en -er	student
studentska -n -or	(female) student
studera/ -r -de	study
studerande -n -	student
studiebidrag -et -	study grant
studiemedel -medlet -	finance for students
studier -na	studies
studieväg -en -ar	course of study
stuga -n -or	cottage
stum -t -ma	dumb, speechless
stå/ -r stod stått	be, be written; stand
stång -en stänger	peg, pole
ställ/a -er -de	put
ställ/a -er -de en fråga	ask a question
ställ/a -er -de sig	stand
ställ/a -er -de till	cause
ställ/a -er -de upp	stand (as a candidate)
stämm/a -er -de	be correct, right
stäng/a -er -de in	shut in
stärkande	invigorating
stökig -t -a	untidy
stör/a stör -de	disturb
störst -a	biggest
störta/ -r -de	overthrow
successivt	gradually
sudda/ -r -de ut	erase
sup -en -ar	dram
surströmming -en	fermented herring

suverän -t -a	fantastic
svamp -en -ar	mushroom, fungi
svara/ -r -de	answer
svart -a	black
svensk -en -ar	Swede
svensk	Swedish *(adj.)*
svenska	Swedish (language)
svenskkunskaper -na	knowledge of Swedish
Sverige	Sweden
svordom -en -ar	oath, swearword
svår -t -a	difficult
svägerska -n -or	sister-in-law
sväng/a -er -de av	turn off
sy/ -r -dde	sew
syd-	southern
synd	shame
synnerligen	most, extremely
syskon -et -	brother or sister, sibling
System(bolag)et	liquor store
system -et -	system
syster -n systrar	sister
så kalla/d -t -de	so-called
så småningom	eventually
så . . . som	as . . . as
sångare -n -	singer, vocalist
såvitt	as far as
säg/a -er sa(de) sagt	say, tell
säker -t säkra	sure, certain
säkert	certainly
sälj/a -er sålde	sell
sällan	seldom, rarely
säng -en -ar	bed
sängkant -en -er	edge of the bed
särskilt	especially
sätt -et -	way
sätt/a -er satte satt	place, put
sätt/a -er satte igång	start
sätt/a -er satte sig	sit down
söder	south
södra	southern
sök/a -er -te	seek, attempt, apply
söndag	Sunday
sönder -	broken
ta/ -r tog tagit	take
ta/ -r tog igen sig	recover, rest
ta/ -r tog in på	put up at, stay at
ta/ -r tog på sig skulden	take the blame on oneself
ta/ -r tog itu med	deal with
tack	thanks, please
tack så mycket	thank you very much
tacka/ -r -de ja	accept
tag (ett)	while
tak -et -	roof
takt -en - er	pace
tal -et -	speech
tala/ -r -de	speak
talang -en -er	talent
tand -en tänder	tooth
tandborste -n -ar	toothbrush
tandläkare -n -	dentist
tanka/ -r -de	fill up (with fuel)
tavla -n -or	noticeboard, blackboard, picture
taxi -n	taxi
te -et	tea
telefonlur -en -ar	telephone receiver
telefonsamtal -et -	telephone call
temperatur -en -er	temperature
tenta/ -r -de	take an exam
teoretisk -t -a	theoretical
teve -n -ar	TV, television
tia -n -or	10 kronor note
tid -en -er	time
tidig -t -a	early
tidigare	earlier
tidning -en -ar	newspaper

tig/a -er teg	be silent
tigg/a -er -de	beg
till	to
till följd av	as a result of
till och med (t o m)	even, to, until
till slut	finally
tillbaka	back
tillgång -en -ar	access, asset
tillkalla/ -r -de	send for
tillverka/ -r -de	manufacture, produce
tillägg/a -er tillade	add
tillåt/en -et -na	permitted
timme -n -ar	hour
timmer timret	timber
tinning -en -ar	temple
tio	ten
tisdag	Tuesday
titta/ -r -de	look
tjej -en -er	girl
tjock -t -a	thick, fat
tjugo	twenty
tjusig -t -a	gorgeous
tjänare!	hi!
toalett -en -er	toilet
toffla -n -or	slipper
tolv	twelve
tonåring -en -ar	teenager
torka/ -r -de	dry
torn -et -	tower
torsdag	Thursday
torv -en	peat
tradition -en -er	tradition
traditionell -t -a	traditional
trafikljus -et -	traffic light
trakt -en -er	area
transportmedel -medlet -	means of transport
trave -n -ar	pile
tre	three
tredje	third
trettio	thirty
trettiotal	about thirty
tretton	thirteen
treva/ -r -de efter	grope for
trevlig -t -a	pleasant, nice
trivas trivs trivdes	get on well
tro/ -r -dde	believe
tron -en -er	throne
trosor -na	knickers
trots	despite
trots att	although
tryck/a -er -te	press
trygg -t -a	safe, secure
tråkig -t -a	boring; a shame, pity
träd -et	tree
trädgräns -en -er	tree line
trädgård -en -ar	garden
trädstam -men -mar	tree trunk
träffa/ -r -de	meet
träffas träffas träffades	meet (reciprocal)
träkyrka -n -or	wooden church
träna/ -r -de	train
träningsoverall -en -er	tracksuit
trög -t -a	stiff
tröja -n -or	sweater
trött trött -a	tired
trötta/ -r -de	tire (*trans.*)
tröttna/ -r -de	grow tired
tunn tunt tunna	thin
tunnelbana -n -or	underground, tube
tunnelbanekiosk -en -er	kiosk in tube station
tunnelbanetåg -et -	tube train
tur och retur	return ticket
turist -en -er	tourist
turkisk -t -a	Turkish
tvivel tvivlet	doubt
två	two
tvärs över	right (straight) across
tvärtom	vice versa

tvätt -en	washing
tvätta/ -r -de	wash
tyck/a -er -te	think, consider
Tyskland	Germany
tystlåten -et -na	quiet
tyvärr	alas
tå -n -r	toe
tåg -et -	train; march, procession
tågluffa/ -r -de	go interrailing
täck/a -er -te	cover
täckjacka -n -or	quilted jacket
tälta/ -r -de	put up a tent, camp
tänd/a -er -e	light, put on a light
tänk/a -er -te	think
ugn -en -ar	oven
under	below, beneath, under
underbar -t -a	wonderful, marvellous
underhållning -en	entertainment
underkläder -na	underclothes
undersök/a -er -te	investigate
undervisa/ -r -de	teach
undervisning -en	teaching, tuition
undra/ -r -de	wonder
undvik/a -er undvek	avoid
ungdom -en -ar	youth, young person
ungefär	about
universitet -et -	university
upp	up
uppdelning -en -ar	division
uppe	up (location)
uppenbarligen	clearly
uppgift -en -er	detail
upphör/a -hör -hörde	cease
upplysning -en -ar	information
upplyst - -a	illuminated
upprepa/ -r -de	repeat
uppror -et -	revolt
uppsats -en -er	essay
uppskatta/ -r -de	appreciate
ur -et -	clock
urdålig -t -a	really awful
urinprov -et -	urine test
ursprungligen	originally
ut	out (direction)
ut ur	out of
utan	without, but
utanför	outside
utbilda/ -r -de sig	train
utbildning -en -ar	education
ute	out (location)
utekafé -et -er	pavement cafe
utflykt -en -er	excursion
utförlig -t -a	detailed, full
utförsåkning -en	downhill skiing
uthyres	to let
utländsk -t -a	foreign
utlänning -en -ar	foreigner
utmärkt	excellent
utnyttja/ -r -de	exploit
utomhus	outdoor(s)
utomlands	abroad
utrikesnyheter -na	foreign news
utrustning -en	equipment
utsatt	allowed, set
utställning -en -ar	display, exhibition
uttala/ -r -de	pronounce
utvandra/ -r -de	emigrate
utvandrare -n -	emigrant
utvandring -en -ar	emigration
vacker -t -a	beautiful
vad	what
vad som helst	anything at all
vagn -en -ar	carriage
vak/en -et -na	awake
vakna/ -r -de	wake up (*intrans.*)

Valborg(smässoafton) Walpurgis Eve (30 April)
valdeltagande -t turnout (in election)
vandra/ -r -de wander, hike, walk
vanlig -t -a normal, common, usual
var where
vara -n -or product
vara bråttom be urgent
vara fena på be fantastic at
vara klar med complete
vara är var varit be
varandra each other
vardag -en -ar weekday
vardagsrum -met - living room
vare sig . . . eller . . . either . . . or . . .
varför why
varg -en -ar wolf
varifrån where from
varje every
varken . . . eller . . . neither . . . nor . . .
varm -t -a hot
vars whose
varsågod here you are, please
vart where (direction)
varuhus -et - department store
vatten vattnet water
vattenkraft -en hydroelectric power
vecka -n -or week
veckoslut -et - weekend
vederhäftig -t -a reliable
vegetation -en -er vegetation
vem who
Venedig Venice
verka/ -r -de seem
verkligen really
verkställ/a -er -de carry out
verkställande direktör managing director
vet/a vet visste vetat know
vetenskap -en -er science
vetenskapsman -nen -män scientist
vi we
vid by, next to, at
vigsel -n vigslar marriage
viktig -t -a important
vild vilt -a wild
vildmark -en -er wilderness
vilja vill ville velat want (to)
vilken vilket vilka which, what
vilse lost
vin -et -er wine
vind -en -ar wind
vindrutetorkare -n - windscreen wiper
vinn/a -er vann win
vinter -n vintrar winter
visa/ -r -de show
vispgrädde -n whipping cream
viss -t -a certain
viss/en [illegible] -na off colour
visserligen admittedly
visst of course
vista/s vistas -des stay be
vore were
vuxen (en) vuxna adult
vykort -et - picture postcard
våga/ -r -de dare
våning -en -ar floor, apartment
vår -en -ar spring
vår -t -a our
vårdcentral -en -er clinic, health centre
väck/a -er -te rouse, awaken (*trans.*)
väckarklocka -n -or alarm clock
väckning -en -ar morning alarm call

väderleksrapport -en -er	weather report	**yrkesliv -et**	the world of work
väg -en -ar	road, way	**yrkesorientera/d -t -de**	skill-oriented
vägg -en -ar	wall	**yta -n -or**	area, surface
vaj/a -er -de	swerve to avoid	**ytterkläder -na**	outdoor clothes
väl	surely, I hope, I suppose	**ytterligare**	further
		zoo (ett)	zoo
välbetal/d -t -da	well-paid	**zoologi -n**	zoology
väldig -t -a	enormous, mighty, vast	**å -n -ar**	river
		åk/a -er -te	go, travel
väldigt	really, very	**ålder -n -åldrar**	age
välj/a -er valde	choose	**ångra/ -r -de sig**	regret
väljare -n -	elector, voter	**år -et**	year
väljarkår -en	electorate	**årligen**	annually
välkomm/en -et		**återvänd/a -er -e**	return
välkomna	welcome	**åtta**	eight
välsmakande	pleasant-tasting	**åttio**	eighty
vän -nen -ner	friend	**äg/a -er -de**	own
vänj/a -er vande sig	get used to	**ägare -n -**	owner
vänlig -t -a	friendly	**ägg -et -**	egg
vänster	left	**äggsmörgås -en -ar**	egg sandwich
vänta/ -r -de	wait	**ägo**	ownership
värld -en -ar	world	**äkta**	genuine, real
världskrig -et -	world war	**älg -en -ar**	elk
värme -n	heat	**älgko -n -r**	elk cow
väska -n -or	suitcase	**älgjakt -en -er**	elk hunt
väst-	western	**älska/ -r -de**	love
väster	west	**älsklingsställe -t -n**	favourite place
västra	western	**älv -en -ar**	river
väx/a -er -te	grow (*intrans.*)	**ämne -t -n**	subject
växande	growing	**än**	than
växel -n	small change	**ändra/ -r -de på**	change
växel -n växlar	gear	**ändring -en -ar**	change
växla/ -r -de	change (money, gear)	**ändå**	nevertheless
		äng -en -ar	meadow
växlande molnighet	varying cloud cover	**ännu**	yet, still
		äntligen	at last
växt -en -er	plant	**äpple -t -n**	apple
växtart -en -er	species of plant	**ät/a -er åt**	eat
yrke -t -n	occupation, profession	**ättika -n**	vinegar
		ö -n -ar	island
		öde -	deserted

ödemark -en -er	wilderness	**östra**	eastern
öga -t ögon	eye	**över**	across, above
ögonblick -et -	moment	**överallt**	everywhere
öka/ -r -de	increase, grow	**övergå/ -r övergick (i)**	convert (to)
ökning -en -ar	increase	**överlev/a -er -de**	survive
öl -et	beer	**övermorgon**	day after tomorrow
önska/ -r -de	wish	**övernatta/ -r -de**	stay the night
öpp/en -et -na	open	**översättning -en -ar**	translation
öra -t öron	ear	**övrig -t -a**	other
öst-	eastern	**övertyga/ -r -de**	convince
öster	east		
Östersjön	the Baltic		

Concise English–Swedish glossary

a little	**lite (grann)**
a while	**ett tag**
a, one	**en** (N-words)
across	**över**
actually	**faktiskt**
address	**adress -en -er**
afford	**ha/-r -de haft råd med**
afraid	**rädd -a**
after	**efter**
afternoon	**eftermiddag -en -ar**
afterwards	**efteråt**
age	**ålder -n åldrar**
ago	**för . . . sedan**
agree with	**håll/a -er höll med**
alike	**likadan -t -a**
all	**all -t -a, hela**
all the time	**jämt**
almost	**nära, nästan**
alone	**ensam -t -ma**
along	**längs**
already	**redan**
also	**också**
always	**alltid**
American	**amerikansk -t -a**
among	**bland**
and	**och**
answer	**svara/ -r -de**
anything at all	**vad som helst**
anyway	**i alla fall**
apple	**äpple -t -n**
approximately	**ungefär**
April	**april**
aquavit	**snaps -en -ar**
area	**område -t -n**
armchair	**fåtölj -en -er**
arrive	**anländ/a -er -e**
as	**eftersom**
as . . . as	**så . . . som**
as . . . as	**lika . . . som**
ask	**be/ -r bad bett**
ask a question	**ställ/a -er -de en fråga**
ask someone's permission	**be/ -r bad om lov**
at home	**hemma**
at most	**högst**
at present	**just nu**
at, in	**på**
attractive	**snygg -t -a**
August	**augusti**
avoid	**smit/a -er smet**
awake	**vak/en -et -na**
awaken (*trans.*)	**väck/a -er -te**
away (direction)	**bort**
away (location)	**borta**
awfully	**hemskt**
back	**tillbaka**
bad	**dålig -t -a**
Baltic	**Östersjön, Baltikum**
bank	**bank -en -er**
bathroom	**badrum -met -**
be	**vara är var varit**

be (located)	**ligg/a -er låg legat**
be (written)	**stå/ -r stod stått**
be (become)	**bli/ -r blev**
be (exist)	**finnas finns fanns**
be able	**få/ -r fick fått**
be acceptable	**dug/a -er dög**
be allowed	**få/ -r fick fått**
be born	**föd/as -s -des**
be called	**het/a -er hette hetat**
be familiar with	**känn/a -er -de till**
be in a hurry	**ha bråttom**
be painful	**gör/a gör gjorde ont**
be right (about)	**ha rätt (i)**
be valid, apply	**gäll/a -er -de**
beach	**strand -en stränder**
beautiful	**skön -t -a, vacker-t vackra**
because	**för, för att**
because of	**på grund av**
bed	**säng -en -ar**
bedroom	**sovrum -met -**
beer	**öl -et**
before	**förr**
begin	**börja/ -r -de**
beginning	**början**
believe	**tro/ -r -dde**
below	**under**
beside	**bredvid**
besides	**dessutom**
between	**mellan**
big	**stor -t -a**
biggest	**störst -a**
biscuit	**kex -et -**
bite	**bit/a -er bet**
black	**svart - -a**
blue	**blå blått blå(a)**
boat	**båt -en -ar**
book	**bok -en böcker**
bookshop	**bokhandel -n bokhandlar**
boring	**tråkig -t -a**
borrow	**låna/ -r -de**
both	**båda**
both . . . and	**både . . . och**

boy	**pojke -n -ar**
bra	**bh (behå) -n -ar**
bread	**bröd -et -**
broad	**bred brett breda**
break, pause	**rast -en -er**
breakfast	**frukost -en -ar**
bridge	**bro -n -ar**
broad	**bred brett breda**
broken	**sönder -**
brother	**bror brodern bröder**
brother or sister (sibling)	**syskon -et -**
build	**bygg/a -er -de**
building	**byggnad -en -er**
bun	**bulle -n -ar**
bus	**buss -en -ar**
businessman	**affärsman -nen -män**
but	**men**
butter	**smör -et**
buy	**köp/a -er -te**
by all means	**för all del**
by the way	**förresten**
cafeteria	**kafeteria -n -or**
cake	**kaka -n -or**
call	**kalla/ -r -de**
can, be able	**kunna kan kunde kunnat**
car	**bil -en -ar**
careful	**försiktig -t -a**
carefully	**försiktigt**
catch	**hinn/a -er hann (med)**
certainly	**säkert**
chair	**stol -en -ar**
change	**förändra/ -r -de, ändra/ -r -de**
change	**ändring -en -ar**
change (money, gear)	**växla/ -r -de**
change (train)	**byte -t -n**
cheap	**billig -t -a**
check	**kolla/ -r -de**
cheese	**ost -en -ar**
child	**barn -et -**

chips	**pommes frites**	cut	**skära skär skar skurit**
choose	**välj/a -er valde**	dad	**pappa -n -or**
church	**kyrka -n -or**	daily paper	**dagstidning -en -ar**
cigarette	**cigarett -en -er**	dangerous	**farlig -t -a**
cinema	**bio(graf) -en -er**	Danish	**dansk -t -a**
clean	**ren -t -a**	dare	**våga/ -r -de**
clearly	**uppenbarligen**	daring	**djärv -t -a**
clock	**ur -et -**	dark	**mörk -t -a**
clothes	**kläder -na**	daughter	**dotter -n döttrar**
coast	**kust -en -er**	day	**dag -en -ar**
coffee	**kaffe -t**	day, 24 hours	**dygn -et -**
coffee shop	**konditori -et -er**	December	**december**
cold	**kall -t -a**	decide	**bestämm/a -er bestämde**
cold	**kyla -n**	decide to	**beslut/a -er beslöt sig för**
collect	**samla/ -r -de**	deep	**djup -t -a**
come	**komm/a -er kom kommit**	definitely	**absolut**
come inside	**stig/a -er steg in**	Denmark	**Danmark**
comfortable	**bekväm -t -a**	department store	**varuhus -et -**
company	**bolag -et -, företag -et -**	depict	**skildra/ -r -de**
complete	**avsluta/ -r -de**	describe	**beskriv/a -er beskrev**
comprise	**omfatta/ -r -de**	description	**beskrivning -en -ar**
consist	**bestå/ -r bestod bestått**	desk	**skrivbord -et -**
contain	**innehåll/a -er -höll**	despite	**trots**
continue	**fortsätt/a -er -satte -satt**	dessert spoon	**matsked -en -ar**
contribution	**insats -en -er**	detail	**detalj -en -er**
correspond (by letter)	**brevväxla/ -r -de**	detest	**avsky/ -r -dde**
cost	**kosta/ -r -de**	dictionary	**ordbok -en -böcker**
cost	**kostnad -en -er**	die	**dö/ -r dog**
cottage	**stuga -n -or**	die (an unnatural death)	**omkomm/a -er -kom**
country	**land -et -**	difference	**skillnad -en -er**
countryside	**landsbygd -en**	different (from)	**olik -t -a**
course	**kurs -en -er**	difficult	**svår -t -a**
cousin	**kusin -en -er**	dinner	**middag -en -ar**
cream	**grädde -n**	dirty	**skitig -t -a**
cream cake	**bakelse -n -r**	disappear	**försvinn/a -er försvann**
create	**skapa/ -r -de**	disappointed	**besvik/en -et -na**
credit card	**kreditkort -et -**	dish (course)	**rätt -en -er**
crispbread	**knäckebröd -et -**	disturb	**stör/a stör -de**
crisps	**potatischips**	do, make	**gör/a gör gjorde**
cup	**kopp -en -ar**	doctor	**läkare -n -**

double room	**dubbelrum -met -**	evil	**ond ont onda**
down (direction)	**ner**	expensive, dear	**dyr -t -a**
down (location)	**nere**	explain	**förklara/ -r -de**
dress	**klä/-r -dde sig**	fact	**faktum faktum/ faktumet faktum/fakta**
drink	**drick/a -er drack**		
drink coffee	**fika/ -r -de**		
drive	**köra/ kör -de**	factory	**fabrik -en -er**
driver	**förare -n -**	fall	**ramla/ -r -de**
dry	**torka/ -r -de**	fall in love with	**bli kär i**
each other	**varandra**	family	**familj -en -er**
earlier	**förut, tidigare**	far	**långt**
early	**tidig -t -a**	farm	**(bond)gård -en -ar**
Easter	**påsk -en**	fast	**fasta/ -r -de**
easy	**lätt - -a**	fat(ty)	**fet -t -a**
eat	**ät/a -er åt**	February	**februari**
egg	**ägg -et -**	feel	**känn/a -er kände**
eight	**åtta**	feel sick	**må/ -r -dde illa**
either	**heller**	female	**kvinnlig -t -a**
either . . . or	**antingen . . . eller**	fetch	**hämta/ -r -de**
eleven	**elva**	few	**få**
employ	**anställ/a -er -de**	figure	**siffra -n -or**
employee	**anställd -a**	figure	**figur -en -er**
end	**slut -et -**	finally	**till slut**
engineer	**ingenjör -en -er**	find	**hitta/ -r -de**
English (adj.)	**engelsk -t -a**	fine	**fin -t -a**
		finger	**finger fingret fingrar**
English (language)	**engelska**		
		finish	**sluta/ -r -de**
English(man)	**engelsman -nen engelsmän**	finished	**slut -et -**
		Finn	**finne -n -ar**
enjoy	**njut/a -er njöt**	fire	**eld -en -ar**
enormous	**enorm -t -a**	firm	**firma -n -or**
enormous	**väldig -t -a**	first	**först**
entertainment	**underhållning -en**	five	**fem**
entrance	**ingång -en**	fix	**fixa/ -r -de**
environment	**miljö -n -er**	flat	**lägenhet -en -er**
equipment	**utrustning -en**	flee	**fly/ -r -dde**
Europe	**Europa**	floor	**golv -et -**
evening	**kväll -en -ar**	flower	**blomma -n -or**
evening (early)	**afton -en aftnar**	fly	**flyg/a -er flög**
evening newspaper	**kvällstidning -en -ar**	follow	**följ/a -er -de**
		food	**mat -en**
eventually	**så småningom**	foot	**fot -en fötter**
every	**varje**	foreign	**främmande -**
everywhere	**överallt**	foreigner	**utlänning -en -ar**

forest	**skog -en -ar**
forget	**glömm/a -er glömde**
forward	**fram**
four	**fyra**
free (gratis)	**gratis -**
French	**fransk -t -a**
French bread	**franskbröd -et -**
fresh	**frisk -t -a**
Friday	**fredag**
friend	**vän -nen -ner**
friendly	**vänlig -t -a**
from	**från**
from there	**därifrån**
frozen	**frus/en -et -na**
fruit	**frukt -en -er**
fry	**stek/a -er -te**
fun	**kul**
fun(ny)	**rolig -t -a**
further	**ytterligare**
future	**framtid -en**
gather together	**samla/s samlas samlades**
genuine	**äkta**
Germany	**Tyskland**
get	**få/ -r fick fått**
get hold of	**få/ -r fick tag på**
get married	**gift/a -er -e sig**
get on well	**trivas trivs trivdes**
get to know	**lär/a lär lärde känna**
get up	**stig/a -er steg upp**
get used to	**vänj/a -er vande sig**
get, acquire	**skaffa/ -r -de (sig)**
gigantic	**jättelik -t -a**
girl	**flicka -n -or**
give someone your regards	**hälsa/ -r -de någon**
glass	**glas -et -**
go off, disappear	**stick/a -er stack**
go (travel)	**åk/a -er -te**
go (walk)	**gå/ -r gick gått**
good	**bra, god gott -a**
goodbye	**adjö**
government	**regering -en -ar**
grandmother	**mormor -modern -mödrar**
Great Britain	**Storbritannien**
grey	**grå grått grå(a)**
ground	**mark -en -er**
group	**grupp -en -er**
grow (*intrans.*)	**väx/a -er -te**
grow cold	**kallna/ -r -de**
grow tired	**tröttna/ -r -de**
growing	**växande**
guess	**gissa/ -r -de**
guest	**gäst -en -er**
half	**halv, hälft -en -er**
hand	**hand -en händer**
happen (chance)	**råka/ -r -de**
happen (occur)	**händ/a -er hände**
happy	**glad glatt glada**
harbour	**hamn -en -ar**
hard	**hård hårt hårda**
hard work	**jobbig -t -a**
hate	**hata/ -r -de**
have	**ha/ -r -de haft**
have fun	**ha roligt**
have to	**måste**
he	**han**
head	**huvud -et -en**
headache	**huvudvärk -en**
health	**hälsa -n**
hear	**hör/a hör -de**
heat	**värme -n**
hello	**hej**
help	**hjälp -en**
help	**hjälp/a -er -te**
her(s)	**hennes**
here	**hit**
here	**här**
here you are	**varsågod**
herring	**sill -en -ar**
hi!	**tjänare!**
high, tall (of things)	**hög -t -a**
him	**honom**
his	**hans**
hit	**slå/ -r slog slagit**

holiday	**semester -n -en semesterar, helg - en, -er**
home	**hem -met -**
hope	**hoppa/s hoppas -des**
hospital	**sjukhus -et -**
hot	**varm -t -a**
hotel	**hotell -et -**
hour	**timme -n -ar**
house	**hus -et -**
how	**hur**
how do you do?	**goddag**
how long	**hur länge**
hurry up	**sno/ -r -dde sig**
husband	**man -nen män**
I	**jag**
idea	**idé -n -er**
identification	**legitimation -en**
if	**om**
ignore	**låtsa/s -des inte om**
immediate	**omedelbar -t -a**
immediately	**genast, omedelbart**
impressed	**imponerad -t -de**
in	**i**
in (direction)	**in**
in (location)	**inne**
in detail	**ingående**
in the vicinity of	**i närheten av**
increase	**ökning -en -ar**
increase, grow	**öka/ -r -de**
incredibly	**fantastiskt**
Indian	**indier -n -**
indoor(s)	**inomhus**
inform	**meddela/ -r -de**
inhabitant	**invånare -n -**
injure, hurt	**skada/ -r -de**
instead	**i stället för**
interested in	**intresserad av**
interesting	**intressant - -a**
into	**in i/in på**
introduce	**introducera/ -r -de**
investigate	**undersök/a -er -te**
invite, offer	**bjud/a -er bjöd**
Irishman	**irländare -n -**

island	**ö -n -ar**
it	**den (N-words)**
it	**det (T-words)**
jam, marmalade	**marmelad -en**
January	**januari**
jetty	**brygga -n -or**
job	**jobb -et -, arbete -t -n**
juicy	**saftig -t -a**
July	**juli**
June	**juni**
keep	**håll/a -er höll**
kilogramme	**kilo -t -**
kitchen	**kök -et -**
kitchen table	**köksbord -et -**
knock, tap	**knacka/ -r -de**
know	**veta vet visste vetat**
knowledge	**kunskap -en -er**
labour	**arbetskraft -en**
lake	**sjö -n -ar**
language	**språk -et -**
later	**senare**
latest, recent	**senast -e**
lay, put	**lägg/a -er lade lagt**
learn	**få/ -r fick reda på**
leave	**lämna/ -r -de**
left	**vänster**
leg	**ben -et -**
lend	**låna/ -r -de**
letter	**brev -et -**
letter box	**brevlåda -n -or**
library	**bibliotek -et -**
lie, be	**ligg/a -er låg legat**
lift	**hiss -en -ar**
lift	**lyft/a -er -e**
light	**ljus -t -a**
light	**tänd/a -er -e**
like	**gilla/ -r -de**
line	**rad -en -er**
liquor store	**Systembolaget**
listen	**lyssna/ -r -de**
litre	**liter -n**
little	**liten litet små**
live	**bo/ -r -dde**
live	**lev/a -er -de**

living room **vardagsrum -met -**
local authority **kommun -en -er**
lonely **ensam -t -ma**
long **lång -t -a**
look **titta/ -r -de**
look (e.g. look pretty) **se/ -r såg . . . ut**
look for **leta/r -de efter**
look up **slå/ -r slog upp**
lose **förlora/ -r -de**
lost **vilse**
love **kärlek -en**
love **älska/ -r -de**
low **låg -t -a**
luggage **bagage -t**
lunch **lunch -en -er**
machine **maskin -en -er**
majority **flertal -et**
make **gör/a gör gjorde**
make an appointment **beställ/a -er -de tid**
male **manlig -t -a**
manage **klara/ -r -de (sig)**
manufacture **tillverka/ -r -de**
many **många**
map **karta -n -or**
March **mars**
married **gift -a**
May **maj**
me **mig**
mean **betyd/a -er -de betytt**
meat **kött -et**
medicine **medicin -en -er**
meet **möt/a -er -te, träffa/ -r -de**
meet (together) **träffa/s träffas -des**
meeting **möte -t -n -**
member **medlem -men -mar**
mend **laga/ -r -de**
metre **meter -n -**
middle-aged **medelålders -**
midnight **midnatt**
Midsummer **midsommar -en somrar**
mild **mild milt milda**
milk **mjölk -en**
million **miljon -en -er**
moment **ögonblick -et -**
Monday **måndag**
money **pengar -na**
month **månad -en -er**
more **fler; mer**
morning **morgon -en morgnar, förmiddag -en -ar**
most **mest**
mostly **för det mesta**
mother **mor modern mödrar**
motorist **bilist -en -er**
mountain **berg -et -; fjäll -et -**
mouth **mun munnen munnar**
much, a lot **mycket**
mum **morsa -n**
mummy **mamma -n -or**
museum **museum museet museer**
mushroom fungi **svamp -en -ar**
music **musik -en**
must **måste -**
name **namn -et -**
narrow **smal -t -a**
naturally, of course **naturligtvis**
nature **natur -en -er**
necessary **nödvändig -t -a**
need **behöv/a -er -de**
neither . . . nor . . . **varken . . . eller . . ., vare sig . . . eller . . .**
never **aldrig**
new **ny nytt nya**
news **nyheter -na**
newspaper **tidning -en -ar**
next **nästa**
night **natt -en nätter**
nine **nio**
nineteen **nitton**
no **nej**

no, none, no one	**ing/en -et -a**
noisy	**höglju/dd -tt -dda**
normal	**vanlig -t -a**
north	**norr -a; nord -**
northern	**norra**
Northern Ireland	**Nordirland**
Norway	**Norge**
not	**ej, inte**
not at all	**inte alls**
not care about	**strunta/ -r -de i**
not very	**inte särskilt**
not, non-	**icke**
not . . . either	**inte . . . heller**
note	**anteckning -en -ar**
note pad	**kollegieblock -et**
nothing	**ingenting**
notice	**märk/a -er -te**
November	**november**
now	**nu**
now and then	**då och då**
now then	**då så**
nowadays	**nuförtiden; numera**
number	**nummer numret -**
number (of)	**antal -et**
object	**föremål -et -**
occupation	**yrke -t -n**
occur	**inträffa/ -r -de**
October	**oktober**
of course	**förstås, (ja)visst**
office	**kontor -et -**
often	**ofta**
oil	**olja -n -or**
old	**gammal -t gamla**
old-fashioned	**gammaldags -**
on business	**i affärer**
on the other hand	**däremot**
on the telephone	**i telefon**
one	**ett (T-words)**
one	**en (N-words)**
one	**man**
one krona coin	**enkrona -n -or**
only	**bara, endast**
open	**öpp/en -et -na**
or	**eller**
order, book	**beställ/a -er -de**
organise	**ordna/ -r -de**
originally	**ursprungligen**
other	**annan annat andra**
otherwise	**annars**
ought to, should	**böra bör borde bort**
our	**vår -t -a**
out (direction)	**ut**
out (location)	**ute**
out of	**ut ur**
outdoor clothes	**ytterkläder -na**
outdoor(s)	**utomhus**
outside	**utanför**
own	**eg/en -et -na**
owner	**ägare -n -**
ownership	**ägo**
pack	**packa/ -r -de**
page	**sida -n -or**
pain	**smärta -n -or**
park	**park -en -er**
part	**del -en -ar**
party	**fest -en -er**
passport	**pass -et -**
past	**förbi**
pattern	**monster monstret -**
peach	**persika -n -or**
pear	**päron -et -**
people	**folk -et -**
perhaps	**kanske**
period	**period -en -er**
permitted	**tillåt/en -et -na**
person	**människa -n -or, person -en -er**
photo	**foto -t -n**
pick	**plocka/ -r -de**
picture	**tavla -n -or**
piece of news	**nyhet -en -er**
pillow	**kudde -n -ar**
place, put	**sätt/a -er satte satt**
place, seat	**plats -en -er**
platform	**plattform -en -er, spår -et -**
play	**spelat -r -de**

please ... tack; varsågod och ...
pleasant trevlig
pocket ficka -n -or
police(man) polis -en -er
poor fattig -t -a
popular populär -t -a
portion portion -en -er
possibly möjligen
post office postkontor -et -
postcard vykort -et -
potato potatis -en -/-ar
pour häll/a -er -de
power makt -en -er
practically praktiskt taget
precisely just
prefer ... to ... föredra/ -r -drog ... framför ...
preferably helst
present present -en -er
press tryck/a -er -te
price pris -et -
problem problem -et -
product produkt -en -er, vara -n -or
programme program -met -
prohibited förbjud/en -et -na
promise lova/ -r -de
pronounce uttala/ -r -de
properly ordentligt
prove bevisa/ -r -de
province landskap -et -
public holiday allmän helgdag
put ställ/a -er-de
put up at, stay at ta/ -r tog in på
quarter (area of town) stadsdel -en -ar
question fråga -n -or
queue kö -n -er
quick snabb -t -a
quickly fort
quiet tystlåt/en -et -na
railway station järnvägsstation -en -er
rain regn -et
rarely sällan
rather (fairly) ganska
reach sträck/a -er -te
read läs/a -er -te
ready, complete färdig -t -a
real riktig -t -a, äkta
really egentligen, verkligen
reasonable, nice, friendly hygglig -t -a
recently nyligen
recipe recept -et -
recover, rest ta/ -r tog igen sig
red röd rött röda
refrigerator kylskåp -et -
relaxation avkoppling -en
religion religion -en -er
remain, still exist finnas finnas, fanns, kvar
remember komm/a -er kom ihåg
repeat upprepa/ -r -de
represent representera/ -r -de
representative representant -en -er
respectively respektive
restaurant restaurang -en -er
return återvänd/a -er -e
return ticket tur och retur
rich rik -t -a
right höger; rätt -en
right across tvärs över
right rätt
ring ring/a -er -de
river älv -en -ar, å -n -ar
road, way väg -en -ar
roof tak -et -
room rum rummet -
round kring; rund runt runda
run spring/a -er sprang
running rinnande
sad, sorry ledsen ledset ledsna
safe, secure trygg -t -a
sandwich smörgås -en -ar

Saturday	**lördag**
sauna bath	**bastu -n -r**
sausage	**korv -en -ar**
save	**spara/ -r -de**
say, tell	**säg/a -er sade sagt**
Scandinavia	**Norden, Skandinavien**
Scandinavian	**nordisk -t -a**
schnapps	**brännvin -et**
school	**skola -n -or**
Scot	**skotte -n -ar**
Scotland	**Skottland**
second	**andra**
see	**se/ -r såg sett**
seem	**verka/ -r -de**
seldom, rarely	**sällan**
self	**själv -t -a**
sell	**sälj/a -er sålde**
send	**skick/a -r -de**
send for	**tillkalla/ -r -de**
September	**september**
serious	**allvarlig -t -a**
serve	**servera/ -r -de**
set the table	**duka/ -r -de**
seven	**sju**
shame	**synd**
share	**dela/ -r -de med sig**
she	**hon**
shirt	**skjorta -n -or**
shoe	**sko -n -r**
shop	**handla/ -r -de**
shop	**affär -en -er**
short	**kort - -a**
show	**visa/ -r -de**
shower	**dusch -en -ar**
shut	**stäng/a -er -de**
side road	**avtagsväg -en -ar**
simple	**enkel -t enkla**
sing	**sjung/a -er sjöng**
single	**enkel -t -a**
single room	**enkelrum -met -**
sink	**sjunk/a -er sjönk**
sister	**syster -n systrar**
sister-in-law	**svägerska -n -or**
sit	**sitt/a -er satt**
sit down	**slå/ -r slog sig ner, sätt/a -er satte sig**
six	**sex**
skirt	**kjol -en -ar**
slacks	**långbyxor -na**
slice	**skiva -n -or**
slow	**långsam -t -ma**
smoke	**rök/a -er -te**
smoking	**rökning -en**
smörgåsbord	**smörgåsbord -et -**
snow	**snö -n**
so-called	**så kalla/d -t kallade**
sofa	**soffa -n -or**
soft drink	**läsk -en**
solid	**rejäl -t -a**
solve	**lös/a -er -te**
sometimes	**ibland**
son	**son -en söner**
sorry	**förlåt**
sort	**sort -en -er**
south	**söder**
southern	**syd-; södra**
speak	**tala -r -de**
speech	**tal -et -**
spend	**ge/ -r gav ut**
spirits	**sprit -en**
spoon	**sked -en -ar**
sport	**idrott -en**
spring	**vår -en -ar**
stand	**ställ/a -er -de sig**
start	**starta/ -r -de**
start	**börja/ -r -de, sätt/a -er satte igång (med)**
stay the night	**övernatta/ -r -de**
stay, be (somewhere)	**vista/s -s -des**
step inside	**stig/a -er steg in**
still	**fortfarande -**
Stockholmer	**stockholmare -n -**
stomach	**mage -n -ar**
stomach ache	**ont i magen**
stop	**stanna/ -r -de**
stop (doing something)	**sluta/ -r -de, låt/a -er lät bli**

stop, prevent	**stoppa/ -r -de**
straight	**rak -t -a**
strange	**konstig -t -a**
strawberry	**jordgubbe -n -ar**
stress	**stress -en**
stripe	**rand -en ränder**
striped	**randig -t -a**
student	**student -en -er**
studies	**studier -na**
study	**arbetsrum -met -**
study	**studera/ -r -de**
study	**plugg/a -r -de**
stupid	**dum -t dumma**
subject	**ämne -t -n**
sudden	**plötslig -t -a**
suffer	**lid/a -er led**
sugar	**socker sockret**
suggest	**föreslå/ -r föreslog**
suitcase	**väska -n -or**
summer	**sommar -en somrar**
summer holiday	**sommarlov -et -**
sun	**sol -en -ar**
Sunday	**söndag**
sure, certain	**säker -t säkra**
surroundings	**omgivning -en -ar**
sweater	**tröja -n -or**
Swede	**svensk -en -ar**
Sweden	**Sverige**
Swedish (*adj.*)	**svensk -t -a**
Swedish (language)	**svenska -n**
sweet course	**efterrätt -en -er**
sweets	**godis -et -**
swim, bathe	**bada/ -r -de**
swimming pool	**simbassäng -en -er**
table	**bord -et -**
take	**ta/ -r tog tagit**
take notes	**anteckna/ -r -de**
talk	**prata/ -r -de**
tall (of people)	**lång -t -a**
taste	**smaka/ -r -de**
tax	**skatt -en -er**
tea	**te -et**
teach	**lär/a lär -de, undervisa/ -r -de**
teacher	**lärare -n -**
teenager	**tonåring -en -ar**
telephone call	**telefonsamtal -et -**
temperature	**temperatur -en -er**
ten	**tio**
ten kronor coin	**tia -n -or**
terrible	**otäck -t -a**
terribly	**förfärligt, förskräckligt**
than	**än**
thank you very much	**tack så mycket**
thanks	**tack**
that	**att**
that (one)	**den där**
the following	**följande**
the other night	**häromkvallen**
the previous	**föregående**
the same	**samma**
the whole, all	**hela**
their	**deras**
them	**dem**
then	**då**
then (after that)	**sedan**
there	**där**
there (direction)	**dit**
they	**de**
thick	**tjock -t -a**
thin (person)	**mager -t magra**
thin (thing)	**tunn tunt tunna**
thing	**grej -en -er**
think	**tänk/a -er -te**
think (consider)	**tyck/a -er -te**
think (ponder)	**fundera/ -r -de**
this	**den här**
this morning (earlier)	**imorse**
three	**tre**
through	**genom**
Thursday	**torsdag**
ticket	**biljett -en -er**
tights	**strumpbyxor -na**
timber	**timmer timret**
time	**tid -en -er**

time	**gång -en -er**	unknown	**okän/d -t -da**
time to	**dags att**	unpack	**packa/ -r -de upp**
timetable	**schema -t -n**	unpleasant	**obehaglig -t -a**
tired	**trött trött -a**	untidy	**stökig -t -a**
to	**till**	unusual	**ovanlig -t -a**
to let	**uthyres**	up	**upp**
today	**idag**	up (location)	**uppe**
toe	**tå -n -r**	us	**oss**
together	**ihop**	use	**använd/a -er -e**
toilet	**toalett -en -er**	usually (do something)	**bruka/ -r -de**
tomorrow	**imorgon**	vice versa	**tvärtom**
tomorrow morning	**imorgon bitti**	village	**by -n -ar**
tonight	**i natt**	visit	**besök/a -er -te, hälsa/ -r -de på**
tourist	**turist -en -er**	visitor	**besökare -n -**
town	**stad -en stader**	wage	**lön -en -er**
town centre	**centrum**	wait	**vänta/ -r -de**
trade	**handel -n**	wake up (*intrans.*)	**vakna/ -r -de**
traditional	**traditionell -t -a**	walk	**promenad -en -er**
train	**träna/-r -de, utbilda/ -r -de sig**	walk	**gå/ -r gick gått**
train (railway)	**tåg -et -**	wander, hike	**vandra/ -r -de**
translation	**översättning -en -ar**	want (to)	**vilja vill ville velat**
travel	**res/a -er -te**	wash	**tvätta/ -r -de**
traveller's cheque	**resecheck -en -ar**	washing	**tvätt -en**
trouble	**besvär -et**	water	**vatten vattnet**
trousers	**byxor -na**	way	**sätt -et -**
truck	**lastbil -en -ar**	we	**vi**
trust	**lita/ -r -de på**	wear	**bär/a bär bar**
tube train	**tunnelbanetåg -et -**	Wednesday	**onsdag**
Tuesday	**tisdag**	week	**vecka -n -or**
turn off	**sväng/a -er -de av**	weekday	**vardag -en -ar**
TV, television	**teve -n -ar**	weekend	**veckoslut -et, helg -en -er**
twelve	**tolv**	welcome	**välkomm/en -et välkomna**
two	**två**	western	**väst-; västra**
ugly	**ful -t -a**	what	**vad**
uncomfortable	**obekväm -t -a**	what time?	**hur dags?**
underclothes	**underkläder -na**	when	**när**
underground	**tunnelbana -n -or**	where	**där**
understand	**begrip/a -er begrep, förstå/ -r förstod**	where	**var**
unemployed	**arbetslös -t -a**	where (direction)	**vart**
unfortunately	**tyvärr**	where . . . from	**varifrån**

which, that **som**
which, what **vilken vilket vilka**
while **medan**
who **vem**
whose **vars**
why **varför**
wife **hustru -n -r**
wild **vild vilt vilda**
wilderness **ödemark -en -er**
will, shall **skola skall skulle skolat**
willingly **gärna**
win **vinn/a -er vann**
winter **vinter -n vintrar**
wish **önska/ -r -de**
with **med**
without **utan**
wonderful **härlig -t -a**
word **ord -et -**
work **arbeta/ -r -den jobba/ -r -de**
work (function) **fungera/ -r -de**
work **arbete -t -n**
world **värld -en -ar**
worry about **bry/ -r -dde sig om**
write **skriv/a -er skrev**
wrong **fel -**
year **år -et -**
yes **ja**
yesterday **igår**
yet **ännu**
you (object) **dig**
you (object) **er**
you (pl.) **ni**
you (sing.) **du**

Grammatical index

Numbers refer to lessons in the book. **Swedish** words are in **bold** type, *English* words are in *italics*.